# Environmental Discourse and Practice

# Environmental Discourse and Practice

Lisa M. Benton and John Rennie Short

First published 1999

Blackwell Publishers Ltd
108 Cowley Road
Oxford OX4 1JF
UK

Blackwell Publishers Inc.
350 Main Street
Malden, Massachusetts 02148
USA

*British Library Cataloguing in Publication Data*

A CIP catalogue record for this book is available from the British Library.

*Library of Congress Cataloging-in-Publication Data*

Benton, Lisa M.
    Environmental discourse and practice / Lisa M. Benton and John Rennie Short.
        p.    cm.
    Includes bibliographical references and index.
    ISBN 0–631–21113–6 (hardcover).  — ISBN 0–631–21114–4 (pbk.)
    1. Environmentalism—History.   2. Environmentalism—United Sates—History.   Environmental
management—Social aspects. I. Short, John R. II. Title.
GE 195.B464   1999
363.7′05′09—dc21                                                                          98–34506
                                                                                              CIP

Typeset in Sabon on 10.5/12pt
by Pure Tech India Ltd., Pondicherry
http://www.puretech.com
Printed in Great Britain by TJ International, Padstow, Cornwall

This book is printed on acid-free paper

*To our Brothers and Sisters*:
Karen, Kevin, Michael, and Michelle

# Contents

# List of Figures

# List of Tables

# Introduction

Suddenly the idea flashed through my head that there was a unity in this complication – that the relation of one resource to another was not the end of the story. Here were no longer a lot of different, independent, and often antagonistic questions, each on its own separate island, as we had been in the habit of thinking. In place of them, here was one single question with many parts. Seen in this new light, all these separate questions fitted into and made up one central problem of the use of the earth for the good of man.

Gifford Pinchot, *Breaking New Ground*, 1947: 320

Societies take up space as well as time. This occupancy of territory provides the material needs of life. But it also gives wider meaning and purpose to life. The physical environment provides not only food, clothing, and shelter but symbolic significance, religious resonance, and cultural meaning. In this book we will look at the stories used to explain, justify, and describe humanity–environment relationships. We will term these stories environmental discourses.

## Definitions

Let us define the term discourse more clearly. A simple definition is: a framework that includes whole sets of ideas, words, concepts, and practices. Discourses are the general context in which ideas take on a specific meaning and inform particular practices. A discourse is a set of widely held ideas that a society relies on to make sense of the world, a set of general beliefs about the nature of reality.

We can think of a hierarchy of discourse; the more encompassing concept we will term metadiscourse.

The term discourse is closely linked to two other ideas: paradigm and problematic. The term paradigm was first used by the philosopher of science T. S. Kuhn (1922–96) to refer to a conceptual schema that defines both objects and methods of investigation. Paradigms, like discourses, set new questions as well as provide new answers. What was considered important in one paradigm is considered insignificant in another.

The term problematic was used by the French philosopher Louis Althusser (1918–90) to refer to systems of concepts that define both the problems set for intellectual endeavor and the means to provide and verify the answers. One of Althusser's students at the Ecole Normale Supérieure in Paris was the historian Michel Foucault (1926–84). The term discourse is most often associated with Foucault. In a series of books he studied the discourses that defined madness, illness, punishment, and sexuality.

The dictionary defines environment as "surrounding; surrounding circumstances of life of person or society." In contemporary society, the word "environment" has often become synonymous with nature or the natural world. We use the term more according to the dictionary definition.

Environmental discourses are thus explanations of the world around us. They are deep structures which pattern thought, belief and practices, and allow us to understand why human–environmental relationships take the forms that they do. The notion of environmental discourse gives theoretical structure to this book.

Discourses are never static and rarely stable. They change and modify over time, both affecting human–environment relations and being shaped in turn by the changes in these relations. At any one time there may be multiple and competing discourses in a process of flux. In tables 0.1 and 0.2 we counterpoise two environmental metadiscourses that provide a rich contrast. The ecological metadiscourse is found in both the modern and postmodern eras while the technological metadiscourse emerged with the scientific revolution and the rise of capitalism. Environmental discourses are less innocent statements of the physical world and more politicized representations. In this book we will look at the emergence of the technological metadiscourse discourse and challenges to its hegemony.

By using environmental discourses, we seek to show that environment is as much a social construct as a physical presence "out there." By exploring the notion of discourse, we highlight the social production of space, place, and the environment. We challenge the assumption that environment is merely a physical entity and resist the categorization of it in only scientific terms. Instead we argue that the environment is also a product of our social institutions. The environment plays an active role in cultural representation, political discourse, and national identity. The "natural world" is socially produced. The environment is as much constructed as it is discovered, catalogued, identified, and classified. Environmental truths are made rather than found. We see the environment less as a backdrop to social action and more as a narrative whose meaning is changing, unstable, and

**Table 0.1** The ecological metadiscourse (pre-modern and post- modern)

| | |
|---|---|
| Time: | is cyclical |
| | life is lived in cycles |
| Place: | has significance and meaning |
| | a spiritual and historical attachment |
| Causation: | divine |
| Economy: | sustainable, meets basic needs of food, shelter and clothing |
| People and Society: | holistic (people and nature are one) |
| | biocentric outlook (both non-living and living have instrinsic value) |
| | take only what you need from the environment |
| | respect nature and give thanks |
| | acknowledge dependency on environment collective |
| | protect the common spaces |
| | believe in obligation to future generations |
| | society constrained by natural laws and limits |
| Humanity–Environment Relationship: | encourages stewardship of environment |
| | awareness that humans need the earth but can easily exploit it |
| | explicit respect for environment |
| | realization of interdependence promotes concern for ecological integrity |

**Table 0.2** The technological metadiscourse

| | |
|---|---|
| Time: | is linear (measured in hours, days, months, years) |
| Place: | is relative and separate |
| | a practical attachment |
| Causation: | scientific reasoning |
| Economy: | accumulation; growth is both necessary and good |
| People and Society: | anthropocentric outlook |
| | (a hierarchy of living beings; humans are at the top of hierarchy) |
| | nature is an object; it is not "alive" |
| | non-living have no value |
| | nature and culture are opposite and detached |
| | privilege individual rights and freedoms |
| | tragedy of the common spaces |
| | society not constrained by natural laws or limits |
| | technological optimism (technology solves problems, makes life better) |
| | progress is equated with continued technological advances and economic growth |
| Humanity–Environment Relationship: | encourages subduing of environment, improving or controlling nature |
| | intense use of earth's resources; exploitative |
| | humanity's separateness from environment leads to disregard for ecological integrity |
| | environmental degradation acceptable price to pay for progress |
| | environment important if "use value" exists |

subject to contestation, negotiation, and conflict. In this book we extend the concept of environment beyond the traditional limits of environmental analysis.

## Discourses in the US

The relationship between people and the environment is complex and fascinating. There has been a great deal written recently about this relationship at the global level. Environmental issues have become part of the global talk that now dominates. Global warming and the greenhouse effect have now joined the dictionary of frequently used words. And with this usage has come an awareness of the links that tie the entire planet and the total human population. While we are acutely aware of the importance of this global perspective, in this book we take a narrower look, with a sharper focus on just one country, the US. We explicitly focus on the USA because we believe it is imperative to ground a discussion of environmental discourses in a particular place, especially since many of the elements which comprise these discourses are connected to ideas about national identity and cultural identity. This is a dynamic story with both ecological relations and social ideas shifting, changing, and swirling through time and across space.

There are many discourses below the level of metadiscourse. This book considers discourses of wilderness, countryside, and city. Each of these broad discourses is composed of beliefs, concepts, dualisms, and paradoxes which have shifted definitions and meanings over time. In many instances, one discourse has defined or influenced the meaning of the other two.

The first environmental discourse is that of the idea of wilderness. Americans have tended to see the wilderness as pristine, somehow untouched by culture or human society. It has been something to conquer and to exploit. In fact, in 1835, the astute observer Alexis de Tocqueville remarked, "The American people see themselves marching through the wilderness, drying up marshes, diverting rivers, peopling the wilds and subduing nature. It is not just occasionally that their imagination catches a glimpse of this magnificent vision, it is always flitting before their mind."[1] There has also been a strong and pervasive desire to save the wilderness, to preserve it, as a place of spiritual restoration. Preserving the wilderness has emerged as a major environmental discourse as the twentieth century draws to a close, although as we shall see in a number of chapters it is less a preservation and more a construction of wilderness.

Another contradictory discourse is inherent in attitudes toward what we term the rural. More recently, transformation of the wilderness into countryside has been seen as both an economic enterprise and a moral act. Transforming the wildernes into something productive has been an overriding theme in the settlement of the United States. As Benjamin Franklin wrote, "agriculture is the great business of this country."[2] Over the years, this transformative process intensified and integrated mechanization and technologies. On the other hand, there has been an emerging critique of the environmental consequences of commercial agriculture. For example, Rachel Carson's famous 1962 book *Silent Spring*, examines the detrimental effects of high-tech farming practices, including the application of pesticides such as DDT. There have been tremendous gains made in the productivity of American agriculture and many nations now rely on its continued productivity for their food needs. Many people take it for granted that agricultural regions will remain highly productive, fertile areas. However, as we approach the twenty-first century, an emerging environmental discourse is concern for the long-term ecological integrity of rural America.

The third environmental discourse we explore is the idea of the city. Cities embody order, culture, and civilization. They are places in which the most noble of human activities occur; they are expressions of humanity at its best. Cities have also been seen to represent the worst of humanity: amorality, chaos, and the mob. This has been made more profound by the continued worshipping of the wilderness, which subtly implies a disdain of the urban. However, we show that the modern urban environmental movement is articulating a discourse that overturns assumptions that the environmental protection is only concerned with "the wilderness," and argues that there is much nature in that most humanized landscape, the city.

### The Organization of This Book

We aim to uncover the discourses outlined above in two distinct, but interconnected ways. First, in part I "Environmental Discourses in History," we use a broad historical approach in order to discover the role of environmental discourses in creating stories about national origins and the shaping of national identity. We explore the changing geographies and competing meanings of the environment. The changing relationship between people and their environments runs through the history of the occupancy of the land and the unfolding definitions of national identity. An environmental historical geography also sheds light on the broader history and deeper meaning of the USA. This is a huge topic but we make no apologies for its inclusion. An historical perspective, however broad, is an important prerequisite for subsequent discussions. However, this book is not intended to be a detailed documentation of American history from an environmental perspective. Other scholars such as Roderick Nash, Benjamin Kline, Max Oelschlager, Joseph Petulla, and Donald Worster have done excellent work in this regard. We do feel, however, it is imperative to be sensitive to the historical perspective, so we focus on the more important defining moments in history which mark profound shifts in the configuration of humanity–environment relations.

In chapter 1 we critically evaluate the discourse of the New World as pristine wilderness. In chapter 2 we look at the effects of colonial encounters on the way the environment was used, valued, and described. Chapter 3 considers the acquisition of land/loss of land and the way this gain/loss altered human–environment relations. Chapter 4 discusses the nineteenth century reactions to the dominant ideas and practices of environmental use and the emergence of an alternative environmental discourse. This theme is brought up to the present day in chapter 5, which details the more recent shifts in environmental awareness and consciousness and considers the importance of the emergence and practice of the Environmental Protection Agency. In chapter 6 we consider how many of the defining moments described in the previous chapters unfold in a specific location. We document the history of Lake Onondaga in New York State. This chapter anchors the the discussion both in space as well as time and provides an illustration of how environmental history takes place. The lake has been a site of contestation for the two markedly different environmental discourses.

Second, in part II, "Environmental Discourses in Practice," we explore the ways these discourses are practiced in specific places, affect politics and policies, and shape social values. We examine the ambiguous character of environmental discourses in the late twentieth century, both in terms of physical space and discursive space. We sharpen our focus in a series of case studies that connect the discourses to particular places and specific themes. In chapter 7 we examine how an environmental sensitivity, in its various forms, has entered broader debates about politics, economic growth and the consumer economy. This chapter makes some assessments of the most recent environmental discourses. In chapter 8 we critically evaluate a range of more radical environmental discourses, including deep ecology, social ecology, and ecofeminism. In chapter 9 we consider the history of the national parks as a window on many of the historical themes discussed in part I, and look to some of the more recent debates about the parks as a study in the "social construction of nature." How we have perceived national parks reflects issues of equity and distribution, reveals power relationships, and says something about how our culture determines its identity. Chapter 10 focuses on how and why environmental discourses have influenced debates outside traditional environmental policy. We use the debate surrounding the North American Free Trade Agreement (NAFTA) as illustration. Some of the ambiguity of national identity and global responsibility is captured in the analysis of the relationship between environmentalists and free traders. Chapter 11 explores the ambiguities inherent in the growth mentality and commodity marketing of environmental organizations. In a postscript we discuss the implications of an environmental awareness in the world's most consumerist culture. We argue that the environment has become one of the new metanarratives of the next millennium, influencing national and personal identity, political action, and cultural representation.

The argument of the book is simple: in part I we show how a premodern ecological metadiscourse was replaced by a technological metadiscourse, which in turn was challenged by a postmodern ecological metadiscourse; in part II we look at some of the sites, consequences, and paradoxes of this recent challenge.

Let us state what the book is not. It is not a physical science text. There are numerous texts which provide a good introduction to environmental science or environmental studies using an earth sciences approach. Our emphasis is different. We do not consider the environment a subject of study that belongs in the domain only of natural and physical scientists or policy analysts. While we believe that there is "nature" that is independent of human thought, we are concerned with the meaning of the environment, what it represents, what it signifies. We are more concerned with social constructions than with biotic facts. As social scientists we seek to reclaim the study of the environment by giving it a humanistic perspective.

Another caveat: this book will not develop ideas and arguments that are hidden behind opaque terminology and jargon. We are committed to the accessibility of ideas, to widening debate and discussion so that it is more inclusive. Some of the ideas found in this book are familiar to the small but growing group of scholars who focus on environmental history and philosophy. We aim to introduce many of these exciting ideas to scholars, students, and engaged minds outside the academy. We believe that sophisticated, complex ideas can be discussed in a clear, straight-forward style. To this end we will not burden the narrative with weighty references; instead we have used chapter endnotes, where appropriate, and have provided a Guide to Further Reading for each chapter.

## NOTES

1   A. de Tocqueville, *Democracy in America* (New York: Penguin, 1991), 96.
2   *The Works of Benjamin Franklin*, 12 vols, ed. John Bigelow (New York: Putnams, 1904), 3: 142.

Part I

# Environmental Discourses in History

# 1

# Imagining a New World

I went to America with prepossessions by no means unfavorable, and indeed rather indulged in many of those allusive ideas, with respect to the purity of government and the primitive happiness of the people, which I had early imbibed in my native country, where unfortunately, discontent at home enhances a very distant temptation, and the western world has long been looked to as a retreat from real or imaginary oppression.

Thomas Moore, 1803

## A New World

One of the most powerful and enduring images of the American condition prior to 1492 is of a vast, unchanging wilderness lightly populated with indigenous people. The picture of an undisturbed, pristine world is encapsulated in the very use of the term New World, a world where the European imagination could, depending on the mood of the observer, see evidence of either Arcadia or Utopia. The New World became a mirror to some of the worst fears and greatest dreams of the Old World. The New World was not so much discovered as invented.

The basic image has shifted in detail over the years. One view, particularly strong in the eighteenth, nineteenth and early twentieth centuries, saw the "Indians" as "primitive men, to whom ambition, time and money mean nothing."[1] This Classical view saw white settlement of the continent as the coming of civilization and the defeat of barbarism, and beheld the New World as a place with more future than past. Although modified over the years it still holds an important place in the triumphalist conception of the United States and undergirds many discourses, from manifest destiny to US exceptionalism and the early traditions of the movie genre of the western. It has not, however, gone uncontested. Another view, which has always been a part of the conceptualization of the New World but which has gained more prominence in the last 50 years, is the Romantic view, which sees white settlement as a fall from grace and 1492 as something to grieve over rather than something to celebrate. In this view the New World was a paradise inhabited by the earliest ecological heroes living in harmony with nature. Even such an august body as the Smithsonian as late as 1991 was involved with an exhibition on the Columbian encounter that subscribed to this popular Romantic outlook. The acting deputy director wrote that

> pre-Columbian America was still the First Eden, a pristine natural kingdom. The native people were transparent in the landscape, living as natural elements of the ecosphere. Their world, the New World of Columbus, was a world of barely perceptible human disturbance.[2]

The coming of white settlement, in this perspective, represents the crushing of nature and the slaughter of the innocents. The contest between Classical and Romantic views is part of the continuing debate about national identity and the meaning of the United States.[3]

Although they differ in the moral meaning of 1492 both views subscribe to the notion of a basically undisturbed wilderness before the coming of the whites. It has proved to be an attractive picture, combining as it does notions of Paradise, a Garden of Eden and a land ripe with potential for both good or evil. This New World is the world of European imaginings and longings.

## A Dynamic World

There is now a great deal of evidence suggesting that the ecosystems in the United States, as elsewhere, were not like a Garden of Eden, fixed in structure from the moment of inception. Recent ecological analysis reveals ecosystems subject to frequent alteration and disturbance.

The New World, just like the Old, experienced the major ecological changes, the warming and freezing of the Ice Ages, that shaped and reshaped the land. In the last 10,000 years, since the last glacial advances of the Pleistocene, the climate of the New World and the Old has shown warmer and more stable temperatures against a background of warm and cold cycles lasting between 20 and 100 years.

The broad-scale division of the land into vegetation types, woodlands in the east, grasslands in the interior and desert in the southwest, was also subject to change. The boundaries between them constantly shifted in line with climatic change and human action. Even within these broad categories there were changes. Over 5,000 years ago the hemlock in the northeast was almost wiped out by pathogenic organisms; it took over 500 years to recover. Fire, hurricanes, storms, and diseases were all active participants in the making of the landscape. But the most important participant was human.

## The First Settlers

The first settlers to the New World came not from the east but from the northwest. The land was first populated by groups of people coming over from the Eurasian landmass. In the past decades archaeological evidence from scattered sites and outright speculation has tended to push the first human migrations further into prehistory. Some suggest that migrating bands of hunters may have followed animals across the Bering Strait as early as 40,000 years ago. Genetic data, however, do not allow any link beyond 15,000 years ago. There was a land bridge between Eurasia and America from 65,000 to 13,500 BP, although it would have been quite difficult to push through the great glacial mass that squatted over much of the northern lands. About 14,000 years ago global warming caused this ice mass to recede, creating an ice-free corridor through the Yukon from Alaska into the interior of the New World. We have evidence that bands of people moved through this corridor, and within 3,000 years people had settled throughout the continent. They were hunters, foragers, and gatherers living off the land. They hunted the large Ice Age mammals, such as the musk-ox, the short-faced bear, the lionlike saber-toothed cat, the stag-moose, the gigantic woolly mammoth, the mastodon, and the great sloth. This was a slow-moving but not static society. There is evidence of technological developments in the quality and quantity of stone tools that were used, the most sophisticated appearing among the so-called Clovis hunters, named after a find in Clovis, New Mexico, who over 10,000 years ago were using specialized bifacial points, well-made scrapers and knives.[4]

The biggest change in this early history came with the domestication of plants. About 3,000 years ago squash and maize were grown, and we have found evidence of pottery technology, bows, and arrows. For the past 2,000 years a greater differentiation took place in the people–environment relationship as people began to control plant growth for agricultural purposes and intensified the hunting of animals. They needed to know the climate, topography, and botany as much as the migration routes of the animals. New forms of knowledge and environmental practices emerged as the people developed a more intimate relationship with the land. Local environments became the basis for material culture, which in turn affected the physical environment. People–environment relationships began to differ according to geographic location. A number of broad categories can be identified (see figure 1.1):

- Northwest Coast
- Woodlands
- Southwest
- Far West
- Plains

**Figure 1.1**   Culture areas of North America (Syracuse University cartography lab)

## Northwest Coast

The great shift from hunting to farming-fishing-hunting occurred between 5,000 and 6,000 years ago on the Northwest Coast, an ecosystem well-endowed with game and fish. The prodigious material base allowed an affluent life supported by plentiful salmon and rich game. A relatively dense settlement of villages composed of numbers of nuclear families grew up along the coastline and inlets. Tribes included the Chinook, Salish, and Yakima. Villages had monumental wooden sculptures: giant totem poles richly worked and exquisitely carved in cedarwood. A society emerged obsessed with caste and wealth, and ostentatious displays of wealth were ritualized. Powerful chiefs would kill slaves to show their power and wealth. The potlatch ritual involved the giving of gifts and the destruction of valuable objects. These occurrences illustrate that conspicuous displays of wealth and power in North America predated the coming of consumer capitalism.

### Woodlands

East of the Mississippi and north to the subarctic was the great forest. Three different types of societies emerged from the woodlands.

The hearth of subsequent migration and cultural diffusion was in the southeast in the Mississippi and Ohio basins. In this area farming techniques were known but not practiced to a large extent until only 1,200 years ago because game was plentiful and adequate enough to support the population. The defining feature of this region was the construction of mounds. From 2,500 years ago until AD 1600 a succession of building projects can be identified from the effigy mounds of the Adena period (2500 BP to 2000 BP) to the burial mounds of the Hopewell period (2000 BP to 1700 BP) and finally to the grand temple mounds of the Mississippian period (AD 700 to AD 1200). In this final period large towns were built with plazas, temples, and substantial populations. The town of Cahokia near St Louis, Missouri had a population estimated at almost 30,000 in AD 1300.

Along the Atlantic Seaboard were Algonquin-speaking people living in over 200 villages from the mouth of Chesapeake Bay to Cape Lookout. Agriculture had developed into a sophisticated practice. Maize, beans, squash, tobacco, potatoes and corn were cultivated in well-tended gardens in villages. The early English colonist John White described the town of Secota at the mouth of the Pamlico river as he remembered it in 1585:

> The houses are farther apart and have gardens, in which they grow tobacco. They also have groves of trees where they hunt deer, and fields where they sow corn.... They also have a large plot where they meet with neighbors to celebrate solemn feasts, and a place where they make merry when the feast is ended. These people live happily together without envy or greed. They hold their feasts at night, when they make large fires to light them and show their joy.[5]

In the northern area small settlements of hunting-fishing and farming groups were widely scattered through the region. There was a variety of Algonquin tribes, including the Abnaki, Massachusetts, and Mahican. In the twelfth and thirteenth centuries AD another group of peoples came into this region from the south. They brought with them knowledge of agriculture and grew squash, beans, and maize. They were subsequently called the Iroquois by the Europeans, but called themselves the Ho-de-na-sau-nee (People of the Longhouse). They lived in long, bark-covered dwellings housing matrilinearly related families. In the fifteenth and sixteenth centuries five tribes – the Seneca, Mohawk, Oneida, Cayuga, and Onondaga – created a federation centered in what is now upstate New York. In the eighteenth century the Tuscarora joined the league. The Iroquois became a dominant power in the region, and their power stretched west to the Mississippi and east to the Atlantic. When the British and French came to settle they had to deal with the fearsome presence and power of this federation.

### Southwest

About 2,000 years ago people in the southwest region acquired farming skills, which they added to their hunting and foraging techniques. The Mogollon peoples of southern New Mexico were the first to develop agriculture and a distinctive black-on-white pottery. In southern Arizona the Hohokam people learned to irrigate the desert. In northern New Mexico and Arizona and southern Utah and Colorado the Anasazi people went through a number of stages. The first was called Basketmaker and involved maize farming without pottery. From AD 700 to AD 1300 the Pueblo period involved dwellings of large apartment-like complexes of stone or thick adobe walls. After the 1300 climatic change Pueblo farmers left their homeland to migrate south and east. The Hopi are the contemporary descendants of the Anasazi and Pueblo farmers.

The Navajo and the Apache were later immigrants to the southwest. They came from the much more recent Athapaskan language stock and probably arrived in this region from the plains between AD 1200 and AD 1500. They were hunters and gatherers but learned agricultural techniques from the Pueblo farmers.

### Far West

In the Great Basin and California from about 5000 BC to AD 1800 people lived by hunting and foraging. Great Basin tribes, such as the Paiute, lived in family groups that led a nomadic existence and took advantage of seasonal availability of seeds, roots, small animals, and insects. In the more benign climates of coastal California tribes such as the Pomo lived in small villages and lived by hunting, fishing, and gathering. They were expert basketmakers.

### Plains

The people of the plains hunted large animals. When the Ice Age mammals disappeared they hunted bison. Later, farmers migrated up the Missouri river and occupied large fortified villages. Tribes such as the Mandan grew maize, squash, and sunflowers. The Columbian encounter had a dramatic effect on this area. The coming of the horse transformed mobility and hunting prowess. By 1800 many tribes in the northern plains, including the Cheyenne and Blackfeet, gave up farming to pursue the buffalo.

This cursory examination shows a rich variety of material cultures and a dynamic adaptation to a changing environment. Before the coming of

Europeans, the New World had been the site of successive waves of immigrant groups across the Bering Strait, the development of agriculture in the east and southwest, and the constant rise and fall of cultures, population movement, and cultural diffusion. From the decline of the great mound builders in the southeast and the mysterious disappearance of the Anasazi people to the movement northward of the Iroquois and the southern movement of the Apache and Navajo, the land had gone through constant change. The New World was not a static unchanging Eden; it was the site of constant ecological change and cultural diffusion.

This brief summary also highlights that the term Native American is a concept of aggregation; it lumps together a variety of language groups, distinct and different cultural groups, and tribal affiliations that numbered in the thousands. Although the term is heard widely and will be used at times in this book it is important to note that there is no single unitary Native-American identity. The stereotypical presentation of the horse-riding Plains Indian is only a fragment of a much more complex picture. By 1500 there were almost 2,000 separate cultures; almost 80 different language groups existed in the Pacific northwest alone.

There was a rich variety of adaptation to the many environments of North America. These environments provided the framework for material living and cultural expression, and human practices in turn shaped the environment. There is now a large body of evidence that points to the role of human action, in a variety of forms, in shaping the pre-Columbian landscape. This action took a variety of forms. Throughout the woodlands there was tree clearance for agriculture. Early European travelers noted cultivated fields for two miles around an Onondagan town in what is now upstate New York. Maize, corn, and squash all required cleared land. The use of fire in the woodlands and plains was extensive and served a variety of purposes: suppressing underwood to improve hunting and travel, eliminating weeds, creating optimal growing conditions for different species (such as the sun-tolerant berry bushes), producing pastures for deer and buffalo and driving game. Native Americans set fire to the forest and the prairie in an attempt to yield greater advantage over their environment. Human-induced fires created new landscapes. The extensive use of fires was a major factor in the maintenance of the prairies' parklike structure.[6]

Pre-Columbian America was a landscape with the imprint of human action and design. It was a landscape that was modified and changed, shaped and managed. Vegetation was cleared for farming, fire was extensively used in the woodlands and plains, villages and towns were constructed, routeways were made and maintained, mounds were excavated. Rather than "a world of barely perceptible human disturbance" the pre-Columbian world was a richly humanized landscape. Cahokia, the town of the woodlands culture, was the largest city in the United States only surpassed by Philadelphia in 1800. The great burial mound at Poverty Point in Louisiana was one of the largest human artifacts in North America until well into the nineteenth century. Even the "natural" vegetation was a response to human presence: the prairies were partly maintained by the use of fire, while even in the great forest certain vegetation types were encouraged by fire and agricultural practices. The forest was now more open than it would have been, and this encouraged fire-resistant, sun-tolerant species such as strawberries and blackberries.

Sometimes explicit, sometimes subtle, the landscape of the New World bore the design of human action.

### The Pristine Myth and the Demographic Holocaust

The first settlers modified the extent and composition of the forest, created and expanded grasslands, constructed cultivated plots, used fire extensively and studded the surface of the earth with their villages and towns. Compared to the present day, the human impact was slight. There were far fewer people with much less technological power at their disposal to transform nature. Every person could see the stars on a clear night, and the basic rhythms of life were set by the changing seasons and the rising and setting of the sun. A common contemporary misperception, however, is the myth of a great, pristine wilderness untouched by humans before the coming of the Europeans. This myth has persisted for a variety of reasons.

For many of the early European settlers the term *wilderness* was used to justify and ennoble the colonial experience. The Puritans of New England envisioned themselves as a chosen people sent forth, like the great biblical story they used as metaphor and guiding narrative, to do God's work in a wilderness. In the southwest the Spaniards saw themselves as bringing light in the form of Roman Catholicism to a barbarous people. The celebration of the coming of civilization required a place without history to give resonance to the Classical notion of light replacing dark, a new page turned, a fresh start made, and a new adventure undertaken. A pristine wilderness fulfilled this rhetorical requirement.

The twentieth-century misperception also has its roots in the nineteenth century. There were many nineteenth-century Romantics who looked at the coming of an urban-industrial order as something to grieve over. Against this spectre they posed the image of a pure wilderness undefiled until the coming of the Europeans. The painter George Catlin (1796–1872), for example, suggested in 1833 that before everything was lost the wildernesses should be

> preserved in their pristine beauty and wildness, in a magnificent park, where the world could see for ages to come, the native Indian in his classic attire... in all the wild and freshness of their nature's beauty.[7]

For Romantics like Thoreau and Emerson as well as Catlin the pristine wilderness was a powerful image to counterpoise against the urban-industrial order. Their beliefs, rhetoric, and imagery have percolated down to the present.

The early settlers came across the Bering Strait before the domestication of animals. This revolution in people–nature relations happened later, but only in the Eurasia and Africa. The people of the New World did not live beside domesticated animals and so did not develop an immunity to the many diseases transmitted by domestic animals, such as smallpox, measles, and chickenpox. In the Old World generations of people living in close proximity to their animals eventually led to genetic resistance to many of the fatal consequences of such diseases. In effect, there were two separate disease zones in the world: the eastern and western hemispheres. The Europeans brought many things to the Columbian encounter, but the most fatal was the least known at the time – their germs and diseases.

Population estimates are always hazy, especially further back in time. However, estimates of the New World total population indicate almost 54 million people. The entry of the Europeans led to a demographic holocaust. Slaughter, maltreatment and especially Old World diseases wrought havoc. By 1650 the population had fallen to 5.6 million. The figures for North America are much smaller, but the decline is just as precipitous: from 3.8 million in 1492 to 1 million in 1800. This demographic disaster had many consequences. It was a tragedy of epic proportions as entire populations succumbed to disease and death. The Europeans, less affected by the diseases, had great power in the eyes of the indigenous population, and the resulting crisis of faith within indigenous belief systems did a great deal to spread the Christian doctrine. The population decline also had an effect on the landscape. If the figures are correct then almost three out of every four in the population were wiped out. In the 200 years following contact in 1492, populations declined drastically everywhere and disappeared completely in some areas.

This demographic collapse had several environmental consequences: there was a reduction in burning, the forest recovered, fields were abandoned and the plains retreated. The human imprint was reduced. By the eighteenth and nineteenth centuries the Europeans, as they moved into the interior of the continent, saw a regenerated forest and a much-reduced Indian population. Strange as it may seem there was more "wilderness" in the 1750s than there was in 1492. What nineteenth-century observers noted, and their perspectives have been the dominant discourse of the early years, was not so much a natural wilderness but a regenerated wilderness, less a product of transparent culture than the result of a dramatic decline in the indigenous population. The images of these observers became part of the taken-for-granted view of precontact America.[8]

## The Ties That Bind

It is misleading to speak of a Native-American religion in the singular. Joseph Campbell makes a distinction between the "way of the seeded earth" of the agricultural peoples, particularly strong in the southwest, and the hunting peoples with their "way of the animal powers" and their much stronger shamanistic traditions.[9] Even this demarcation was never fixed as peoples migrated and different religious beliefs were transformed in the ferment of constant cultural contact. There were even distinct and complex traditions between and within tribes. Despite these differences, however, we can identify elements of a broad perspective on people–environment relations that were built into the fabric of belief systems.[10]

The environment provided the basis of material life and cultural expression. Artifacts came from local fauna and flora, and foods were grown or hunted locally. There was an intimate connection between environment and cultural expression that was manifested in myriad ways, from the seasonality of social rituals to the type of foods eaten and prized and to the type of clothes worn. An ecological consciousness was built into the everyday fabric and expression of social life. But the environment was more than just a provider of the material necessities and luxuries of life. Native-American cosmology was rooted in an animistic conception of the world. Demons, gods and spirits inhabited the world; the spirit world was embodied as well as reflected in the trees, the plants, the animals, the air and the sky. Spirits in the natural world provided comfort as well as irritation, a source of constant interaction, a reminder of the interconnected-ness of life. "Nature," noted Leon Shenandoah, Chief of the Onondaga, "that's our religion, our way of life."[11] The environment connected people to the great mysteries of life. Nature was the ground of being, powerful and present, an integral part of the mystic connections between the different planes of existence. One commentator stated, "The moccasin is more than something to keep the foot warm and dry: it is symbolic of that sacred relation and interaction with the plants and animals that the Navajo see as so central to 'reality.'"[12]

The bonds between people and the environment were both sacred and pro-fane, religious and secular. The human–environment relationship was inter-twined in an ethos that encompassed spiritual essence and subsistence practice. The resulting paradox of participating in the world but also exploiting it was appeased by myths and rituals. The "way of the animal powers," for example, involved a celebration of the hunted animals to atone for the guilt that the hunters felt for killing them and to reconcile the conflict between the hunter and hunted by reaffirming the spiritual ties that bound them together in the same cosmos.

The relationship to nature was not abstract but localized. Specific sites and particular trees and animals were invested with spiritual meaning. Identity was bound up with selective place not general space. Place had deep significance: it was the source of identity, a connection to the past, the present and the future. As Paula Gunn Allen noted,

> We are the land. . . . More than remembered, the earth is the mind of the people as we are the mind of the earth. The land is not really the place (separate from ourselves) where we act out the dreams of our isolated destinies. It is not a means of survival, a setting for our affairs, a resource on which we draw in order to keep our own art of functioning. It is not the ever "Other" which supplies us with a sense of "I." It is rather a part of our being, dynamic, significant, real. It is ourselves.[13]

Places were not just occupied space; they were an integral part of the stories of creation, mythic narratives, and everyday tales of the position of a people in the wider sphere of things. Place gave meaning and identity. Where you were was the same as who you were. In Cherokee the word for land, *Eloheh*, also means history, culture, and religion. As Audrey Shenandoah, Clan Mother of the Onondaga Nation expressed, "In our language we don't have a word for what everybody calls nature because our ancestors and our tradition are so involved as one with what is called nature, our environment."[14]

The great European land grab was a huge blow to Native Americans. Not only was it a loss of the basis for material life, it was also a loss of meaning, of identity. It was the loss of the central hub of their world, their place in the cosmos. Native Americans were rooted in place. The loss of land was not a loss of real estate, but the loss of cosmic significance. Contemporary Native-American land claims are not just about reclaiming property but about regaining identity, dignity, and a place of significance in the world.

Native-American environmental discourses, the dominant one being the ecological metanarrative, contained a strong sense of the connection of all things. All living things were tied in a web of communion that connected material provision and spiritual reciprocity. The practices of daily life, such as the weaving of a basket or the construction of a dwelling, as well as the more formal rituals, celebrated these connections. The shape and meaning of the interlinked world was reaffirmed and repeated in the material necessities of life as well as in the formal religious ceremonies.

The kinship between Native Americans and their wider world involved obligations and responsibilities to the environment and future generations. Native-American discourses reflected the wonder of creation but also the responsibility of human beings. Chief Oren Lyons, an Onondagan, has written of the long-term responsibility for "the seventh generation" as a guide for human action. "Respect the proper manner so that the seventh generation will have a place to live." His words encapsulate an ecological consciousness that connects the human to the natural, the present to the past.[15]

## The Invented Indian

The environmental discourses of pre-Columbian America have all but disappeared. They survive in fragments but primarily as historical reconstructions. These reconstructions, however, are not innocent. They were counterpoised to the dominant and dominating Anglo-American cultures. Native Americans have been compared and contrasted through the rival images of ignoble and noble savage. One was a block to progress, the other a contrast to all that was wrong in contemporary society.

Neither were the reconstructions unchanging. For much of the colonial period and the early life of the Republic, Native Americans were depicted as a counterpoint to progress, civilization, and the forward march of history. Indians were a footnote to the upward trajectory of a confident and buoyant civilization. In the dominant Classical view, with its belief in progress and the superiority of Western civilization, Native Americans and their culture provided a reminder of a more savage age. However, with the gnawing doubts about the superiority and long-term sustainability of Western civilization there arose the Romantic view, which framed progress and civilization as, at best, mixed blessings. An integral part of the Romantic vision was a construction of the noble savage, a gentler, kinder, and more ecologically aware and environmentally responsible Native American who contrasted favorably with a greedy, corrupt, and materialistic Anglo-American society.

The movement from a Classical to a Romantic view can be seen in the changing perspectives reported in the *National Geographic*. For over 100 years this popular journal has reported on the various peoples and cultures of the world for the US public. A survey of articles devoted to Native-American topics tells us much about changing attitudes. Articles in 1898, 1907, and 1915 shared a common view of Native Americans as primitive, the savage other who with help and education could be brought into the mainstream of society. The author of the 1898 piece noted with some surprise, "by law, they are allowed to become citizens of the United States, but they have failed to avail themselves of this privilege." There is scorn for the communal ownership of land and the inability to use the mineral resources on "native" land. The terms *primitive* and *uncivilized* littered the pages. The 1907 article described Native Americans as "primitive men, to whom ambition, time and money mean nothing." Recent articles reflect a very different attitude. The terms *primitive* and *savage* do not appear, and the Native American, once the savage, is now the ecological hero. A 1976 article noted: "He lives on the land; but he does not destroy it. This distinction supports the fundamental ethic that we call conservation today." A special issue of the *National Geographic* in 1991 was devoted to articles on America before Columbus, with the dominant themes of the cultural sophistication and environmental responsibility of precontact populations. The Native Americans had become something to celebrate and emulate rather than to pity and marginalize.[16]

Native-American practices and beliefs have been not so much described and recorded as invented and imagined. The Classicists could ignore cultural complexity and sophistication, whereas the Romantics did not discuss Indian slavery and environmental damage before the coming of the whites. Much Native-American identity is a construction of the dominating Anglo-American cultures.[17]

Native Americans have been described from the outside for specific purposes that reflect more the mood, time, and place of the commentators than an accurate portrayal. However, the mirror metaphor is inappropriate because it ignores the active participation and appropriation of cultural themes by Native Americans. Let us elaborate with reference to the myth of Mother Earth.

A number of commentators have noted the importance of Mother Earth as a major Native-American goddess. After a careful analysis Sam Gill, an academic specializing in Native-American religions, could find little evidence of a dominant

Mother Earth figure in Native-American cosmology. The myth appeared to have arisen more from nineteenth- and early twentieth-century Anglo-American commentators, such as Edward Taylor in his classic work, *Primitive Culture*, published in 1873, and repeated as fact by subsequent scholars and writers. In effect, argued Gill, there was no such figure in original belief systems; rather, it was a product of western projection, the female embodiment of America being a common conceit from the sixteenth century down to the present day. A strange thing then happened later in the nineteenth century. The Mother Earth figure began to appear in the writings and speeches of Native Americans. Educated in the ways of the whites, Native Americans began to appropriate the myth. For example, Charles A. Eastman, a Sioux born in 1858 and educated at Dartmouth College, began to use the Mother Earth myth in his book on Indian religion, *The Soul of the Indian*, published in 1911. By the 1970s Native-American writers, such as Oren Lyons, used the myth to express their attachment to the land in the words and symbols that the whites could understand, to emphasize the similarities between Anglo-American and Native-American cultures and to highlight the differences and superiority of Native-American beliefs compared to Anglo-American cultures. A product of Anglo-American perceptions had been incorporated by Native America and projected back to influence Anglo-American perceptions of Native America. Rather than a mirror metaphor we need to imagine a number of crazy mirrors bouncing distorted images back and forth.[18]

## The Ecological Indian

Nowhere is the invented Indian as strong as in debates about environmental discourses. The Classical view had Native Americans as too stupid and too backward to develop fully their land and resources. The Romantic tradition, in contrast, posed Native Americans as the ecological hero, close to the land, listening to the land, at one with the environment. In both cases the Native American is used more to evaluate the state of Anglo-America than to describe the reality of Native America. It is the Romantic conception that dominates contemporary debates about both Native Americans and environmental ethics. Environmental sensitivity has been associated with "traditional" Native-American beliefs and practices, and Native Americans have been praised and commended for their environmental awareness. The reality of Native-American beliefs and practices now seem beside the point as Native-American activists have taken on the language of ecological awareness in much the same way that the symbol of Mother Earth was appropriated. We probably cannot tell which mirror is reflecting whose image. What we can be certain about is the pivotal position of perceived Native-American beliefs as an important element in the modern environmental movement.

How can you buy or sell the sky? The land? The idea is strange to us. If we do not own the freshness of the air and the sparkle of the water, how can you buy them?

Every part of this earth is sacred to my people. Every shining pine needle, every sandy shore, every mist in the dark woods, every meadow, every humming insect. All are holy in the memory and experience of my people.[. . .]

This we know: the earth does not belong to man, man belongs to the earth. All things are connected like the blood that unites us all. Man did not weave the web of life, he is merely a strand in it. Whatever he does to the web, he does to himself.

One thing we know: Our God is also your God. The earth is precious to Him and to harm the earth is to heap contempt on its Creator.

These words are attributed to Chief Seattle in response to President Franklin Pierce's commitment to buy the land of Chief Seattle's tribe. The speech was part of an oral address given in 1854 (some have it cited it as 1855) in the chief's native language of Suquamish. It was translated at the time and subsequently written up from these notes by Henry Smith in 1887. Smith's version was amended by William Arrowsmith and then rewritten by Ted Perry as the script of a film entitled *Home*, made in 1972 by the Southern Baptist Convention. In other words the widely reproduced phrases are the product of a number of different rewrites by a variety of people with a range of purposes.[19]

As history, the speech is lost, the "original" words disappearing into the air as soon as they were spoken. We now have no idea what the chief actually said. The oral message became embodied in other, different discourses and subject to multiple reinterpretations. We hesitate to use the word original, even with the knowing, nudging quotation marks. The only words we have available to us today are the subsequent written reinterpretations. There is no *original* original.

This speech is quoted in readers, textbooks, and magazines. It is often used as an historical statement, as if the words written were the ones actually spoken. It appears as fact and is endorsed as right. It has become an often-quoted part of the discourse of environmentalism, a rallying cry, a poignant reminder, a beacon of hope, an articulation of a dream.[20]

Three themes run through the speech:

- the environment is a spiritual resource more than an economic entity,
- there is a web of connection between all things, and
- occupancy of the earth is a religious bond with responsibilities and obligations.

This speech and its themes are an important part of the contemporary environmental movement. It should not strike us as strange that a contemporary social movement calls up an imagined past. Whenever the present is troublesome and the future is uncertain the past is used as a refuge to give explanatory shelter and an emotional resting place. But there is something much richer, much deeper at work here. A nostalgia fills the modern world. A sense of loss. A grief for something that is past, over, and only available in tiny fragments, whose fleeting appearance serves to reinforce the feeling of loss. A sense of disconnection from our environment. A sense of homelessness. What the imaginative reconstruction of the ecological Indian involves is not so much a faithful record of the past but more of a contemporary grief and an intimation of a better future. The use of an idealized Native-American past is less a work of careful historical reconstruction and much more a lament for the present and a model for the future.

## FURTHER READING

Billard, J. B., ed., 1993. *The World of the American Indian*. Washington DC: National Geographic Society.

Booth, A. and H. Jacobs, 1990. "The Ties That Bind." *Environmental Ethics* 12: 27–43.

Clifton, J., ed., 1990. *The Invented Indian*. New Brunswick and London: Transaction.

Denevan, W. M. 1992. "The Pristine Myth: The Landscape of the Americas in 1492." *Annals of the Association of American Geographers* 82(3): 369–85.

Gill, S., 1987. *Mother Earth: An American Story*. Chicago and London: University of Chicago Press.

Honour, H., 1975. *The New Golden Land: European Images of America from the Discoveries to the Present Time*. New York: Random.

Vescey, C. and R. Venables, eds, 1980. *American Indian Environments: Ecological Issues in Native American History*. Syracuse, NY: Syracuse University Press.

Weatherford, J., 1991. *Native Roots. How the Indians Enriched America*. New York: Crown.

## NOTES

1  "North American Indians," *National Geographic* (July 1907): 469–84. Quote from p. 484.

2  S. Shetler, "Three Faces of Eden," in *Seeds of Change: A Quincentennial Commemoration*, H. J. Viola and C. Margolis, eds, (Washington, D.C.: Smithsonian Institution Press, 1991), 226.

3  Witness the furore over an art exhibition. In 1991 when the National Museum of American Art in Washington, DC mounted an exhibition entitled *The West as America* with a critical commentary the reaction was harsh. Critics referred to political correctness.

4  R. S. McNeish, "Early Man in the New World," *American Scientist*, 64 (1976): 31–76.

5  *A Brief and True Report of the New Found Land of Virginia*. (London, 1588).

6  For a review of the immense ecological literature, see Gordon Whitney's 1994 book *From Coastal Wilderness to Fruited Plain* (Cambridge University Press), especially chapters 1–5. For a specific example see C. M. Cowell, "Presettlement Piedmont Forests: Patterns of Composition and Disturbance in Central Georgia," *Annals of the Association of American Geographers* 85 (1) (1995): 65–83.

7  Quoted in L. C. Mitchell, *Witnesses to A Vanishing America* (Princeton, N. J.: Princeton University Press, 1981).

8  W. M. Denevan, *The Native Populations of the Americas in 1492*, 2nd edn (Madison: University of Wisconsin Press, 1992). See also his 1992 paper, "The Pristine Myth:

The Landscape of the Americas in 1492," *Annals of the Association of American Geographers* 82: 369–85.

9    Joseph Campbell, *The Historical Atlas of World Mythology* (New York: Harper and Row, 1988).

10   For a range of material see A. Booth and H. Jacobs, "The Ties That Bind," *Environmental Ethics* 12 (1990): 27–43; W. H. Capps, ed., *Seeing with a Native Eye* (New York: Harper and Row 1976); J. D. Hughes, *American Indian Ecology* (El Paso: Western Press, 1983); B. Tedlock and B. Tedlock, *Teachings from the American Earth: Indian Religion and Philosophy* (New York: Liveright, 1975); C. Vescey and R. Venables, eds, *American Indian Environments; Ecological Issues in Native American History* (Syracuse, N.Y.: Syracuse University Press, 1980).

11   Quoted in Vescey and Venables, *American Indian Environments*, 2.

12   Quoted in Capps, *Seeing with a Native Eye*, 22.

13   Paula Gunn Allen, "Iyani: It Goes This Way," in *The Remembered Earth*, Geary Hobson ed., (Albuquerque: Red Earth Press, 1979).

14   R. Nolan, *Syracuse Post-Standard*, January 15, 1990, 3.

15   Oren Lyons, "An Iroquois Perspective," in *American Indian Environments: Ecological Issues in Native American History*, C. Vescey and R. Venables eds, (Syracuse, N.Y.: Syracuse University Press, 1980), 173.

16   C. H. Fitch, "The Five Civilized Tribes and the Survey of Indian Territory," *National Geographic* (December 1989): 481–91; F. K. Lane, "From the War-Path to the Plow," *National Geographic* (January 1915): 73–87; N. S. Momaday, "A First American Views His Land," *National Geographic* (July 1976): 13–18; "North American Indians," *National Geographic* (July 1907): 469–84; "1491, America before Columbus," *National Geographic* (October 1992): 4–99.

17   A book edited by James Clifton had the provocative title of *The Invented Indian* (New Brunswick and London: Transaction Publishers, 1990). The articles in this book highlight the constructed nature of Native-American identity.

18   Sam Gill *Mother Earth: An American Story* (Chicago and London: University of Chicago Press, 1987).

19   Carolyn Merchant wrote, "Many of the words which resonate with modern ecological consciousness are not the original words, but contain phrases and flourishes designed to appeal to ecological idealism and the Christian religion." *Radical Ecology* (London: Routledge 1992): 122.

20   For just one example of the speech's use, see the very popular book Al Gore's *Earth in the Balance* (New York: Houghton Mifflin, 1992), 259.

# 2

# Colonial Encounters

In the history of North America, there was no single, colonial encounter. There was a whole series of colonial encounters involving different groups in a range of locations at different times. There was a rich variety: on one side the mix included Spanish Dominicans in search of converts, Dutch and French fur traders, indentured workers and slaves, theocratic English Puritans, Scots-Irish settlers, land-hungry farmers from many countries; on the other side was a mosaic of different Native Americans; the Iroquois Confederacy, the Apache, the farmers of the southwest and the agriculturalists of the eastern coast. From the fifteenth century to the twentieth century the various groups reacted to each other in a series of exchanges and interactions, trades and barters, accommodations and resistances, victories and defeats. These encounters produced a change in the dominant environmental discourse; a shift from an ecological to a technological metadiscourse.

## Competing Empires

Jamestown (1607), Quebec (1608), and Santa Fe (1609) were founded within the space of two years of each other, and they mark the presence of the three dominant European powers in North America. For much of the period from the fifteenth to the eighteenth century the three largest competing European empires in North America were Spain, France, and England (Britain from 1707). Their attempts at colonization, their interaction with each other, and their contact with the Native-American population did much to shape environmental practice and belief in the New World. Before examining the different geopolitics of each of these empires and the factors that kept them apart it is important to consider the beliefs that united them (see table 2.1).

**Table 2.1**   Characteristics of colonial environmental discourses

The New World had unlimited, inexhaustible resources
   ⟶ conflicts for control of those resources

Classical view of the wilderness:
   wilderness presented a physical threat to security (basic survival)
   wilderness represented moral chaos (moral resonance)
      ⟶ deforestation, settlement

Ecological Imperialism
   ⟶ replace native plants, animals with Old World species

Mercantilism
   ⟶ export resources to Europe
   ⟶ exploit labor power (Indian)

Environment commodified through exchange value
   ⟶ appropriate land as individual property

Let us consider three of these discursive elements:

- mercantilism,
- the commodification of nature and
- a classical view of wilderness.

The first, a common adherence to mercantilist doctrine, was an economic ideology claiming that the main business of the state is to stimulate national economic interests. Foreign trade was believed to be the main method of increasing national wealth. Initially the accumulation of gold and silver was thought the best way to increase national wealth. The emphasis evolved, however, toward a belief in the importance of raw materials and the export of manufactured goods. The state did everything in its power to achieve a favorable balance of trade. Mercantilists believed that the world's total wealth was fixed. As with a giant pie, any increase in one nation's slice of wealth was achieved at the expense of the others. The English merchant and director of the East India Company Thomas Munn counseled his countrymen in 1622: "We must ever observe this rule: to sell more to strangers yearly than we consume of theirs in value."[1] For mercantilists, colonies provided the best method of national wealth. Colonial holdings gave monopoly power over territories. Colonies were like branch plants of the national economy, providers of commodities and purchasers of manufactured goods. In well-protected colonies the supply of minerals and raw materials was safe from foreign control, and the colonial market was secure from foreign competition. The great expansion of European powers from the sixteenth century onward was driven by the mercantilist image of holding territory that would provide valuable commodities, offer secure markets, increase national wealth and enhance national standing. Mercantile capitalism was the driving force behind European overseas expansion and at the root of imperial rivalry in Europe and around the world.

The second shared characteristic of a European environmental discourse was a commodification of nature in the New World. The precontact societies were precapitalist. This is not to assume some kind of unchanging golden age. In chapter 1 we have shown that the image of a static, pristine Arcadia does not fit the historical reality. There was an accumulation of wealth, trade and barter, but the primary relationship to the physical environment was for subsistence rather than profit. In his discussion of commodities and commodification in his great work *Capital*, Karl Marx made a distinction between the use value and the exchange value of an item of goods. The use value meets human need and wants. Thus clothing provides warmth while housing gives shelter. The exchange value is the value of the goods in market relations. In precapitalist societies it is the use value of goods that determines human-environment relations. Beaver were hunted to provide clothing to give warmth. The beaver was honored and revered as well as hunted. But when beaver pelts became commodified, it was the exchange value rather than the use value that determined hunting practices. Social sanctions and taboos on hunting activities were replaced by market forces as primary determining elements in human–environment relations. When resources become commodities, local economies are more connected to world market systems than regional barter systems, and the nexus of the capitalist market competes with the power of local customs in shaping human action and interaction. The most important commodification during colonization involved land. The Europeans were land hungry, and they laid claim to vast tracts of land. What had been a communal resource became a private appropriation, a source of individual wealth and individual aggrandizement. European imperialism in the New World involved the privatization of land, the commodification of nature, new perceptions of nature, and created very different forms of human interaction with the physical environment from those found in the precapitalist, precontact world.

The third belief uniting the various Europeans in the New World was a Classical view of wilderness. When William Bradford stepped off the *Mayflower* onto the New England shore in 1620 he saw a "hideous and desolate wilderness, fall [sic] of wild beasts and wild men."[2] The competing empires shared this perception of the New World as wilderness. For the early Europeans in the New World the term "wilderness" did not mean unpopulated, free of people. Wilderness had a particular moral connotation. It signified a place of savagery, the locale of uncivilized people. The people of the wilderness had no legitimate right to the land in the eyes of the Europeans. The term "wilderness" was thus used to invoke the image of a land vacant of legitimate authority and hence subject to the power and authority of European monarchies and republics. This Classical view depicted the New World as a wilderness to fear and to subdue. The wilderness and especially the forests that greeted the earliest travelers in the east and south were dangerous places. Words like dreadful, gloomy, uncouth, melancholy, and beast-haunted were used as epithets for forest in a seventeenth-century

English dictionary. The danger came in a number of forms: the wild animals of the forest, the people of the forest, and the effect of wilderness itself. The term "bewilderment" captures the notion that contact with the wilderness was dangerous. For the early Europeans in the New World the wilderness was a real and palpable threat to survival. Settlements were abandoned, communities starved, people died. The wilderness became a symbol for disorder, a metaphor for evil.

The defeat of the wilderness involved basic survival, but it also had a moral resonance. The Europeans all shared the same Christian metaphor of doing God's work by creating a garden from the wilderness and an evangelical concept of bringing the true faith to the ignorant, light to the dark, of transforming the dark wilderness into the bright sun of the enlightened Christian doctrine. The people of the wilderness were in darkness, the unredeemed. The defeat of the wilderness was a process of commodification, but by creating a garden from the wild it was also an act of devotion sanctioned by interpretations of Christian doctrine. There were alternative visions. In New England the dominant themes were struck by such writers as Michael Wigglesworth, who in 1662 described New England before the coming of the Europeans as

> A waste and howling wilderness
> Where none inhabited
> But hellish fiends and brutish men.[3]

There were also the observations of Roger Williams, another New England cleric, who several years earlier in 1643 reversed the argument by making an Indian say,

> We wear no cloaths, have many Gods
> And yet our sinnes are lesse:
> You are Barbarians, Pagan Wild,
> Your land's the wilderness.[4]

The sentiments of Wigglesworth rather than of Williams dominated colonial environmental discourses. The poems of Wigglesworth were enormously popular whereas Williams was banished from Massachusetts in 1635 for doctrinal differences with the local Puritans. His banishment indicates how out of step he was with contemporary opinions and beliefs.

We can examine the major differences between the colonial powers competing for territory, trade and power in the New World by sketching very lightly the broad story of each in turn. Figure 2.1 depicts their geographical extent in 1713. Remember, however, the experience was never a singular one, the Europeans were continually interacting with the Native-American populations and each other in the struggle for control and dominance.

### The northern borders of New Spain

The Spaniards moved up from the south. North America was on the rim of their empire of New Spain centered in South and Latin America. The earliest

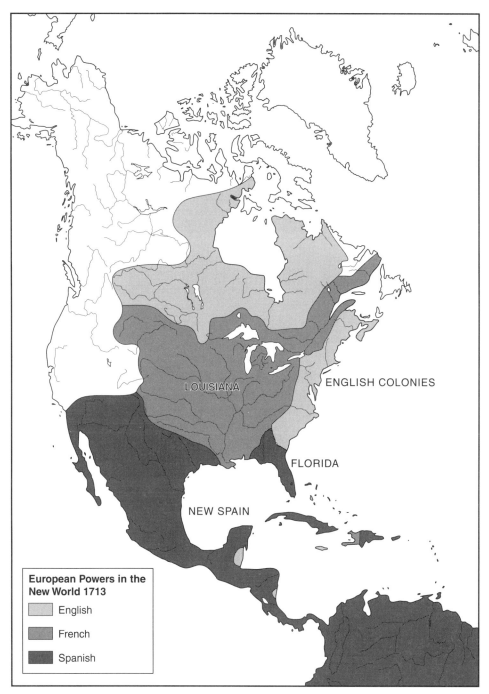

**Figure 2.1** European powers in the New World 1713 (Syracuse University cartography lab)

explorations and incursions northward were fueled by the lure of quick wealth and the need to find slaves. By the early sixteenth century deaths of the indigenous peoples in the mines and plantations of Central America and the Caribbean created a need for more sources of slave labor. The promise of huge wealth to be made from slaves, gold, and precious metals was an idea firmly held in the minds of most Spanish explorers and adventurers. As one soldier put it, Spaniards had left Europe "to serve God and his Majesty, to give light to those who were in darkness and to grow rich as all men desire to do."[5]

The first encounters involved such explorers as Ponce de Leon (1513), Alvarez de Piñeda (1519), and Pedro de Quejo (1525), who traveled from islands in the Caribbean and came to what is now Florida, the shorelines of the Gulf of Mexico and the Atlantic Seaboard. In 1521, in an act resonant of things to come, Spanish ships dropped anchor just north of present-day Charleston, South Carolina, captured some of the local inhabitants and brought them as slaves to the island of Española.

Early contact was limited to coastal regions. The interior remained terra incognita. In the spring of 1528 a party of almost 400 Spaniards, under the leadership of Pánfilo de Narváez, landed at what is now Tampa Bay, Florida with a license from the Spanish Crown to "explore, conquer and settle." The expedition proved disastrous. Narváez split up the group, and 300 men traveled along the coast and the remainder in ships sailed close by. The parties got lost from each other and never met up. The ships searched for almost a year and then returned to New Spain. The land party headed north and encountered illness and attacks from the Apalachees after the Spaniards had taken their chief as a hostage. The remaining Spaniards made five makeshift barges and sailed along the coast of the Gulf of Mexico seeking a return to New Spain. In November 1528 two of the barges were washed up after a storm near Galveston, Texas. Four of the survivors, Alvar Núñez Cabeza de Vaca, Andreas Dorantes, Alfonso de Castillo and Esteban, the slave of Dorantes, tried to return to their countrymen by moving through the interior. Cabeza de Vaca and his three companions took eight years to return to New Spain, moving west and south and passing from tribe to tribe dependent on the generosity and knowledge of the Native Americans. Posing as holy men and healers they received food, shelter, and directions from the local inhabitants. Cabeza de Vaca knew he was approaching New Spain when he came upon territory emptied of people who had fled to escape the slave-raiding parties from the south. In 1536 Spaniards seeking slaves in northwestern Sinoloa in Mexico came across Cabeza de Vaca and Esteban with an Indian retinue numbering in the hundreds. Cabeza returned to New Spain, and embellished accounts of his travels soon circulated as exaggerated rumors. The published accounts of his travels were printed in Spain in 1542 with just enough references to treasure and wealth to tantalize the adventurous and stimulate the greedy.

Later expeditions included Hernando de Soto's (1539–43) journey into the southeastern United States, Coronado's (1540–42) travels into the southwest and up into present-day Kansas and Juan Rodríguez Cabrillo's (1542–3) adventures along the California coast. When Cabrillo's party came ashore at present-day San Diego the indigenous population fled. The next day, after assuring the locals of their friendly intent and giving presents, they discovered that the local people had learned from the people of the interior, where Coronado had traveled, that "men like us were traveling about, bearded, clothed and armed... killing many Indians, and... for this reason they were afraid."[6] They had every reason to be afraid. The Spaniards were after gold, slaves, and converts. The needs or rights of the local populations were rarely given much attention or regard.

After the initial encounters the Spanish presence in North America was limited to the southwest and Florida. Neither place provided the wealth of Central and South America. The northern frontier of New Spain was a difficult enterprise facing recalcitrant natives and large-scale resistance. It was defended as a means to protect the richer territories of New Spain from English and French incursions and as a way to claim ownership of vast lands. Almost half a million Spaniards had emigrated to the New World by 1650, but there were only 1,500 in Florida and 3,000 in New Mexico. The two colonies were a drain on the Spanish Crown and relations between the locals and the Spaniards were marked by distrust, fear, and conflict.

The Spanish presence consisted of missions, presidios, and pueblos. In the seventeenth and eighteenth centuries, religious orders such as the Franciscans established, with Crown blessing, missions for the propagation of the Christian message. The missions were also economic centers, relying on Indian labor to grow maize, beans, grains, vegetables, and tobacco and raise livestock, which was sold locally and exported to New Spain. The body of the Indian proved just as important as the soul. The presidios established a military presence to quell uprisings and secure the Hispanic order. The pueblos were the civil communities involved in agriculture and trade. The indigenous societies determined which Spanish institutions would succeed or fail. Where there were settled farmers the pueblos and missions were important, but when there was resistance the presidios were the dominant institution.

At the heart of the whole system was the exploitation of Indian labor power. Agricultural production was based on the use of unpaid or, at best, very cheap Indian labor. It is not surprising that there was resistance. The history is one of continual sporadic resistance and reimposition of control. In 1680, for example, the Pueblos of New Mexico rose in revolt; missions were destroyed, priests were killed and almost 400 of the 2,500 colonists died in the fighting. The Spanish reimposed their control only to have yet another revolt break out in 1696. By the end of the eighteenth century some measure of stability had been reached due in no small part to the success of Indian resistance against the harsher elements of Spanish control and to the mutual recognition that peace could bring benefits to both Spaniards and Indians.

The last colonial enterprise of the Spaniards was in California. Between 1769 and 1823 Franciscans built 21 missions, each a day's ride apart, from San Diego in the south to San Francisco in the north. Four military presidios in San Diego,

Monterey, Santa Barbara, and San Francisco protected the missions where Indian labor was again used to grow crops and raise livestock. This was the last venture for the Spanish Crown because with Mexican independence in 1821 Spain lost its foothold in North America. On April 11, 1822 the Spanish flag above the plaza in Monterey was lowered for the last time.

The growth, extent, and shifting of boundaries of the Spanish Empire were shaped by native resistance and rivalry with other European powers. The purpose of Spanish entry into New Mexico and Florida was to defend their territory against the French and English. Entry into California was to thwart Russian and English expansion. In 1819 Spain yielded claims to Oregon and British Columbia to the United States in order to retain Texas.

The Hispanic legacy remains an important part of the character of the United States particularly in the west and southwest. The persistence of the Spanish language, the importance of Spanish mission-style architecture as well as the enduring presence of Spanish settlement patterns and water rights systems all provide a reminder, sometimes weak, often strong, of an Hispanic influence.

### The French move south

The French had been traveling to North America from the early sixteenth century. The great fisheries off the northeast coast attracted hundreds of French fishermen. Seasonal work camps along the shorelines in Labrador, the Gulf of St Lawrence, and Newfoundland were established where the cod were unloaded, gutted, and salted. Some of the fishermen traded for furs, and the fur trade became an important factor in explaining the French presence. By the middle of the seventeenth century that trade was centered in the Gulf of St Lawrence. Montreal, founded in 1642, was a major trading post. By the end of the century French commercial influence extended into the upper Midwest and by the middle of the eighteenth century extended into the interior. The two major routes of the fur trade were from the upper Midwest through the Gulf of St Lawrence and southward from the upper Midwest down the Mississippi through New Orleans. A series of forts and posts, such as Fort Detroit, were the transaction hubs between traders and trappers, French and Indian.

Before the Treaty of Utrecht was signed between France and Great Britain in 1713, French settlement was restricted to the lower St Lawrence and the Bay of Fundy (Acadia). After the treaty, Great Britain gained control of Acadia. Doubting the loyalty of the French-speaking Acadians during the 1755–8 conflicts, the British expelled them. Some of them moved to the mouth of the Mississippi, where they became known as Cajuns.

France, on the other hand, sought to reestablish a presence in North America after the treaty. In 1717 a merchant company was granted title to Louisiana to establish 6,000 settlers and 3,000 slaves. In 1718 the company founded the city of New Orleans. Large estates were granted and a plantation economy was established in which slave labor was used to grow rice, tobacco, and indigo.

Further up the Mississippi small agricultural settlements formed tiny pinpricks of French presence in the midst of vast country.

France laid claim to a vast region, with the geopolitical aim to pin the English along the coast and resist their inland encroachment. Although claim was made the French presence was small. Concentrated along the lower St Lawrence were 60,000 French, and in what is now the United States there were probably no more than 10,000 people in the continental interior and along the Mississippi. In the Seven Years' War France lost most of its territory. The French army's surrender in 1760 marked the end of extravagant claims to continental territory, but the French presence did not die. In Canada its continuity eventually led to an official bilingual society. In the United States the French imprint was less distinct but lives on in land division patterns in Green Bay, St Louis, the lower Mississippi, and in the street pattern and layout of New Orleans.

### England and Britain in North America: An Empire Won

In 1606 King James I of England (the VI of Scotland) granted patents to the London and Plymouth Companies for land on the eastern seaboard of North America. The territory between 38° and 41° North was included in both grants, but neither company was permitted to make a settlement within 100 miles of the other. Grants in 1609 and 1620 made the division between the Virginia Company of London and the Plymouth Council for New England along the 40° North line of latitude. No mention was made of the rights of the indigenous people. The main purpose of the land grants was to establish a claim against the other European powers, particularly Spain and France. Throughout the seventeenth century and even into the eighteenth century the English Crown gave grants of huge tracts of territory to the Plymouth Colony (1630), Lord Baltimore (1632), the Earl of Clarendon (1665), William Penn (1682), and James Oglethorpe (1732).

While the Crown was motivated by the mercantilist doctrine and the desire to carve out a sphere of influence to compete with its European competitors, the diversity of people involved and their varied aims and objectives meant that there was not one English colony but several, including theocratic communities in New England, experiments in religious toleration in Pennsylvania, and Oglethorpe's founding of Georgia as a fresh start for debtors. The image of the intolerant Puritans, the canny sensibilities of the Quakers and the stark contrasts of the opulence and poverty of the southern planters and their slaves, although stereotypical, help outline some of the major differences in style and character. Despite their differences the colonies were bound by their connection to the Atlantic economy. The environment was commodified along the eastern seaboard and tied to the rhythms and demands of a wider economy. In the south tobacco became an important crop, and while the stony soils of New England limited agricultural production for export, the city of Boston emerged as a significant northern trading center. In the middle colonies grain was the principal export.

The colonies were part of a wider trading system, involving the great triangular connection of slaves from Africa, rum and sugar from the West Indies, and the export and reexport of such products as rum, sugar, grain, rice, and tobacco. The very success of the colonial adventure created problems. The Crown wanted the monopoly of trade so that items such as tobacco were to be sent only to Britain, which would then reexport them to Europe. By 1750 North America accounted for one third of Britain's export trade. By the eighteenth century the colonists had become practiced in evading British trading laws. When Britain was at war with France US traders still traded with the French sugar islands in the Caribbean. In terms of trade, the interests of Britain and the American colonists were moving apart.

As the native population declined, in some cases precipitously, the immigrant population increased dramatically. From 1700 to 1750 the colonial population increased fivefold to more than 1 million. There was a land hunger, and the "empty" wilderness beyond the Appalachians cast a beckoning wave to the immigrants of the New World. To secure alliances with the Indians, in 1763 Britain proclaimed a boundary running the length of the Appalachian watershed. West of this line colonists were barred from purchasing or settling. The Royal Proclamation was observed more in the breach than in the letter of the law. The breaching of this line and the westward march became part of the myth and practice of the fledgling republic to come.

### Rivalry, Alliances, and Contact

North America, unlike Central or South America where Spain had an established hegemony, was keenly disputed amongst the European powers. The North American colonies became both setting and reason for interimperial rivalry. Settlements were established and claims made in order to head off the claims of rivals. In a pamphlet published in 1756 Benjamin Franklin proposed the settling of two western colonies in North America. He reasoned that it would ensure frontier security, stop French Canada and French Louisiana from joining up and pinning the British in the coastal region, and ensure the "great increase of Englishmen, English trade and English power."

The continent became a chessboard where move was met by countermove as each sought to maximize their position and weaken their enemies. The Spanish, for example, moved into the southwest to counter the French and English and later advanced into California in the last quarter of the eighteenth century to head off Russian and British claims.

Rivalry extended into open conflict. The French and Indian Wars of 1689–1713, 1739–54 and 1755–63 involving primarily France and England/Britain were part of the ongoing struggle for continental dominance. The treaties between the powers demarcated the respective spheres of influence. After the Treaty of Utrecht (1713) the continent was divided, as shown in figure 2.1. By 1762, Britain was at war with Spain as well as with France. Victory and defeat

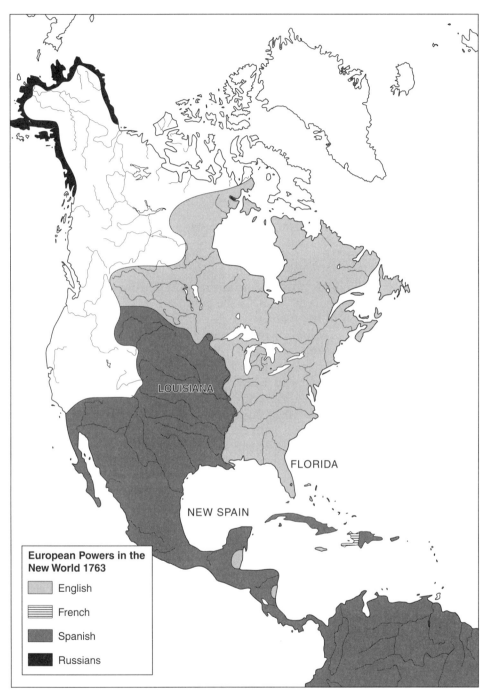

**Figure 2.2** European powers in the New World 1763 (Syracuse University cartography lab)

were reflected in the gain and loss of colonial holdings. The British victory involved the gaining of vast territories in the interior from France and the acquisition of Florida from Spain. Under the Treaty of Paris, signed in 1763, the British gained Florida from Spain and control of French territory throughout North America (figure 2.2). By 1763 Britain and Spain were the major imperial powers with vast claims to territory. The imperial cartographies divided up the territory on the map, but on the ground imperial power was more difficult to maintain and ensure.

Native Americans were an integral part of colonial rivalries. Their resistance or accommodation was a vital part of colonial strategy. In a letter to Cadwaller Colden in 1753 Benjamin Franklin argued persuasively for a better-regulated trade with the Indians because

> furnishing the Indians with goods at the cheapest rate without aiming at profit, as is done by Massachusetts; by which means I think we must vastly undersell the French, and thereby attach the Indians more firmly to the British interest.[7]

For the colonists the Indians provided access to valuable commodities, such as beaver skins, as well as powerful allies. In the pamphlet of 1756 Franklin argued for further colonization of the interior because "the gaining of the back Indian trade from the French...would of itself greatly weaken our enemies."[8] Trade with the Indians was a source of wealth while political alliances provided an important source of military might. The British and French competed for Indian allies throughout the northeast and midwest.

Native Americans were also a source of power in their own right. The powerful Iroquois, for example, saw an upsurge of their power in the colonial period and consistently blocked colonial annexation of western New York until after the War of Independence. French influence was limited in the region because the British successfully used the Iroquois as their allies; Montreal was first palisaded in the 1680s against the Iroquois, and French settlements in the lower St Lawrence always had a wary eye on the Iroquois.

But Native Americans not only resisted European colonists; they also had their own agendas. The competing colonial powers were a dangerous presence for Native Americans, but also a resource that, handled warily, could be used to defeat old enemies and strengthen existing positions. The Iroquois, for example, brokered their geopolitical position between British and French interests to extend their influence, gain better trade arrangements, and defeat their traditional enemies – the Huron, Mahican, Neutral, Erie and Susquehannock. The Europeans could also be used in common purpose against traditional enemies. In the southwest the Ute and the Pueblo shared an alliance with the Spaniards against the Apache, Navajo, and Comanche. The colonial encounter was a not a traditional chessboard with two players. We need to imagine a multidimensional chess game with numerous players. Some were more powerful than others but, just as pawn swaps can determine a chess game's outcome, the smaller, weaker players also had a role to play.

Traditional historiography treated the Indians as mere temporary obstacles eventually overcome by the more powerful Europeans. Much contemporary scholarship, however, has stressed the bravery of Indian resistance. More sophisticated analyses, however, transcend this simple division to see a complicated struggle for power, and wealth, and influence taking place all across the continent with a rich variety of peoples and diverse strategies.

In broad historical terms the European encroachment into North America took a familiar pattern of exploration, gathering of border and coastal resources, barter with local populations, plunder of commodities and valuable resources, establishment of commercial/political/religious outposts, imperial imposition of formal control, implantation of permanent settlers, and creation of imperial colonies involving a range of institutions including law, military, commerce, and religion. For Native Americans the story was one of initial contact, incorporation into an Atlantic commercial economy and European imperial rivalries. Ultimately, and notwithstanding the persistence of Native resistance, the Europeans won and the Indians lost. In their colonization of the lower Mississippi the French, for example, defeated the Natchez, who between 1729 and 1731 were dispersed, many as slaves to St Dominique. Some Native Americans survived defeat, relocation, and cultural trauma. Others disappeared. The Europeans gained control over vast territories, and the Indians lost land, power, and prestige. The loss was resisted in some places longer than others, and the loss was greater amongst some people than others, but these are finer calibrations to a more general story of victory and defeat. One side won and the other lost.

The colonial encounters can be seen as a series of processes: ecological transformation, market making, land taking, boundary setting, state forming, and self shaping. We will discuss the ecological effects in the next section of this chapter. The other processes are self-explanatory: market making involved the incorporation of barter economies into commercial economies, the dominance of exchange values over use values and the incorporation of Native Americans and settlers into a wider capitalist economy. Land taking involved the transfer of land from Native Americans to Europeans through annexation, treaty negotiations, purchase, and simple conquest. Boundary setting involved a whole range of demarcations from the delimitation of imperial spheres of influence, the geographical and cultural distinctions between wild and settled, us and them, to the measurement and division of the land into units to be sold, traded, and purchased. State forming involved the gradual imposition of centralist authority over large tracts of territory, and the move from wilderness, to frontier, to territory both embodied and reflected different forms and levels of governance. Finally, self shaping was the process whereby distinctive peoples and regions emerged from this crucible of diversity. Historical geographer Donald Meinig identified five regional societies along the Atlantic Seaboard in c.1750 with distinctive peoples, economies, and cultural landscapes: Greater New England, Hudson Valley, Greater Pennsylvania, Greater Virginia, and Greater South Carolina. The unique combination of global and regional forces produced this mosaic of distinctive societies that in some cases have survived the later processes of homogenization.

## The Environmental Impacts

The Columbian encounter is one of the most significant episodes in the environmental history of the world. The contact between the two hemispheres led to an exchange and interchange of plants and animals that changed the carrying capacity of the land, and the fundamental integrity of many ecosystems. American plants such as corn and potatoes enriched the diet of the Old World while chili peppers gave spice and pineapples sweetness. Turkeys, tomatoes, sunflowers, and peanuts were other staples of the New World. Tobacco was a gift that came with the price that all habit-forming, dangerous drugs exact. Imported from the Old World were hens, cattle, pigs, and horses as well as sugarcane and wheat. The entire world was transformed. New plants and animals raised food production to levels that sustained enormous population increases. Ecosystems were forever changed as new crops, plants and animals were introduced throughout the world.

There was also the mass transportation of peoples from Europe and Africa to North America. Over 10 million slaves were shipped from Africa to the Americas. Disease transfer came in the wake of population relocation and contact. Smallpox, measles, and typhus ravaged the populations of the New World. Epidemics reduced the overall population in the first 100 years of contact. The deaths and subsequent discouragement of the survivors were significant reasons behind the success of the European colonizers. The indigenous peoples were killed off, and those who survived were naturally dispirited by mass deaths. The vector of disease was not all one way. There is some evidence to suggest that syphilis was brought back to Europe by those who had taken part in the very first voyages of Columbus. The commander of the *Pinta*, Martín Alonso Pinzón, died soon after his arrival in Spain of what was in all likelihood syphilis. There is no record of syphilis before this time. The first recorded epidemic of the disease took place in Italy at the end of the fifteenth century and by the seventeenth century had become a common disease throughout Europe.

Environmental practices were modified by contact and incorporation into an exchange economy. Part of the French and Dutch incursions into the northeast were to gain control of the fur trade. Beaver populations numbered in the millions. Native Americans had always hunted beaver for food and fur, but the hunt was bound by rules and regulations that linked people and animal in an ecological and spiritual balance. The hunter was also the keeper of the game, bound by cosmological ties, sanctions, and taboos to keep a rough balance. Now the hunting of beaver became a trade, an economic arrangement, a way to obtain material goods. Hunting methods became more efficient with the use of snare wire and steel traps. There was increasing competition amongst the indigenous people to trap and sell beavers. The beavers were hunted in the millions and traded with the whites for knives, axes, hooks, kettles, guns, and alcohol. The overhunting was caused not simply by economic pressure but, as Calvin Martin has demonstrated, by the coming apart of all those religious constraints that had imposed some kind of order and balance to human-people relations in the traditional society.

In many Native American communities, moral sanctions against overhunting disappeared in the wake of the collapse of traditional society in the aftermath of a series of epidemics. Diseases had ruptured the fabric of the indigenous societies, and alcohol made things worse. The contact with whites had unraveled the old belief systems, and they no longer provided comfort and support in a world changing so abruptly. The old ways were under attack. The ecological metadiscourse was challenged. The new commercial order promised and provided material goods. Given incentives and shorn of sanctions Native Americans hunted down the beaver in an unrestrained slaughter.

Changes also came in land use and settlement. It would be too simplistic to make a sharp division between indigenous peoples and European settlers. Especially in the early years of colonialism, settlers and Indians shared the same space, both existed by hunting and farming and in many communities the early settlers relied upon the local populations for environmental knowledge, sustenance, and support. The Thanksgiving holiday in the United States reaffirms the importance of native goods such as corn and turkey and the comfort afforded to the Puritans by Native Americans. However, with time and the press of further immigration and colonialism came the great land transfer from indigenous to European peoples. This occurred through sale, conquest, and appropriation. It was a change from collective use to private possession, the use of the things on the land to the ownership of land itself. Land became one of the single most important commodities, bought and sold, numbered and measured, bounded and surveyed. Fields and fences replaced the open forest.

Land use practices were also changing. For the Europeans the New World presented a seemingly limitless supply of land. Whereas labor and capital was scarce, land was plentiful, and there was always more just over the horizon. The emphasis was on the of managing scarce labor and capital. Farming techniques paid less attention to careful husbandry. Overgrazing and poor cultivation techniques led to soil erosion. The pressure to produce for the wider economy, in association with limited ecological knowledge and the cheap supply of land reinforced wasteful practices. Tobacco growers in the south would exhaust the soil within four years and then move on to a new piece of land. In New England overgrazing and overcultivation of grain placed pressure on delicate ecosystems. The market demand reinforced the ecological destruction. Tobacco farmers would plant on the thin hillsides to meet the demand in Britain for tobacco, resulting in erosion of the soil, which in turn led to new hillsides being cleared and cultivated. Declining fertility in New England fields would lead to new forests being cleared, new fields being created. And so, as historian William Cronon has noted, ecological and economic imperialism reinforced each other. Farming, timber extraction, and fishing all experienced the same cycle of economic demand leading to environmental destruction. Driven by the market and with limited knowledge of local ecosystems the colonists did a great deal of damage. As early as 1705 Robert Beverley was criticizing his fellow Virginians for their "alterations" to the land that were not improvements but rather resulted in environmental damage. When they first came to the areas English colonists found the rivers alive with herring, bass, and perch. Compared to England it was a cornucopia. A number of observers wrote of "unbelievable" amounts of fish and rivers alive with fish. Even with the natural tendency to exaggerate the persistence and repetition of the claims gives some credibility to the vast numbers of fish. But by the late 1600s fish were disappearing. There were, however, some early conservation measures. The legislature of colonial Virginia, for example, enacted fish conservation measures in 1680 to preserve fish stock. The spearing and snagging of fish moving upstream was prohibited during the principal spawning season between March and November. Worried by the continued decline of fish, the legislature enacted laws from 1759 to 1772 that made it easier for fish to make their way upstream. Mill owners were required to make ten-foot openings in their mill dams, and later more clearly specified fish ladders were required. Despite the legislation the fish stocks declined. Agricultural run-off was choking the rivers, and more efficient commercial fishing downstream reduced the numbers further. Even with conservation measures the decline of the fish stock was not halted, because these measures were rarely enacted, policed, or enforced. When they were, the results were disappointing. The framers of the fish protection measures in Virginia did not know that agricultural runoff was choking the rivers.

Environmental damage was caused by many factors: lack of knowledge, the demands of the market, and a stubborn perception that the westward push was the permanent solution to problems of scarcity and environmental management. The western horizon was always beckoning the colonists. Beyond the frontier lay a land of perpetual promise and endless opportunities. The New World of European imaginings was always on the other side of the frontier.

## FURTHER READING

Billington, R. A. 1974. *Westward Expansion: A History of the American Frontier*, 4th edn. New York: Macmillan.

Boorstin, D. J. 1958. *The Americans: The Colonial Experience*. New York: Random House.

Cronon, W. 1983. *Changes in the Land: Indians, Colonists and the Ecology of New England*. New York: Hill and Wang.

Crosby, A. W., Jr. 1972. *The Columbian Exchange: Biological and Cultural Consequences of 1492*. Westport, Conn.: Greenwood.

——1986. *Ecological Imperialism: The Biological Expansion of Europe 900–1900*. Cambridge: Cambridge University Press.

Cumming, W. P., R. A. Skelton, and D. B. Quinn. 1972. *The Discovery of North America*. New York: Heritage.

Jennings, F. 1975. *The Invasion of America: Indians, Colonialism and the Cant of Conquest*. Chapel Hill: University of North Carolina Press.

Limerick, P. 1987. *The Legacy of Conquest*. New York: Norton.

Martin, C. 1978. *Keepers of The Game*. Berkeley and Los Angeles: University of California Press.

Meinig, D. W. 1986. *The Shaping of America. Volume 1: Atlantic America 1492–1800*. New Haven and London: Yale University Press.

Morgan T. 1993. *Wilderness at Dawn: The Settling of the North American Continent*. New York: Simon and Schuster.

Weber, D. 1992. *The Spanish Frontier in North America*. New Haven and London: Yale University Press.

## NOTES

1  Quoted in George Rude, *Europe in the Eighteenth Century* (London: Weidenfeld and Nicholson, 1972), 267.

2  William Bradford, *Of Plymouth Plantation 1620–1647*, ed. by S. E. Morison (New York: A. A. Knopf, 1952), 62.

3  *Proceedings of the Massachusetts Historical Society* 12 (1871): 83–4.

4  *The Complete Writings of Roger Williams*, 7 vols. (New York: Russell and Russell, 1962), 7: 364.

5  Quoted in Carlos Cipolla. *Guns, Sails and Empires* (New York: Pantheon, 1965), 132.

6  Quoted in D. J. Weber, *The Spanish Frontier in North America* (New Haven: Yale University Press, 1992), 41.

7  *The Works of Benjamin Franklin*, ed. John Bigelow, vol. 3 (New York: Putnams, 1904), 142.

8  *Works of Benjamin Franklin*, 156.

# 3

# From Colony to Empire

The Anglo-American government in the acquisition of territory, has for its object not only an extension of the limits of the country, already too great, and the preparing by this means for the dominion of the whole of the New World to which it aspires, but also that of laying up an immense fund of wealth and resources, in lands that are yet wild and uninhabited.

Luis de Onis, 1821[1]

Their one primary and predominant object is to cultivate and settle these prairies, forests and vast waste lands. The striking and peculiar characteristic of American society is, that it is not so much a democracy as a huge commercial company for the discovery, cultivation and capitalization of its enormous territory.

Emile Boutmy, 1891[2]

In much of eastern and central North America, as in other areas of the world including India and the West Indies, the imperial rivalry of the mid-eighteenth century was fought between Britain and France. The turning point was the Anglo-French War of 1755–63. The war started badly for Britain with major defeats, but by 1759 the tide was turning in Britain's favor and by the early 1760s the British had won. In the Treaty of Paris of 1763 France effectively ceased to be a presence in North America.

The very success of the British against the French in North America laid the seeds of subsequent trouble. The war was costly. And in the 1763 Treaty of Paris Britain gained control of extensive territory from France and Spain, but the maintenance of troops to ensure order throughout these vast lands was expensive. Britain looked to taxation from the colonies to cover the costs of the war and the controlling of the extended postwar territory. The colonists were not willing to pay the taxes imposed by a government over 3,000 miles away. "No taxation without representation" became a rallying cry for colonial merchants unwilling to meet Britain's bills. There was also the conflict over land. Britain wanted to hold back western movement and ensure land ownership by its Indian allies. The colonists resisted the arbitrary line drawn by Britain in 1763 along the Appalachian ridge.

Throughout the late 1760s and early 1770s resentment flourished in the colonies against British taxes and central control. The first shots were fired in 1775, the Declaration of Independence was signed in 1776, and the war dragged on for seven more years. In 1783 Britain declared an end to the war. Subsequent British expansion in North America had therefore been halted by a colonial revolution that signaled both the loss of empire and the creation of a new imperial power. However, the environmental discourses which had emerged during the colonial period remained dominant in the new Republic (see table 3.1).

**Table 3.1**    Characteristics of dominant environmental discourse in the early Republic

The New World had unlimited, inexhaustible resources
    ⟶ intensify use of environment
    the wilderness presented a physical threat to security
    the wilderness represented moral chaos
    ⟶ continue to wield the ax, settle the west, clear the forest

Expansionist/manifest destiny
    ⟶ territorial expansion westward
    ⟶ map, survey, catalog the environment
    ⟶ remove the Indian from their lands

Capitalism
    ⟶ commodify the environment
    ⟶ exploit slave labor access to resources

## The Empire Takes Shape

In the early days of the Republic, before the Treaty of 1783 the United States was restricted to a wedge of land jammed against the eastern seaboard of the continent. By 1853 the Republic had expanded to its present position of continental dominance (see figure 3.1). Through purchase, conquest, and annexation the United States extended its dominion.[3] As one historian noted,

> Conceived by the greatest imperial power of the time, colonial America debated not whether it would become an empire, but how.[4]

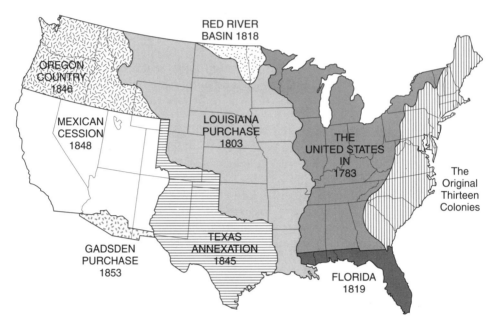

**Figure 3.1**   The Republic takes shape (Syracuse University cartography lab)

Throughout the first half of the nineteenth century the Republic extended its territorial dominance. In the peace agreement of 1783, the land from the boundary of the 13 colonies to the banks of the Mississippi, formerly British, passed over to the control of the United States. In the south, land that is now Alabama and Mississippi came under the control of the states, which ceded them to Congress; Kentucky, Tennessee, and West Virginia emerged from the Appalachian wilderness; and in the north, an area that later would become Illinois, Wisconsin, Michigan, Ohio, and Indiana also came under the control of the states, which, in order to avoid creating colonies of their own, also ceded them to Congress.

The single largest extension was the Louisiana Purchase, a huge area of territory in the center of the continent. France had ceded the territory to Spain in 1762 as a reward for being an ally against the British. In 1800 Spain had returned the territory to France. The land passed to the fledgling Republic in an agreement signed in the spring of 1803. France was eager for the land not to fall into the hands of the British. Napoleon sold the land for $15 million. The Senate approved the purchase in the fall of the same year. The 828,000 square miles of the territory more than doubled the size of the country.

In 1819 the United States purchased Florida from Spain. The final spurt of imperial expansion on the continental landmass took place in the 1840s. In the south and west land was obtained from Mexico. Texas was annexed in 1845, nine years after it had declared independence from Mexico. In 1846 Britain and the United States settled their dispute in the northwest with the Treaty of

Washington, which settled the boundary on the 49th parallel. In the war against Mexico the United States gained the rich prize of California and the New Mexico territory for $15 million. By midway through the nineteenth century the Republic had completed a massive imperial expansion that now covered the continent from the Atlantic to the Pacific, from a boundary with British Canada in the north to the Rio Grande in the south. A land area of approximately 3 million square miles had been wrested from Britain, Spain, France, Mexico and from hundreds of indigenous tribes of Native Americans.

The term *manifest destiny* first appears in the expansionist 1840s. The "destiny" was the belief that the United States had rights to a continental empire. The term first appeared in 1845 in a magazine article by John O'Sullivan. The New York journalist and lawyer advocated territorial expansion:

> Other nations have intruded themselves in a spirit of hostile interference against us, for the avowed object of thwarting our policy and hampering our power, limiting our greatness and checking the fulfillment of our manifest destiny to overspread the continent allotted by providence for the free development of our yearly multiplying millions.[5]

The phrase was picked up in the debate surrounding the expansionism of the 1840s. President James K. Polk gave substance to the claims of manifest destiny. He was a close friend of O'Sullivan and approved the annexation of Texas, endorsed the Oregon settlement with Britain, and engineered the war with Mexico to acquire California and the New Mexico territory. There were, however, limits to manifest destiny. The United States shied away from acquiring all of Mexico and resisted the fight with Britain for dominance in Canada. The belief that the United States had a special mandate for territorial expansion persisted throughout the nineteenth century, was expressed in defense of incursions into Cuba and the Philippines, and later metamorphosed into a justification for US geopolitical dominance after the Second World War.

We often assume an historic inevitability to past events; history leading up to the present in an unbroken, straight line of certainty. If things had turned out differently, a lesser United States would have seen little expansion beyond the Louisiana Purchase, a much reduced Oregon territory and an untouched west and southwest. The lesser United States represented the views of those who saw danger in too great an expansion and counseled against manifest destiny.

## The Practice of Territorial Expansion

There were a number of recurring themes that interweave themselves through the various eras and areas of territorial expansion. We will consider just two: state formation and the so-called Indian problem.

*State formation*

The transformation of territory into states was a long and complicated process. Apart from the 13 original states, Vermont, Kentucky, and Tennessee most of the other states in the Union had to go through a long period of gestation.[6] Initially there was a population requirement of 60,000 before a territory could become a state. This was not, however, a binding rule. Illinois was created in 1818 with only 46,620, and Oregon with only 48,460 was admitted to the Union in 1848. Nevada had a population of 21,140 but was made a state in 1861 because the Union needed the revenues from the gold and silver mines.

The timing of territories to become states was caught up in the issue of slavery. The balance between slave- and nonslave-owning states was a delicate compromise. The Mason-Dixon and Ohio lines marked the geographical division between free and slave states, which were admitted in turn in order to keep the balance in the Senate. Thus, Ohio (1803) was followed by Louisiana (1812), Indiana (1816) was followed by Mississippi (1817), and Illinois (1819) was admitted before Alabama (1819). By 1819 there were 11 free and slave states. The application of Missouri for statehood threatened to disrupt the status quo. The territory had reached the required 60,000 population minimum and asked for admission as a slave state, but this meant that west of the Mississippi there would be a slave state north of the Mason-Dixon line. The Missouri application aroused passions that were to plague the Republic and flare up into Civil War later in the century. The debate raged in Washington and across the country, eventually reaching a compromise. The Missouri Compromise allowed the admission of Missouri as a slave state but banned slavery in other states of the Louisiana Purchase north of latitude 36° 30', and slave and free states had to be admitted in tandem. The compromise patched some consensus across the steadily widening rift in the Republic and meant that states such as Michigan, Wisconsin, Minnesota, Nebraska, Iowa, and the Dakotas would automatically be free states on admission to the Union. Subsequent pairings were Missouri (1821) and Maine (1820), Arkansas (1836) and Michigan (1837), Iowa (1845) and Florida (1846). The legality of the Missouri Compromise was tested in 1857. Dred Scott was a slave whose army officer master took him north of the 36° 30' line and then back to Missouri where Scott then sued for his freedom on the basis that he had been a resident in a "free" area. The case came before a southern-dominated Supreme Court. In its decision in March 1857 the Court ruled that a Negro could not be a citizen of the United States; as a resident of Missouri he was bound by the laws of that state and Congress had no right to deprive citizens of their property. In other words Dred Scott's master had a constitutional right to keep slaves. The Court argued that the Missouri Compromise was thus unconstitutional. The defeat of the South in the Civil War and the proclamation of emancipation made the decision irrelevant and states were no longer admitted on the basis of slave or free. Admission of territories was still not automatic. Utah had to wait 46 years as a territory before becoming a state in 1896. The stumbling point was polygamy, which the Mormon leader and first governor of the territory of Utah, Brigham Young, had made official in 1852, but which did not fit the moral outlook of Victorian America. Punitive federal measures and protracted legal battles were unleashed against the practice. In 1890 to secure the future of their faith the Mormon hierarchy dispensed with polygamy as an act of the faithful. The public morality of residents of Utah was now more in line with the rest of the country. Utah was admitted into the Union in 1896.

New Mexico had the longest wait.[7] Obtained from Spain in 1848, it had two years under military rule and then 62 years as a territory. New Mexico was largely Hispanic and, while this racial category was seen as better than Negro in the dominant racial cosmology of the times, it was not considered ideal for statehood. Behind the arguments was a consistent, implicit, and often explicit racist fear of nonwhites becoming citizens of the Republic. The admission of New Mexico and Arizona in 1912 did not signify a defeat of the racist notions but merely reflected an acceptance of the territories as states in the Union. The admission of Arizona in February, 1912 marked the end of state making in the landmass of the contiguous states.

### The Indian problem

The territory obtained by the Republic was not a vacant land. It was inhabited and was a source of material culture and spiritual significance for the original Americans. The citizens of the Republic called them Indians; they are now more commonly known as Native Americans to distinguish them from those who came later. For the later arrivals, the Native Americans were a recurring problem because of their occupancy of the land. In a letter to Thomas Pownall in 1756 Benjamin Franklin stated the issue most clearly, "I do not believe we shall have a firm peace with the Indians till we have well drubbed them."[8]

For the British, relations with the Native Americans involved pacts and alliances as well as wars and retributions in order to secure broader geopolitical objectives against competing imperial powers on the American continent. For the Republic the Native Americans did not hold such a privileged position. Wars and retributions outweighed pacts and alliances. The new Republic and the many different tribes were less tied by the fear of common enemies and more riven by conflict over the possession and occupancy of land. The dominant perspective within the Republic saw Native Americans as an impediment to development, a barrier to progress, a problem to be solved.

The basic problem for the Republic was what to do with the Indians. Their occupancy of land was seen as a block to progress and their removal justifiable. The land utilization argument, consistently used from the first white settlements throughout the life of the Republic, was that the Indians were hindering the march of progress because their land could be more profitably used by white settlers, miners, and lumber interests. A Virginia congressman advocated the forced dispossession of the Seminole Indians, to do otherwise, he thought, would "condemn one of the beautiful and fertile tracts of the earth to perpetual sterility as the hunting ground of a few savages." Governor William Harrison of the Indiana territory summed it up:

> Is one of the fairest portions of the globe to remain in a state of nature, the haunt of a few wretched savages, when it seems destined by the Creator to give support to a large population and to be the seat of civilization, of science, and true religion?[9]

For the leaders of the Republic the question posed by Governor Harrison was rhetorical. The answer was clear and unequivocal: the Indians had to be cleared from the land. The only remaining question was how. It was taken for granted that Indians could not be allowed to take up land to pursue their traditional ways. This would be to ignore the inexorable rise of progress. Hunting-gathering tribes were easily dismissed. But even such tribes as the Cherokee, which pursued a successful policy of commercial agriculture, were seen as a threat to national sovereignty. If they remained as they were, they would be seen as a Stone Age remnant no longer welcome; if they adapted to the new commercial opportunities, they would be seen as a threat. There was no room for the Indians, no place for them in the new Republic. The official policy and practice was Indian removal.

When Jefferson purchased Louisiana, the vast lands seemed to allow Indian removal without dispossessing them entirely of land. It may not have been their ancestral homeland, but the vast plains west of the Mississippi were seen by Jefferson as "the means of tempting all our Indians on the East side of the Mississippi to remove to the West." The removal was aided by the shift in the balance of power in Indian–white relations in the first three decades of the nineteenth century. Before the great Shawnee leader Tecumseh was killed in in 1813 in battle he had tried to form an alliance of eastern Indians to resist whites and retain their land. Traveling throughout the country, his rhetoric extolled the dangers of whites and the advantages of a great alliance,

> The white men are not friends to the Indians; at first, they only asked for land sufficient for a wigwam; now, nothing will satisfy them but the whole of our hunting grounds, from the rising to the setting sun. [10]

His death in battle marked the end of the vision of a grand alliance. Between 1812 and 1830 Indian power was shattered in the east. The defeat of the Creek in the War of 1812–14 by Andrew Jackson marked a decisive turning point in control over land. The largest Indian confederation was defeated and massive land transfers resulted. A similar tale was told throughout the country. In the southeast, treaties were signed with the Cherokee and the Chickasaw that transferred huge tracts of land. In the Midwest the Miami gave up most of present-day Indiana for $55,000 and an annual payment of $25,000. Jackson's presidency was marked by an aggressive Indian policy. In 1830 the Removal Act was signed by Congress that allowed the president to move any eastern tribe west across the Mississippi. A year later the French writer Alexis de Tocqueville stood on the banks of the great river at Memphis and witnessed the act in operation as he recorded the heart-rending sight of Choctaws being moved west:

> The Indians and their families with them, and they brought in their train the wounded and the sick, with children newly born and old men upon the verge of death. They possessed neither tents nor wagons, but only their arms and some provisions.... no cry, no sob, all were silent. [11]

Indian removal was a series of forced expulsions. In 1838 16,000 Cherokees were moved west. Almost 4,000 died in what has become known as the Trail of Tears, which stretched from their original homeland to the Indian Territory of what is now Oklahoma. Over 60,000 Indians were forced westward; including such tribes as the Choctaw, Seminole, and Creek and in the north the Shawnee, Miami, Ottowa, Huron, and Delaware were removed. But removal was not without resistance. The Seminole of Florida had already been removed once. In 1816 they were pushed from the north of the state to the central area. In 1834 when they were threatened with removal yet again they resisted. The Seminole War proved costly; in seven years of guerrilla warfare the US Army lost 1,500 troops and spent almost $30 million. The war was never concluded; only in 1934 was a truce signed with a small band of descendants. The Seminole War was the Vietnam War of the 1830s; an unsuccessful campaign waged in an hostile environment with no clear sense of victory and a public very critical of the conduct of the war. The cost of the imperial mantle could be high, but the price paid by the Indians was even higher.

Indian removal cleared the way for white settlement in an ongoing process as the frontier kept moving west. The Winnebago of Wisconsin were evicted from their land first in the 1820s. But as the frontier moved toward them they were relocated again and again. In total they signed seven land turnover treaties. They were displaced finally to Crow Creek Reservation in South Dakota.

Removal was associated with resettlement. The federal government was committed in principle to purchasing the desired land from the Indians and providing land and expenses for their necessary resettlement. Indians were shunted west, but the demand for land kept building up behind them. Land allocated to them was continually encroached upon by squatters, speculators, and railroad magnates. Even the land formally designated as Indian Territory was not protected from white incursions after the gold rush of 1848 led to a scramble for lands. In one of the darker moments of US history, the federal government abandoned its treaty obligations.

The push west was relentless, but there was resistance. In 1862 the Santee Sioux rose in open rebellion in Minnesota. The struggle was so fierce that 23 counties were deserted by whites for many years to come. Control over the northern Plains Indians was a long drawn-out affair for the US Army. Red Cloud of the Oglala Sioux had harassed the US Army into a stalemate, and a treaty was signed in 1868 in which the United States abandoned its forts and the Sioux were "given" land in South Dakota, Wyoming, and Montana. The discovery of gold in the Black Hills renewed white interest. The refusal of the Sioux to sell this land was the background to one of the last major conflicts. The defeat of Custer at the battle of the Little Big Horn in May 1876 was the last great victory for the Indians. The rest of the century is a sad story of flickering resistance; the Nez Percé's epic flight toward Canada and Geronimo's sturdy resistance in the southwest. By 1871 the US Congress abolished the right of tribes to make treaties. The Indians were a defeated people. Many looked to the spiritual faith of their ancestors: the teachings of Smohalla, which encouraged a return to Indian ways, swept through the Plains; a young Paiute, named Wovoka, called for ritual dance. It was called the Ghost Dance, and it promised to bring back the buffalo, the comfort of the old ways, and the destruction of whites in an apocalyptic end. The Ghost Dance frightened many whites, and in 1890, a group of 350 Sioux were rounded up at a military camp at Wounded Knee, South Dakota. In the tense atmosphere a gun was fired and the army opened fire. Almost 300 Indians and 25 soldiers were killed, most of them in "friendly fire." Wounded Knee marked the end of the long formal resistance of Native Americans. Soon the superintendent of the census would record that, on the basis of the 1890 census, the frontier had closed. The US government had achieved hegemony over the Native peoples and the land. This victory and defeat was also embodied in environmental discourses.

### The Ecology of Territorial Expansion

The main spoils of imperial expansion into the North American continent was land. It initially came under the control of the government and was in the public domain. From 1781 to 1802 the states ceded almost 266 million acres to the public domain, most of it in the Northwest Territory, now the states of Ohio, Indiana, Illinois, Michigan, and Wisconsin. In 1803 the Louisiana Purchase added another 529 million acres. More territory came later: Florida in 1829, the Pacific northwest in 1846, the far west in 1848, all the way through to the purchase of Alaska from Russia in 1867. The federal government got great bargains. President Jefferson, although himself an unsuccessful businessman, bought the Louisiana Purchase for five cents an acre; Florida was purchased for 17 cents an acre; most of California for four and a half cents an acre. Under the Gadsden Purchase of 1853 the United States received 18 million acres from Mexico for 52 cents an acre, and Alaska was purchased for just under two cents an acre. It was the greatest bargain basement in land of all time.

Consistent with the prevailing environmental discourse, this vast public domain was measured, surveyed, and subdivided prior to sale. Land sales were seen as an important source of federal revenue, the primary vehicle for creating an agrarian democracy and the necessary means to colonize the huge territory. At the outset they were also used to pay off soldiers. More than 60 million acres of land were granted for military services prior to 1855. For example, Abraham Lincoln received a land warrant for service in the Black Hawk Indian War. Land was also given to railroad companies: over 94 million acres were set aside along the iron trails that linked the country together. Railroad companies in turn sold off the land and promoted westward expansion. The biggest single transfer, a staggering 280 million acres, was from the public domain to homesteads. In a series of acts the federal government made it easier for people to purchase land. The price and minimum lot size was steadily reduced through the first half of the nineteenth century. In 1800 the minimum purchase was 640 acres; by the Homestead Act of 1862 this had been reduced to 160 acres. In 1796 the land was priced at $2 an acre, but by the Homestead Act land was freely available. However, land transfers slowed down before all of the land was sold. The resultant legacy was that by the twentieth century the United States had one of the largest public domains of any capitalist society, almost 400 million acres. As we will see in subsequent chapters this was to provide the basis for one of the largest national park and national forest systems in the world.

These huge transfers of land involved the creation of an agricultural landscape. Grasslands and plains were now individually appropriated. Where deer and buffalo once roamed, cattle grazed and land was plowed. Farms studded the landscape, and the economy of places was tied less to immediate needs and more to the rhythms of eastern cities and world markets. The land was incorporated into a calculus of profitability, and ecological management was concerned with individual profit rather than collective subsistence.

Agriculture, according to Benjamin Franklin was, "the great Business of the Continent." The land was turned into an agrarian landscape as farmers sought to eke a living from the great bounty of nature. There were almost half a million European-stock farmers in the United States in 1800. By 1850 there were 1.5 million and almost 6 million by 1900. The number of farmers peaked in the 1930s at under 7 million. The settlers were attracted by the promise of good land: railway companies offered land and the federal government provided easy access. After the Homestead Act of 1862 4.4 million farms were created.

They were not all a success, in part because of the variability of weather across the great continent. Further west rainfall was more uncertain, and techniques learned in the wetter east were less effective. John Wesley Powell suggested that federal land policy be more sensitive to this issue and called for the creation of self-governing river basins as the best way to develop the west. Powell was defeated by the machinations of developers and politicians. There were many other critiques of American agriculture. In 1859 Baron Justus von Liebig noted that

> The American farmer despoils his field without the least attempt at method in the process. When it ceases to yield him sufficiently abundant crops, he simply quits it and, with his seeds and plants, betakes himself to a fresh field.[12]

The baron went on to castigate the American farmer for the grossest vandalism in the management of the land. It was a charge often leveled and often accurate. From early exploitation, to the Dust Bowls of the 1930s, to the heavy use of chemicals in the present era many agricultural practices have caused environmental degradation. The lack of good agricultural practices has had a major environmental impact and been the cause of extensive criticism.[13] Compared to Europe, where land was in short supply, the early extensive farming practices of the United States were often wasteful. As crop yield declined cultivators moved on to fresh land. In the nineteenth century US farmers had half of the wheat yields of their European counterparts. Soil exhaustion was a recurring problem as US farmers had neither the skills nor the means to follow the more labor-intensive practices followed in Europe. Continual cropping reduced the organic material in the soil, led to a decrease in soil fertility and accelerated soil erosion. The loss of soil was to be a recurring problem especially as western expansion pushed agriculture into more marginal lands. By the 1930s almost 50 million acres of former cropland had been exhausted. In the northeast in the past 50 years, since the high point in the number of farms, the farming frontier has receded as farms have been abandoned and poor land returned to the forest.

The ecosystem of the plains was transformed by the coming of commercial agriculture. The midlatitude grasslands were plowed out, grazed out and mown out. Prairies were converted to cropland, overgrazing led to the decline of the tall-grass prairie, and regular mowing reduced the natural hay meadows.[14] The result was an ecological transformation of major significance.

By the end of the twentieth century agriculture had declined in extent, but yields were maintained by the adoption of intensive methods. The marginal lands were abandoned while the remainder were subject to major inputs of fertilizers, pest controls, and chemical additives. While the nineteenth century had problems of extensive agriculture, the problems of a chemically intensive agriculture began to emerge in the twentieth century. The United States contains some of the world's most efficient agricultural regions. The great corn belt and the massive fruit output of Florida and California are signal achievements, but they have been achieved at a price of chemical dependency, ecological vulnerability, and long-term uncertainty.

### Clearing the forest

Another important ecological change wrought by the new Republic as it moved west and intensified land use was the clearance of the forest. Before 1850 113 million acres of forest were cleared in the east; between 1850 and 1910 another 195 million acres were cleared. Trees were chopped down for fuel, fencing, housing, implements, and the plow. Trees were cut down for maple sugar, for potash, and for the railroad ties upon which lay the iron rails that stretched across the vast land. In Ohio, on average, 100 square miles of virgin forest were cleared every year from 1820 to 1860. A similar tale can be told for the other states. After the Civil War the commercial lumber industry added to the rate of clearance. Between 1870 and 1879 almost 50 million acres of trees were cleared. The assault upon the forest was one of the largest ecological changes on the continent. The conversion of forested area to agricultural region, a total of 350 million acres, resulted in the fragmentation of the woodlands. The remaining forests were restricted to more marginal areas and species changes resulted. Edge habitat species proliferated.[15]

### Commodifying nature

The westward extension of the Republic also involved the increasing commodification of nature. In a very detailed study William Cronon looked at this process, as the market influence of Chicago cast a commercial shadow across the midwest.[16] Cronon carefully documented the way in which the grain, lumber, and meat industries transformed nature into a commodity; he used the term "second nature" to describe how local ecosystems were drawn into market relations, tall-grass prairie was transformed into cornstalk, forest became lumber, and bison were replaced by livestock.

One of the biggest changes was the virtual extinction of the buffalo. At the dawn of the nineteenth century there were approximately 25 million buffalo roaming the great plains – a source of food, materials, and cultural meaning to the Plains Indians. By the beginning of the twentieth there were only about 500. The southern herd was extinguished in 1875, and by 1885 the basic survival of the northern herd was threatened. The buffalo population was declining before the slaughter of the 1870s; drought, competition with horses for food, new diseases, and habitat destruction had all taken their toll. But the human slaughter of these animals was as immense as it was indiscriminate. The slaying of the buffalo was an important prerequisite to the settling of the plains and the introduction of domesticated animals. Cattle replaced the buffalo, ranchers pushed aside Indians and a commercial economy displaced a communal economy.

## The Culture of Territorial Expansion

There was also a cultural response to the great expansion of the Republic and the intensification of land use. The dominant response, at least throughout the nineteenth century and into the first half of the twentieth, was a celebration of the defeat of wilderness. There were many strands to this viewpoint. Most of the early settlers, arrived with a set of preconceptions, shaped in the Old World and by a Classical perspective, that saw the wilderness as a source of danger and ugliness. The wilderness, and especially the forests that covered much of eastern Northern America, were symbols of disorder. The danger of the wilderness came from the people (the savage other), from the beasts of the forest and from the effect of the wilderness in stripping away the civilized veneer that underpinned civil society. The term and idea of *bewilderment* captures the basic premise; contact with the wilderness was not uplifting but had the very real ability to turn civilized people into barbarians. It was a fear expressed throughout the early life of the Republic and became ingrained as the dominant environmental discourse. This fear is best expressed in the work of Nathaniel Hawthorne (1804–64), whose writings are full of the contrast between the civilized towns and the evil, foreboding surrounding forests. In his short story *Young Goodman Brown* the main character leaves his home one night for a walk through the forest:

> He had taken a dreary road, darkened by all the gloomiest trees of the forest, which barely stood aside to let the narrow path creep through and closed immediately behind.

When he reaches the heart of the forest, he discovers the devil's church formed from rocks and trees, where Indians and some whites worshipped. It is a chilling story that touches on recurring Puritan concerns with evil and redemption with a strong coding of the forest as a symbol and place of evil.

Well into the late eighteenth century, mountains, which we now picture in a positive aesthetic light, were portrayed as sites of ugliness, giant sores disrupting the smooth surface of the earth, a symbol of human evil distorting the perfect, smooth round, God-created world.

The fear of the wilderness was sharpened in the early years by the precarious hold that people had on the environment. In the westward expansion, there was a struggle to survive, people did die, settlements were abandoned and many did not succeed. The fear of the wilderness and the celebration of its defeat was a rational, human response to this struggle. The insecurity produced not a love of the wilderness but rather a burning desire to see it transformed into something more manageable, more controlled. Although the patrician de Tocqueville could make the following observations,

> The Americans...may be said not to perceive the mighty forests that surround them till they fall beneath the hatchet. Their eyes are fixed upon another sight.... The American people see themselves marching through wilderness, drying up marshes, diverting rivers, peopling the wilds and subduing nature. It is not just occasionally that their imagination catches a glimpse of this magnificent vision...it is always flitting through their mind.[17]

The wilderness was all the more desolate, counterpoised as it was to the myths of the New World as the Garden of Eden. Adlard Welby, writing about her visit to the Ohio Valley in 1820, captured the disappointment in her phrase, "Instead of a garden I found a wilderness."

The defeat of the wilderness had a moral resonance. The early Puritans embraced the Judeo-Christian notion of doing God's work by creating a garden from the desert as an act of moral redemption and atonement as well as a course in practical economics. This idea was reinforced by the Puritan belief of a chosen people. Adopting much of the rhetoric and environmental ideology of the biblical Jews the Puritans saw themselves as reaffirming the enduring concern with the transformation of the wilderness as a sacred act that provided sustenance and glorified God. To defeat the wilderness was an act of Christian worship that provided the means of life and revealed God's presence. The formal religious overtones were transformed into an ideology of nationalism that saw the citizens of the United States as the chosen people. (American politicians regularly ask that "God Bless America" not as a special dispensation but almost as the deity's first order of business.) In the nineteenth and much of the twentieth centuries the defeat of the wilderness embodied the creation of nation and society. Transforming the wilderness into a settled garden was to make a living, to take part in God's bounty, and to create a truly American society.

Drawing upon a variety of sources, including the brute facts of a commercial society, the Puritan notion of a chosen people doing God's work by making a garden from the wilderness and the Classical distaste for the wild, the dominant environmental discourse of the Republic, until relatively recently, saw the defeat of the wilderness as something to celebrate. The transformation of prairie into pasture, trees into lumber, locations into cities were all part of a huge undertaking that was praised, celebrated, and encouraged. The commodification of nature embodied and defined American national society.

## FURTHER READING

Brown, D. 1970. *Bury My Heart at Wounded Knee*. New York: Holt, Rineheart & Winston.

Conzen, M., ed. 1994. *The Making of the American Landscape*. London: Routledge.

Cronon, W. 1991. *Nature's Metropolis: Chicago and the Great West*. New York and London: Norton.

Limerick, P. N. 1987. *The Legacy of Conquest*. New York: Norton.

Meining, D. W. 1993. *The Shaping of America. Volume 2: Continental America 1800–1867*. New Haven: Yale University Press.

Milner, C. A., C. A. O'Connor, and M. A., Sandweiss, eds, 1994. *The Oxford History of the American West*. New York and Oxford: Oxford University Press.

Morgan, T. 1995. *A Shovel of Stars: The Making of the American West 1800 to the Present*. New York: Simon and Schuster.

Nash, R. 1982. *Wilderness and the American Mind*. New Haven: Yale University Press.

Parkman, F., Jr. 1982. *The Oregon Trail*. (Orig. pub. 1849.) New York: Viking Penguin.

Short, J. R. 1991. *Imagined Country: Society, Culture and Environment* London: Routledge.

Williams, M. 1989. *Americans and Their Forests: An Historical Geography*. Cambridge: Cambridge University Press.

## NOTES

1  Luis de Onis was a Spanish diplomat who negogiated the 1819 treaty between the United States and Spain. His memoir on his experiences was first published in Madrid in 1820 and translated into English the following year. He called the new Republic "a colossal power with huge ambition for territorial expansion and continental domination."

2 Emile Boutmy was a French political scientist who wrote on constitutional law in France, Britain, and the United States.

3 The modes of expansion identified by historical geographer D. W. Meinig include purchase (Louisiana Purchase), assertion of claims and diplomatic compromise (Oregon Territory), military conquest and annexation (East Florida and California), military protectorate and eventual annexation (West Florida), filibuster, i.e., armed independent groups seizing territory (West and East Florida), annexation by request from a foreign state or population (Hawaii), settlers and secession (Texas). D. W. Meining, *The Shaping of America*, vol. 2 (New Haven: Yale University Press, 1993), 203–9.

4 Walter LaFeber, "Foreign Policies of a New Nation," in *From Colony to Empire*, ed. W. A. Williams (New York: Wiley, 1972), 10.

5 The quote is taken from the journal *US Democratic Review* (July 1845): 6. John L. O'Sullivan was the editor of the journal.

6 There were some exceptions. Maine was ceded by Massachusetts and became a state in 1820 without having been a territory. Texas was an independent republic from 1836 to 1845 and then was annexed by the United States as a state. California became a state in 1850 without having been a territory. West Virginia seceded from Virginia during the Civil War and in 1863 was admitted directly into statehood.

7 Arizona had to wait 49 years from when it was created in 1863 from part of New Mexico, for exactly the same reasons. A bill of 1904 called for both Arizona and New Mexico to be admitted as one state. The bill passed the House but failed in the Senate.

8 *The Works of Benjamin Franklin*, 12 vols, ed. John Bigelow (New York: Putnams, 1904), 3: 142.

9 Quoted in A. K. Weinberg, *Manifest Destiny* (Baltimore: The Johns Hopkins Press, 1935), 79–80. See also William Hagan, "Justifying Dispossession of the Indian: The Land Utilization Argument," in *American Indian Environments: Ecological Issues in Native American History*, ed. C. Vescey and R. W. Venables (Syracuse, NY: Syracuse University Press, 1980), 65–80.

10 Quoted in P. Nabokov, ed., *Native-American Testimony* (New York: Penguin, 1991), 96.

11 A. de Tocqueville, *Democracy in America* (New York, 1945), 1: 352.

12 Baron J. von Liebig, *Letters on Modern Agriculture* (London: Walton and Mabberly, 1859), 179.

13 A consistent line of criticism links Baron Liebig to Rachel Carson and Donald Worster.

14 "The disappearance of a major natural unit of vegetation from the face of the earth is an event worthy of causing pain and consideration by any nation. Yet so gradually has the prairie been conquered by the breaking plow, the tractor and the over-crowded herds of man, and so intent has he been upon securing from the soil its last measure of innate fertility, that scant attention has been given to the significance of this endless grassland or the course of its destruction. The prairie provides us with a background against which we may measure the success or failure of our own land management.... It is a slowly evolved, highly complex organic entity, centuries old. It approaches the eternal. Once destroyed it can never be replaced." John Weaver, *North American Prairie* (Lincoln, Neb.: Johnsen, 1954), 325.

15 Despite the destruction of old-growth forests, nature has fought back. The forests of the United States have shown amazing powers of regeneration. After the assault of

the nineteenth century there has been a regrowth. Since 1910, over 82 million acres of land has reverted back to forest in the eastern states.

16  W. Cronon, *Nature's Metropolis: Chicago and the Great West* (New York: Norton, 1991).
17  de Tocqueville, *Democracy in America*, 2: 74.

# *4*

# No Holier Temple

Thousands of tired, nerve-shaken, over-civilized people are beginning to find out that going to the mountains is going home; that wildness is a necessity; and that the mountain parks and reservations are useful not only as fountains of timber and irrigating rivers, but as fountains of life.

John Muir, 1901[1]

Celebrating the defeat of the wilderness was the dominant environmental discourse throughout much of the early life of the Republic up to the middle of the twentieth century, when the notion of preserving the wilderness became just as, if not more, important. This shift did not come overnight and did not go unchallenged. Environmental themes and ideas that we now take for granted were developed often in a hostile environment, contested in fierce debates, and rose only slowly to the prominence they now hold. In this chapter we consider the historical roots of this shift and the emergence of the conservation and preservation movements.

## Regret and Nostalgia

William Cooper made a success on the frontier of New York. In the 1780s and 1790s, as Iroquois land was taken over by the Republic, Cooper acted as an agent for settlers and investors. At one time he owned 750,000 acres. Cooper became a congressman and judge, built an impressive manor house and founded a town that was named after him at the edge of Otsego Lake. Cooperstown is perhaps best known by most Americans now as the home of baseball's Hall of

Fame. Cooper, as was the fashion of the time, had a large family. The twelfth of his 13 children, James Fenimore Cooper (1789–1851), became a writer and one of the earliest American writers to achieve international prominence. Cooper is best known for his Leatherstocking tales. In *The Pioneers* (1823) he introduces the frontier hero Natty Bumppo. Living on the edge of wilderness and civilization Bumppo is the first western hero: honorable, close to nature, and sympathetic to the Indians. He embodies the ambiguity involved in the loss of wilderness. While aiding white settlement Bumppo regrets the loss of the wild. In the other books in the series, *The Last of The Mohicans* (1826), *The Prairie* (1827), *The Pathfinder* (1840), *The Deerslayer* (1841), the Indians are portrayed as noble people and the coming of the frontier as something to regret. Here we see Cooper's political agenda. Uncomfortable with the democratic spirit of the age, the mass of new settlers disturbed his elitist and patrician tendencies. His books were widely read throughout North America and Europe, where, in an ironic twist of fate, they acted as recruiting agents for continued emigration to the United States.

Cooper's novels embody the regret at the passing of the wild. For some the process of empire building, nation-making and environmental transformation was underpinned by a sense of loss, a nagging feeling that something important was being destroyed. This grief was best expressed in transcendental philosophy, Romantic art, and a growing environmental awareness. Let us examine each of these.

### Fountains of Life

Ralph Waldo Emerson (1803–82) was a pivotal figure in the movement know as transcendentalism, which flourished in New England in the 1840s. In some ways it is the philosophical equivalent of Romantic art; it stressed intuition, mind, nature, and self-expression. A combination of Yankee individualism and self-reliance, the movement was more a collection of individuals than an organized program. In his essay "Nature" (1836) Emerson noted,

> If the stars should appear one night in a thousand years, how would men believe and adore; and preserve for many generations the remembrance of the city of God which had been shown! But every night come out these envoys of beauty, and light the universe with their admonishing smile.

Emerson's writings are suffused with a belief that God is revealed in nature and that contact with the rhythms of nature allows us an entry into our truer, better selves. Emerson also became involved in some of the political debates of the time. He wrote to President van Buren in 1839 to protest against the confiscation of Cherokee land, and he spoke out against slavery and for women's rights. While the environmental theme was more implicit than explicit, Emerson is an early example of a nature-sensitive individual. He was a poet, philosopher, and writer whose concern with nature was the backdrop to his other interests. But his writings are a counterpoint to the growing materialism and conformity of US society. Emerson is an early proponent a strain of American individualism, a nature-sensitive, socially concerned individualism that sees in contact with nature a way to know our higher self.

Henry David Thoreau (1817–62) was deeply influenced by Emerson's *Nature*. On July 4, 1845 he moved to a cabin beside Walden Pond just outside Concord, Massachusetts, where he lived for two years. His account of his sojourn was published as *Walden* in 1854 and has since become an American classic. It is a deeply pantheistic reading of the land that everywhere bears the print of God's presence. A profound love of nature and an enduring skepticism runs through this most beautiful of nature accounts in American literature. "Observe the hours of the universe, not of the railroad cars," he told his readers. Thoreau was a social critic as well as a nature watcher. As a protest against the Mexican war he refused to pay his taxes and was jailed for a night. In 1849 he wrote *On The Duty of Civil Disobedience*, which influenced the war resistance movement of the 1960s.

For Thoreau, wildness was the preservation of the world. "Hope and future," he wrote in his 1851 essay "Walking," "for me are not in lawns and cultivated fields, not in towns and cities, but in the impervious and quaking swamps . . . Give me the ocean, desert or the wilderness."

Both Emerson and Thoreau railed against the materialism of their time. They saw a tragic loss in the defeat of the wilderness. Nature was a reflection of spiritual truth, an embodiment of the moral, the good and the sacred. To drain the quaking swamps was to lose a vital element in our relationship to nature and ultimately it meant a loss to ourselves.

The message of Emerson and Thoreau was not widely heeded at the time. Their writings soon fell out of fashion; indeed Thoreau was never really in fashion in his lifetime. Emerson was revived in the 1920s, whereas Thoreau's uncompromising stance against convention and authority found a more welcome audience in the 1960s. Both writers have exercised a considerable influence on US social thought, and today they are seen as authentic voices that outlined and intimated the philosophical basis of the environmental movement and influenced such varied activists as David Brower, Dave Foreman, and many contemporary US nature writers. Emerson and Thoreau articulated ideas for an alternative environmental discourse.

## Constructing Nature

The North American landscape was, by the nineteenth century, being represented in the Romantic tradition. The Romantic landscape genre first emerged in the work of Thomas Cole (1801–48). He was born in Lancashire in England and arrived in the United States as a young man. In 1825 he traveled up the Hudson and contemplated what he later noted as the "perfect beauty." His canvasses depict the physical environment as spectacular, full of grandeur. The landscape was God's handiwork, and the goal of the artist was to reveal the architecture of the Deity. Cole painted scenes from the frontier of his day: upstate New York and western New York, and one of his paintings, *Genesee Scenery* (1847), depicts an area only about 100 miles west of Cooperstown. Cole's pupils, such as Frederick Edwin Church (1826–1900), extended Romantic depictions; in 1857 Church completed his massive *Niagara Falls*, one of the first depictions emphasizing the awe rather than the fear in the great natural feature.

In 1832 George Catlin (1796–1872) set out for the headwaters of the Missouri River. Only a few days before he arrived at Fort Pierre in South Dakota in May he was told and later recounted in his memoirs[2] that an immense herd of buffalo had passed along the river. There were so many of them that they blackened the plains. A party of 500 Sioux Indians rode across the river at noon one day and by the end of the day rode back to the fort with 1,400 buffalo tongues, which they exchanged for a few gallons of whiskey. Catlin was appalled at what he called "this profligate waste." This sense of waste at the loss of the wilderness was the main motivation in Catlin's artistic work.

Catlin was an easterner; he practiced law in Pennsylvania and became a portrait painter depicting the wealthy of Philadelphia and Washington. One day Catlin saw a delegation of Native Americans passing through Philadelphia on their way to Washington. He was electrified by the sight and fascinated by their appearance and the thought that they could be vanishing from the scene. He resolved "by the aid of my brush and my pen, to rescue from oblivion so much of their primitive looks and customs as the industry and ardent enthusiasm of one lifetime could accomplish." Traveling up the Missouri river to Fort Union at the mouth of the Yellowstone river and then back down the river, Catlin painted 135 pictures, including portraits, domestic scenes, landscapes, and hunting scenes. Catlin continued to travel and paint. By 1838 he had painted some 600 portraits of Native Americans. These were shown in the major cities of the east as well as London and Paris. Most of the paintings are now in the Smithsonian.

Catlin was not a great painter. His figures are crudely drawn, but what he lacked in skill he made up in energy. He painted as much as he could and despite the lack of artistic merit, the paintings and drawings provide us with a glimpse of vanished and vanishing culture. Catlin was sensitive to the broad sweep of historical change. He was well aware, decades before most other commentators, that the buffalo would be made extinct and that the Indians would be pressed to extinction. The "melancholy contemplation" of this prospect made him propose the creation of a national park covering the grasslands from Mexico to Lake Winnipeg. This "splendid contemplation" was to be a nation's park protected by the government where Indian, elk, and buffalo could remain in their pristine condition. Catlin not only celebrated the disappearing wilderness, but he also proposed a solution to its demise. The park idea could not resist the forward momentum of westward expansionism, but it was reinvented decades later. In Catlin we have a Romantic artist and an early preservationist.

The west was a rich area for artists. Karl Bodmer (1809–93) traveled in the same areas that Catlin did, painting portraits and depicting battles and encounters between whites and Native Americans. But the grandeur of the west was captured by the Romantic artists; among a large number the most influential were Thomas Moran and Albert Bierstadt.

Thomas Moran (1837–1926) was another Englishman, like Cole born in Lancashire, whose canvasses depict the American landscape. Moran also painted on a huge scale, and his goal was to tell the story of nature. Concerned more with a general impression, Moran thought realism was a prison to the imagination, but he took care over the details of his pictures, often consulting scientists to get the geology and flora correct. Moran painted the spectacular west of the Rockies. He accompanied Ferdinand Hayden's expedition into the Yellowstone in the summer of 1871. His most famous painting, The *Grand Canyon of The Yellowstone* (1872), was based on this trip. This painting and others by Moran, as well as the photographs by W. H. Jackson, were submitted as evidence at the congressional hearings that subsequently led to the declaration of Yellowstone as the nation's first national park. In 1873 Moran joined John Wesley Powell's expedition in the Grand Canyon. He painted watercolors and drew sketches, some of which provided the basis for another grand Romantic painting, *The Chasm of the Colorado* (1873–4) This painting, like the *Grand Canyon*, was purchased by the US government. Moran's huge canvasses were increasingly seen as the official national landscape.

The Romantic representation of American nature drew upon a European tradition, notably a German tradition clearly shown in the work of the great German Romantic artist Caspar David Friedrich (1774–1840). The German influence was at times direct. Albert Bierstadt (1830–1902) was born in Solingen, Germany, but his family moved to Massachusetts. By the early 1850s Bierstadt had his own studio and over the next 20 years established a reputation as the premier painter of the American west. Beginning in 1859, Bierstadt made three trips out west, sometimes accompanying scientific trips, other times accompanied by fellow artists and photographers. He made sketches, drawings, and woodcuts and painted huge canvasses. His paintings of the Rocky Mountains sold well – very well. Bierstadt had become a celebrity artist whose paintings were eagerly sought by the economic elite. As with all successful artists, especially very successful artists, his work was criticized. The grand design did not work for everyone. "We fear," one critic noted, "Mr. Bierstadt has undertaken a subject much beyond his powers. To suggest God's nature on canvas requires a depth of feeling which few artists can bestow... his cold brilliant talent produces work which may impose upon the senses, but does not affect the heart."[3]

By the late 1870s Bierstadt's popularity was waning. The reviews were more negative, and the prices for his paintings began to fall. He had, however, one last great hurrah. In 1886 William Hornaday, chief taxidermist for the Smithsonian Institute, reported that he had found it difficult to find a suitable buffalo specimen. There were few surviving buffalo, and Hornaday went on to decry the wanton destruction of the once-numerous animal. The report was picked up by the popular press and received wide attention. In 1888 Bierstadt completed his massive canvass *The Last of the Buffaloes*. It was submitted for an art exhibit in Paris but was rejected because it was considered too big and not representative enough of contemporary American art. The rejection set off another public debate in the United States. Issues of national pride, the definition of national art and the fate of the buffalo were combined in a media debate, one upshot of which was growing public concern about the fate of the animal. Soon after, the government undertook the first official buffalo census.

The Romantic artists from Cole to Moran and Bierstadt had an enormous influence on the perception of the wilderness. They depicted on huge canvasses the grandeur of pristine nature. In their vision wilderness was not something to be defeated but something to be celebrated. In wilderness was the manifestation of God, the direct opposite to crass materialism and social conformity. Their work shifted the perception of a national landscape. Settled farms and a prostrate nature were no longer the aesthetic zenith. The beautiful were the crags and chasms, grand vistas where human presence was absent, the grand mountains and awesome valleys bereft of human presence.

In Europe the Romantic landscape tradition influenced aesthetic perception. In the United States the tradition also shifted national sentiments. The Romantic artists represented the wild west to the eastern establishment; they gave shape and substance and form to the interior that few had seen. The more remote parts of the United States were depicted primarily in Romantic genres, partly a function of the time they were represented, and this dominant depiction continues to influence popular representations. The real west is often the deserted west, the west of natural grandeur rather than of human presence. From the films of John Ford to the Marlboro ads, the quintessential American landscape has remained the landscape first painted by the Romantics. The wilderness became, in the hands of these artists, the uniquely American landscape. While Europe had ancient cities and medieval cathedrals, the United States had Yellowstone and Yosemite. The very size and grandeur of the American west was distinctive and unique. The increasingly dominant artistic depiction of the US landscape by the nineteenth century – as pristine wilderness – had real effects; from the use of Moran's paintings to convince Congress, to Bierstadt's painting influencing public concern with the buffalo. The Romantics not only depicted the wilderness, they helped to create it.

## Managing Nature: Conservation and Preservation

As economic and population growth continued throughout the nineteenth century there was a backlash. We have already looked at the literary and artistic responses. There was also an explicit environmental awareness, which had two main themes: the preservation of the wild and the conservation of resources.

If the resource conservationists were concerned with the efficient and rational use of the nation's resources, the nature preservationists were concerned with the protection of the nation's wilderness. The most important and lasting achievement of the preservationists was and is the national park system of the United States. The intellectual roots of the preservationists were Romanticism and transcendentalism. The background to the growth of the preservation movement was the rapid economic growth in nineteenth-century United States. More virgin prairie was being brought under the plow, more forests were being chopped down. Many Americans were beginning to value the spiritual quality and beauty of the wilderness just as it was being threatened and destroyed.

### Preservation and the national park movement

On March 1, 1872 President Ulysses S. Grant signed into law the Yellowstone Park Act, thereby sanctioning the creation of the first national park over almost 3,000 square miles in Wyoming. The legislation did not come out of the blue. A major precedent had been set earlier in California. On June 30, 1864 Abraham Lincoln had signed the Yosemite Park Act in the midst of Civil War conflicts. This act covered an area of only 44 square miles. An area covering the Yosemite Valley and the redwoods of Mariposa Grove were turned over to the state with clear use guidelines as public space, resort, and recreation "for all time." The valley had powerful advocates: Horace Greeley, owner and editor of the *New York Tribune* (circulation 300,000) had described the area to his readers as unique and majestic; Bierstadt had painted *The Rocky Mountains* (1863) and *Valley of the Yosemite* (1864); the photographer Carleton E. Watkins had photographed the valley a number of times since 1861. The valley had been represented back east as a beautiful place, a sacred space worthy of saving. The preservationists gained victory with the passage of the Yosemite Park Act and set a powerful precedent for the Yellowstone Park Act.

Like Yosemite, Yellowstone had been represented as a wilderness area in the exploration, aesthetic, and scientific discourses. In 1869 Charles Cook, David Folsom and William Peterson had tramped through the area and reported on the natural scenic wonders. In 1870 another expedition headed by Henry Dana Washburn traveled into the area now designated as national park. It was not so much the act of exploration that created public opinion as the consequent publicity. Articles, lectures and books about the region, written by the expedition's leaders and members were avidly consumed by an eastern elite eager to see an American wilderness west of the Mississippi, a sacred space where national identity could be embodied and honored. In 1871 another expedition set off, approved and funded by Congress and led by Ferdinand Hayden. In his party were the photographer W. H. Jackson and the painter Thomas Moran, whose painting of the Yellowstone was purchased by Congress in 1872. Many of the paintings, photographs, drawings and watercolors were reproduced and distributed to a wider audience and became an important background to the passage of the Yellowstone Park Act as much as the expert scientific advice given by Hayden did. Watercolors, paintings, and drawings were displayed in the Capitol as the legislation was being debated.

The Yellowstone Park Act marked the beginning of the federal system of national parks. In the early years the emphasis was more on scenic monument-alism rather than ecological preservation. Ecology had not yet emerged as a legitimate discourse for policy making. It was easier to persuade Congress to set aside areas of rugged beauty and natural grandeur than places of ecological significance. Wilderness was defined more with reference to grand landscapes than biological purity. The earliest parks were sites of scenic wonder, sites were selected on their visual impact. Scenic nationalism was more important than environmental preservation. Yellowstone was followed by Mount Rainier in 1889, Yosemite, Sequoia, and General Grant in 1890, Crater Lake in 1902, Mesa Verde in 1906 and Glacier National Park in 1910.

The designation of the earliest parks still had to fight against the prevailing discourse which stressed the logic of economic growth. Many political advocates of the latter used the argument of "worthless lands." It was easier to get the legislation passed if the lands were perceived as unusable for farming or lumbering. Many of the earliest parks designated were unsuitable for farming and above the timberline, a line of reasoning that did not explain the Yosemite, Sequoia, and General Grant parks, which had valuable timber stands. But it was always easier for congressional supporters to describe the parklands as places not so much taken out from "productive use" as being "unsuitable for productive use."

The preservation of parks was an evolving issue. Tourism was encouraged and not only by the business interests. To increase accessibility even the most stout defender of the pristine wilderness, such as John Muir, advocated building roads. Cars and trains were initially encouraged because the increased traffic would generate much needed income as well as allow people to see natural wonders. Accessibility was not an issue in the early years when the number of visitors remained few. Many of the parks were so far away from centers of population that only the wealthiest could afford the time and money to travel to them. As the twentieth century progressed, however, more people were able to venture into national parks and the issue of increased accessibility raised problems of preservation. How to combine public access with nature preservation was to become one of the biggest issues revolving around national parks in the second half of the twentieth century. And beyond.

### John Muir

An important figure in the US environmental movement was John Muir (1838–1914), who was born on April 21 in Dunbar, Scotland. He had a strict child-hood; his father, Daniel was a disciplinarian who believed that the only good book was the Bible. In 1849 the Muir family set sail for America, ending up on the Wisconsin frontier and a life of hard labor. On the family farm, Muir took some comfort in the surrounding wilderness and the few books he could get his hands on. Despite his lack of formal training, John Muir was a creative indi-vidual, inventing body temperature measurement devices, self-setting windmills and an automatic horse-feeder. He also went to the University of Wisconsin, where he studied natural sciences.

In 1867, after studying plants in Canada and working in factories in Indiana, he undertook a 1,000–mile hike to the Gulf of Mexico. He wrote about and made sketches of his travels. This event marked his future life path as a traveler, nature observer, and writer. He left the University of Wisconsin, he later remarked, for the University of the Wilderness.

In 1868, after arriving in San Francisco, he traveled through California and settled in the Yosemite Valley, the first area in the country preserved for future generations and a precedent for the national park system. In Yosemite Muir acted as guide to the numerous visitors. He personally invited Ralph Waldo Emerson to visit with him; he later noted that this was one of the high points of his life. Muir learned about transcendentalism not only from books. He hiked in the High Sierra; his observations of glaciers were subsequently published as an article in the *New York Tribune* in 1871. Muir continued to journey into the mountains and to write about his travels. He also began to publicize the need to protect the Sierra and published articles in *Harper's Monthly* and *Scribner's Monthly*, which reached a wide and influential readership. Muir was developing a case and a pressure group for setting aside areas of pristine beauty.

Muir had a deep, almost religious, connection with wilderness. For him, the wild areas were a necessity, a place where people could find spiritual refreshment and emotional rest. He spoke about a divine presence in the wild and described the great forests as God's temples. He propagated this message in lectures and a stream of articles and books that influenced an educated elite throughout the United States. Muir condensed the strong Romantic and nationalist impulses into a clearly defined goal of preserving grand landscapes and rugged scenery.

Protection of the Yosemite was a major preoccupation. The valley, under the control of the state Board of Commissioners, which was under the control of the Southern Pacific Railroad, was under threat from farming and lumbering. After intense lobbying by Muir and others (Muir wrote articles as well as letters) the valley was designated as a national park by Congress in 1890. In 1892 in San Francisco, 26 people, concerned at the lack of protection for land in the Sierra Mountains, gathered to found the Sierra Club "to explore, enjoy and render accessible the mountain regions of the Pacific Coast and to enlist the support of the people of the Sierra Nevada Mountains". As a wilderness preservationist with a powerful pen, a clear message and a consummate ability as a political lobbyist, Muir was the unanimous choice as the club's first president.

Muir became a major figure and the principal spokesman for the preservation of the wilderness. In 1903 President Roosevelt asked him to be his guide in a four-day trip in Yosemite. The two camped out and clearly enjoyed each other's company. Soon Roosevelt was also describing the giant sequoias as temples, and in the coming years he fought to triple the size of the national forest and double the number of national parks.

There were setbacks, the largest being Hetch Hetchy. This valley was the site of a struggle between the political leaders of San Francisco who wanted to flood the valley as a reservoir for the rapidly expanding city and the preservationists. Beginning in 1901 the fight continued until 1913 when President Wilson signed the bill authorizing the flooding of the valley. Muir was distressed by the outcome and in an outburst that condenses the core of his beliefs declared:

> These temple destroyers, devotees of raging commercialism, seem to have perfect contempt for Nature, and instead of lifting their eyes to the God of the Mountains, lift them to the Almighty Dollar. Dam Hetch Hetchy! As well dam for watertanks the people's cathedrals and churches, for no holier temple has ever been consecrated by the heart of man.[4]

Muir died in 1914. His last major battle had seemingly ended in defeat. But for someone who has left such an important legacy it is fitting that we see that even this defeat had its bright consequences. Muir and others had rallied support for saving the valley and mobilized public opinion. The controversy helped in the 1915 appointment of Stephen Mather to the directorship of the national parks and in the passage of the 1916 National Park Service Act, which created the park service as we know it today.

> The extent and vigor of the resistance to San Francisco's plans for Hetch Hetchy constituted tangible evidence for the existence of a wilderness cult. Equally revealing was the fact that very few favored the dam *because* they opposed wilderness. Even the partisans of San Francisco phrased the issue as not between a good (civilization) and an evil (wilderness) but between two goods. While placing material needs first, they still proclaimed their love of unspoiled nature. Previously most Americans had not felt compelled to rationalize the conquest of the wild country in this manner. For three centuries they had chosen civilization without any hesitation. By 1913 they were no longer so sure.[5]

John Muir, the archdruid of this wilderness cult, was a major reason behind this growing uncertainty. By the first decades of the twentieth century, new attitudes to wilderness, a romantic sensibility, had reshaped the dominant discourse in a profound and enduring way.

### "The New Policy Conservation"

The resource conservationists were guided by the rationalist impulse of science; they were the heirs of the Enlightenment; they had a belief that the environment was susceptible to analysis and understanding and ultimately to human management that could ensure long-term sustainability. Although they did not use the phrase they were some of the first proponents of sustainable development, the idea that economic development and sound ecological principles could be combined for "wise use of the land." They placed emphasis on the efficient utilization of resources, especially of the huge public lands with their vast natural wealth of soil, forests, and water. They advocated a thoughtful, wise use of the earth.

The resource conservation movement was intimately connected with the formal establishment of a scientific discourse in US public life. The establishment of land grant colleges gave an institutional basis for the development of a scientific approach to resource use. Departments of agriculture, forestry, husbandry, economics, botany, and geology all emerged and gave an institutional space for scientific discourse. Many of these colleges became the sites for an improved knowledge of the physical environment. The resource conservationists were also connected to the formal establishment of scientific societies, and government bureaucracies. The Department of Agriculture was established in 1837 and the Division of Forestry in 1875. By the end of the nineteenth century there was a flourishing scientific discourse in universities, scientific societies, and government bureaucracies that was advocating a wiser use of resources. These sites drew upon the work of many people. Let us consider two of the most important figures: George Perkins Marsh and Gifford Pinchot.

George Perkins Marsh (1801–82) was born in Woodstock, Vermont into an affluent family. He entered Dartmouth when he was 15 and graduated in 1820 with an education restricted to the classics and the Bible. He became a lawyer and dabbled in various business ventures, including sheep rearing, marble quarrying, and real estate speculation. His life seemed full but never completely connected as he drifted in to and out of various schemes and political campaigns. In 1840 he was elected to Congress on a Whig platform. In 1849 Marsh was appointed ambassador to Turkey. Although not a major appointment and with little money to cut an elegant figure, he spent his time satisfying his natural curiosity. Marsh collected data on a range of natural phenomena, including stream flow, temperature, rainfall, etc. He returned to Washington, DC in 1854 to retry his hand at various schemes. In 1857 he submitted a report to the Vermont legislature that explained the decline of fish in relation to abuse of the land, cutting of trees and overgrazing of the soil.

In 1860 he was appointed ambassador to Italy by President Lincoln and remained in Italy until his death in 1882. There he began and completed his masterwork, *Man and Nature*, first published in 1864, which argued that human impact on the environment could have deleterious effects.[6] This was a radical thought relative to the dominant Classical tradition, which saw human action as essential to the creation of a more civilized state and invariably beneficial. Drawing upon his experiences in Vermont, Turkey, and the Mediterranean world Marsh wrote of the destructiveness of human impact. In *Man and Nature* he drew attention to the unforeseen consequences of human action; floods and landslides, for example, were the direct result of overgrazing. Marsh emphasized the food chain, the importance of forests to soil conservation and the need for sound ecological principles. These are now such taken-for-granted notions that we often forget they had to be developed and presented. Marsh combined a moral concern with arguments about utility and self-preservation. His book is an indictment of unsound practices, the costs of unrestrained growth, and the lack of attention to ecological principles.

Over 1,000 copies of *Man and Nature* were sold. One reviewer in the *Nation* called it "one of the most useful and suggestive books ever published." In the revised version, *The Earth as Modified by Human Action* (1874) Marsh also advocated that

> some large and easily accessible region of American soil should remain as far as possible in its primitive condition, at once a museum for the instruction of students, a garden for the recreation of the lovers of nature, and an asylum where indigenous trees, plants, beasts may dwell and perpetuate their kind.

Marsh's book went through many printings in the last quarter of the nineteenth century and the first decades of the twentieth. Written in an accessible style its careful argument was wrapped in a simple thesis: people modified the earth and the consequences could be disastrous. Marsh gave both a scientific rationality and a moral consideration to human–environment relationships.

George Perkins Marsh was a major influence on the American conservation movement. His ideas, now seemingly so commonplace, are the very core of current popular perceptions of the world. This is his enduring legacy.

Gifford Pinchot (1865–1946) referred to *Man and Nature* as epoch-making. Although born a year after the book was first published, it left a deep and lasting impression. Pinchot, born into the eastern establishment and educated at private schools, traveled widely in Europe. His father, James Pinchot, encouraged the young Pinchot's interest in forestry and urged him to be a professional forester. He entered Yale in 1885, where there was no course in forestry, and unable to find professional schools in the United States, Gifford Pinchot left for Europe in 1895. He studied in Germany and France, where he learned that forests could be scientifically managed to ensure sustainable yields and that the government should control private cutting. On his return to the United States Pinchot put many of his ideas into practice at the Vanderbilt's Biltmore estate in North Carolina. On the 5,000–acre estate in the rolling, wooded hill country in the eastern part of the state Pinchot developed his three main principles – profitable production, constant annual yield, and improvement of the forest – through selective logging that protected young trees as well as mature trees for seeding.

Pinchot was also involved in promoting scientific sustainable management. He prepared an exhibit at the 1893 Chicago World's Fair and wrote a pamphlet on the Biltmore Forest. In addition he and others created a forestry commission, of which Pinchot was the secretary. The president was Charles Sargent of Harvard, who took a different perspective and believed that some areas should be set aside and not forested. The split in opinion led to the divergence of meaning in preservation and conservation, which previously had been used synonymously. Pinchot believed in the efficacy of conservation. In 1898 he was placed in charge of the Division of Forestry in the Department of Agriculture. He was only 32 years of age, but what he lacked in experience he made up for in energy. He became a consummate bureaucrat. By 1901 the division became a bureau providing technical information to private owners as well as managing the forest reserves. Pinchot was successful in promoting his message in this setting. He wrote and spoke widely, always eager to spread the good word. In 1899 he spoke with the governor of New York, Theodore Roosevelt, on the subject of forestry in a meeting that was to mark the beginning of a long and close relationship. When Roosevelt took over the presidency after the assassination of McKinley, he called on Pinchot to develop proposals that he could present to Congress. In his first speech to that body in 1901 Roosevelt noted that "the forest and water problems are perhaps the most vital internal questions of the United States."[7]

Pinchot's success lay in his assocation with Theodore Roosevelt. Roosevelt was a progressive Republican who had a love for the outdoors. Born a rather sickly child, he transformed himself into a figure of virile masculinity reveling in outdoor pursuits and feats of courage and endurance. Upon graduation from Harvard he had wanted to become a naturalist but instead became a rancher in Dakota for a time. In 1898 he organized the first volunteer cavalry regiment (the Rough Riders), saw active service in the war with Spain in Cuba, and returned home a war hero. Elected to the vice-presidency with McKinley, he became president upon the latter's assassination. Roosevelt was a progressive. He called for administrative reform, and his platform of a Square Deal spoke to the growing realization that individual freedoms could only be secured with greater government regulation and control over the huge monopolies that had emerged to dominate the economic life of the country. An integral part of Roosevelt's domestic reform and political platform was his environmental policy. Although strenuously opposed by Congress, Roosevelt managed to push through major pieces of environmental legislation. In Roosevelt's two terms of office 150 million acres were set aside for the national forest reserve; through the Federal Reclamation Service over 1 million acres of arable land were added; five national parks, two national game preserves and 51 wild bird refuges were created. Specific policies included the 1902 Newlands Irrigation Act, which established a policy of water irrigation in the arid west. Although given the scientific endorsement by Pinchot it was resisted especially by western representatives. Roosevelt personally backed the measure and helped its passage through Congress.

Pinchot was an important advisor and counselor to the president and a major driving force in the progressive conservation movement that shaped legislation in the Roosevelt administration. The term conservation, Pinchot later recalled, developed from conversations he had with Overton Price, a colleague in the Forest Service.

> After many other suggestions and long discussions, either Price or I (I'm not sure which and it doesn't really matter) proposed that we apply a new meaning to a word already in the dictionary, and christen the new policy Conservation.[8]

Conservation ideas became associated with the wise use of resources such as national forests, while the term preservation became associated with places like the national parks.

In 1905 the Transfer Act gave Pinchot, as Chief Forester, responsibility for 86 million acres of forestland. With Roosevelt's full support, Pinchot interpreted his powers as broadly as possible. To limit overgrazing he instituted a policy of permits and fees and began to develop a land management program based on land classification and comprehensive surveys, the need to develop resources fully and the basing of entitlements on the maximization of benefit for the greatest number of people rather than for the profit of the few. Roosevelt also established a number of commissions. A report of the Inland Waterways Commission called for planning and development based on entire river basins as the primary unit, a plan later developed more fully during the New Deal's Tennessee Valley Authority; the National Conservation Council began compiling a inventory of the nation's resources under the four categories of water, forest, land, and mineral. Pinchot continued to publicize his views in newspaper columns, press releases and pamphlets. When Congress seemed recalcitrant Pinchot took his arguments to the people. In his 1910 book, *The Fight For Conservation*, he painted a bleak picture of timber and coal resources running out and increasing soil erosion and overgrazing.

With Roosevelt gone from the presidency in 1909, Pinchot had less sway in the centers of power. Although Pinchot was retained as Chief Forester, Taft's appointment of Richard Ballinger as head of the Department of Agriculture meant a change in operations. There was tremendous animosity between Ballinger and Pinchot, and eventually they clashed in a dispute involving land use in Alaska. Pinchot saw himself as defending the public interest against the power of special interest. He lost the political battle, and Taft replaced him as Chief Forester in 1910.

As a private citizen Pinchot continued to publicize his conservation ideas. He called for the wise use of land – a practice of resource development based on careful knowledge, sustained yield, and a comprehensive approach that looked at all resources with an eye on public interest as much as private profit. Pinchot did not leave the political scene forever (he was governor of Pennsylvania and served two terms, 1923–7 and 1931–5), but he never regained the center stage he held under the Roosevelt administration. His ideas, however, percolated into legislation, forestry practice and an environmental approach that came to dominate. In his autobiography Theodore Roosevelt summed up Pinchot's contribution:

Gifford Pinchot is the man to whom the nation owes the most for what has been accomplished as regards the preservation of the natural resources of our country. He led, and indeed during its most vital period embodied, the fight for the preservation through use of our forests. He played one of the leading parts in the effort to make the National Government the chief instrument in developing the irrigation of the arid West. He was the foremost leader in the struggle to coordinate all our social and governmental forces in the effort to secure the adoption of a rational and farseeing policy for securing the conservation of our natural resources.[9]

## Conservation and the Progressive Movement

In a detailed study, the historian Samuel Hays drew attention to the importance of rational planning and efficient development in the progressive conservation movement. He termed it the "gospel of efficiency."[10] From 1890 to 1920 this movement was less concerned, argued Hays, with curbing big business and more concerned with the rational use of the nation's resources. Hays, perhaps, overstated the efficiency rationale. It was important but so was the notion of public interests as opposed to private interests. Pinchot was not a protosocialist, but he was concerned with restraining the power of business interests to get public lands too cheaply and to have unlimited control over them. Pinchot embodied the wise use of the policy of sustained yield. His work was dominated by the gospel of efficiency but also by the notion of long-term national interest overriding short-term private concerns. Today the progressive conservation movement would use the term *sustainable development*; a term that implies resource exploitation over the long term.

The zenith of the conservation movement occured during the Roosevelt administration, when a conservation-minded president and advisors like Pinchot and Newlands shaped the policy agenda and the course of informed public opinion. It was a difficult task persuading a recalcitrant Congress, Western interests, and resource-based business interests that conservation would not diminish profits. Fearful of government control of resources, business interests fought a sustained battle that, following the Roosevelt presidency, they began to dominate. Conservation measures did not disappear – the National Park Service was created in 1916 – but a succession of conservative Republican administrations, including Harding (1921–3), Coolidge (1923–9), and Hoover (1929–33), did little to expand conservation policies. During the years of the conservative Republican ascendancy, the emphasis of government policy was on reducing the national debt, lowering taxes, and aiding business. Conservation measures that dovetailed with business were encouraged: the Forest Service shaped its policies to suit lumber interests, borax mining was approved in the Death Valley National Monument and the Boulder (Hoover) Dam produced power at prices set low so as not to undercut private utilities. At the start of the Depression, President Hoover even considered ceding the land in the public domain to the states. After the crash of 1929, the sluggish economy and low business confidence eventually spiraled down into the Great Depression.

## Conservation and the New Deal

At his inaugural address on March 4, 1933 Franklin Roosevelt said that "the only thing we have to fear is fear itself." Soon after becoming president, Roosevelt embarked on an ambitious set of policy measures to relieve economic distress and hardship. Shaped by the contemporary depression, Roosevelt's administration can be seen as a continuation of the earlier progressive movement because the two administrations shared many similarities. Theodore and Franklin were cousins who shared the same background. It is paradoxical that the two presidents with perhaps the most patrician background are associated with the most progressive measures of the first half of the twentieth century. And although he was not an outdoorsman like his cousin, Franklin was something of a country squire and landowner, who once listed his occupation as "tree farmer." Roosevelt also had experience with the politics and administration of environmental policies; as a senator in New York State legislature he was chair of the Fish and Game Committee and head of the Agriculture Committee. Even the name adopted by FDR, *New Deal*, echoes Theodore Roosevelt's *Square Deal*; there was a shared belief in an increased role for government, reflecting less an ideology and more a practical response to a desperate situation.

Under the New Deal conservation measures were expanded enormously. They were part and parcel of broader social and economic policies. In the first 100 days of the administration, the Civilian Conservation Corps, for example, was established to enlist young unemployed men to stop them from drifting into subversive organizations and to help conserve natural resources. By 1941 some 2.5 million men had passed through these camps; 17 million acres had been planted, dams constructed to stop erosion and vital work done in creating and improving state and federal parks. The Works Public Administration (WPA), established in 1933 under the National Industrial Recovery Act, channeled billions of dollars into reforestation, flood control, sewerage plants, and a host of public building projects. The Public Works Administration (PWA) also gave grants and loans to government authorities and private businesses for the construction of public projects and financed many of the nation's dams.

In addition there were specific measures focused on soil conservation, grazing rights and wildlife, including

- The Soil Conservation Act of 1936, which, building upon the 1933 Agricultural Adjustment Act, provided for the reforestation of formerly marginal areas. This measure was introduced at a time when the dust storms of the midwest and plains were sweeping away millions of tons of topsoil.
- The Taylor Grazing Act of 1934, which placed the public domain under federal regulation and instituted fees for usage. It was a good idea but like lots of ideas the devil was in the implementation. The legislation, to gain the support of western ranchers, set the charges very low and did little to redress the power of the larger ranchers. The large ranchers continued to reap a substantial benefit from federal largesse, a position they held until comparatively recently.
- The Pitman-Robertson Federal Aid in Wildlife Restoration Act of 1937 reallocated the 11–percent excise tax to be applied to wildlife research and land acquisition. In 1939 the US Fish and Wildlife Service was created from existing departments in Agriculture and Commerce.

The preservation impulse was also accommodated during the New Deal. Cheap and plummeting land prices allowed the government to buy land easily and cheaply. There was a vast increase in the national parks: from 14.7 million acres in 1933 to 20.3 million in 1946. Five of the new parks – Olympic, King's Canyon, Big Bend, Isle Royale, and Everglades – were wilderness areas drawn with reference to ecology rather than to the criteria of monumentality and tourism. Everglades could not be compared as a "moving, stirring site" to Yellowstone or Yosemite.

One of the single biggest achievements of the New Deal was the Tennessee Valley Authority (TVA). Historian Samuel Eliot Morison referred to it as "a great and permanent achievement."[11] The TVA embodied many of the objectives and ideas of the commission that had been created by Theodore Roosevelt. The idea that a single river basin should be the object of rational planning and development was adopted directly from the earlier commission's report. The TVA, a giant federal scheme, had a number of objectives: to control the Tennessee river basin by flood control measures, to construct dams to produce cheap electricity, to manufacture and distribute fertilizer, to raise the economic and social well-being of the river basin's inhabitants. Dams and steam plants were built throughout the basin. Six dams were completed before the Second World War and over 30 in total were built; a dozen steam plants and over 1 million acres of land was forested. Cheap electricity was distributed to thousands of people who had had little or no power.[12]

The New Deal consolidated the power of the federal government and embodied many of the principles of the progressive conservation movement. In a wide-ranging package of programs, acts, and measures shaped by consistent belief, inherited ideologies as well as compromises and responses to particular events and circumstances, the New Deal changed the shape and extent of government involvement and environmental legislation. Endeavoring to deal with an economic depression the New Deal created a new role for environmental public policy and practice. It gave us a new environmental discourse that was shaped by the needs of economic growth and a belief in resource conservation. Keynesianism and progressive conservation were combined. In the second half of the twentieth century the issues of economic growth and environmental protection, resolutely combined in the New Deal, would be forced apart and then later recombined in a new environmental discourse that constituted the greening of the United States.

## FURTHER READING

Fox, S. 1981. *John Muir and His Legacy: The American Conservation Movement.* Boston: Little, Brown.

Hays, S. P. 1959. *Conservation and the Gospel of Efficiency: The Progressive Conservation Movement, 1890–1920.* Cambridge, Mass.: Harvard University Press.

—— 1981. "Gifford Pinchot and the American Conservation Movement," in *Technology in America: A History of Individuals and Ideas*, ed. C. W. Purcell, Jr. Cambridge: MIT Press.

Lowenthal, D. 1958. *George Perkins Marsh: Versatile Vermonter*. New York: Columbia University Press.

Nash, R. 1976. *The American Environment: Readings in the History of Conservation*, 2nd edn. Reading, Mass.: Addison- Wesley.

—— 1982. *Wilderness and the American Mind*, 3rd edn. New Haven: Yale University Press.

Strong, D. H. 1988. *Dreamers and Defenders; American Conservationists*, (orig. pub. 1971). Lincoln and London: University of Nebraska Press.

# NOTES

1  John Muir, *Our National Parks* (Boston: Houghton, 1901), 1.

2  George Catlin, *North American Indians: Being Letters and Notes on Their Manners, Customs, and Conditions, Written during Eight Years' Travel among the Wildest Tribes in North America, 1832–1839*, 2 vols (1880).

3  Quoted in A. Hendricks, *Albert Bierstadt: Painter of the American West* (Fort Worth: Amon Carter Museum of Western Art, 1974), 198.

4  John Muir, *The Yosemite* (Boston: Houghton Mifflin, 1912), 261–2.

5  Roderick Nash, *Wilderness and the American Mind* (New Haven: Yale University Press, 1982), 181.

6  George Perkins Marsh, *Man and Nature: or Physical Geography as Modified by Human Action* (New York: Charles Scribner, 1864).

7  Theodore Roosevelt, *State Papers as Governor and President, 1899–1909* (New York: Charles Scribner), 120.

8  Gifford Pinchot, *Breaking New Ground* (New York: Harcourt Brace and World, 1947), 42.

9  Theodore Roosevelt, *An Autobiography* (New York: Macmillan, 1913), 429.

10  Samuel P. Hays, *Conservation and the Gospel of Efficiency: The Progressive Conservation Movement, 1890–1920* (Cambridge, Mass.: Harvard University Press, 1959).

11  Samuel Eliot Morison, *The Oxford History of the American People* (New York: Oxford University Press, 1965), 960.

12  The TVA scheme was controversial because many people resisted relocation to make room for the new dams.

# 5

# A Fierce Green Fire

On August 6, 1945 the Japanese city of Hiroshima was hit by an atomic bomb dropped by the US Air Force. Most of the city was destroyed and over 200,000 people were killed. The deadly cloud that quickly mushroomed over Hiroshima soon became an icon of human power and destructiveness, a symbol of global significance, a harbinger of the postwar world, an unforgettable image for the coming age. The new atomic age gave humankind, for the very first time in history, the prospect of self-induced extinction. The contemporary environmental movement grew up against this terrifying background. At the heart of the postwar environmental movement was the perceived need to protect the earth from human destruction.

## Preserving the Wilderness

If the environmental movement in the USA has had one sustaining image it is the preservation of the wild. Saving the wilderness has been a central and enduring element of environmental thought and practice in the United States for over 100 years. The spirit of John Muir has been upheld by a number of people and a range of organizations.

### Aldo Leopold

One important figure in the twentieth-century preservationist movement actually began his working life as a resource conservationist. Aldo Leopold (1887–1948) graduated with a master's degree from Yale's School of Forestry in 1907 and got a job with the Forest Service, working in New Mexico and Arizona. In 1916 he was placed in charge of planning recreational use in the national forests of the southwest. As a keen hunter he was well qualified to consider hunting concerns and forest management. Leopold was instrumental in getting a wilderness area created in 1924 at the headwaters of the Gila River. In the same year he moved to Wisconsin to become associate director of the Forest Products Laboratory. He resigned shortly thereafter and became a consultant. In 1928 he undertook a survey of game in the Midwest funded by sporting-gun manufacturers. Leopold eventually became a professor of game management at the University of Wisconsin. Leopold's interest widened, and he developed a much broader appreciation of wilderness than just as a setting for game. In 1935 he helped found the Wilderness Society, which was dedicated to expanding and protecting the wilderness areas of the country. He also bought a small farm of 80 acres, where he and his family spent many weekends. He wrote of his experience on the farm and combined his earlier work into one manuscript. One week after the manuscript was accepted for publication, Aldo Leopold died.

*A Sand County Almanac* was first published in 1949. The book is small but has three distinct parts. The first is an almanac of natural history based on his experiences on the farm. Following is a section from July:

> Like other great landowners, I have tenants. They are negligent about rents, but very punctilious about tenures. Indeed at every daybreak from April to July they proclaim their boundaries to each other, and so acknowledge, at least, by inference, their fiefdom to me.... At 3.35 the nearest field sparrow avows, in a clear tenor chant, that he holds the jackpine copse north to the riverbank, and south to the old wagon track. One by one all the other field sparrows, within earshot recite their respective holdings.[1]

These monthly notes have some of the feeling and cadence of Thoreau's *Walden*. The second part, entitled *Sketches Here and There* (renamed the *Quality of Landscape* in some expanded versions of the book), contains observations of Leopold's travels in Wisconsin, Illinois, the southwest, Canada, and Mexico. One of the most interesting pieces is entitled "Thinking Like a Mountain" in which Leopold described a turning point in his life:

> In those days we had never heard of passing up a chance to kill a wolf. In a second we were pumping lead into the pack, but with more excitement than accuracy: how to aim a steep downhill shot is always confusing. When our rifles were empty, the old wolf was down, and a pup was dragging a leg into impassable slide-rocks.
>
> We reached the old wolf in time to watch a fierce green fire dying in her eyes. I realized then, and have known ever since, that there is something known only to her and to the mountain. I was young then, and full of trigger-itch; I thought that fewer wolves meant more deer, that no wolves would mean a hunter's paradise. But after seeing the green fire die, I sensed that neither the wolf nor the mountain agreed with such a view.[2]

The notion of a fierce green fire contains ideas of an animistic religion and the sense of connection found in Native-American religious systems. Leopold had come full circle. The wilderness was now a sacred space for the preservationists – not just a place to save but a place to revere.

The third part of *Sand County Almanac* is entitled *The Upshot*. It deals with what Leopold called philosophical questions. Perhaps the most referenced section is "The Land Ethic." It is short, no more than 30 pages, but it caps Leopold's shift from a concern with resource management to a belief in environmental ethics. The "land" of the land ethic is a general name for what we would now call the environment; it includes soils, water, plants, and animals. Leopold argued that we need to enlarge our connection with the land beyond narrow economic considerations toward a broader ethical concern. The land ethic for Leopold is an emotional and moral as well as scientific standpoint. The land should be more rightly seen as part of a wider definition of community, a connection involving environmental responsibility, environmental obligations, and an environmental ethic:

> a system of conservation based solely on an economic self-interest is hopelessly lopsided. It tends to ignore, and thus eventually to eliminate, many elements in the land community that lack commercial value, but that are (as far we know) essential to its healthy functioning. It assumes, falsely I think, that the parts of the biotic clock will function without the uneconomic parts.[3]

Leopold's writings are important. *A Sand County Almanac* has sold over 1 million copies and influenced a range of environment activists. He shifted the center of gravity in environment debates from people to the environment and gave a moral twist to the preservation movement. Saving wilderness was not just a good science or sound economics, it was the ethical thing to do.

### Saving the Earth

In 1945 writer Rachel Carson submitted a proposal to the *Reader's Digest* for an article on the effects of the synthetic chemical DDT (dichloro-diphenyl-trichloro-ethane). The publisher was not interested. Carson developed the article into a book, *Silent Spring*, which was eventually published in 1962. In Kirkpatrick Sale's concise description of the modern environmental movement in the United States, he put a date on the start of what he called the green revolution: the publication of Rachel Carson's book. The date is arguable, because specific dates tend to slice up long, coherent processes into single instances. What is less contentious, however, is the pivotal importance of the book to the US environmental movement.

Rachel Carson (1907–64) was born in Pennsylvania, the youngest of three children. From an early age she had two loves: writing and science. At the age of ten she won a writing award for a story submitted to a children's magazine.

Later, at the Pennsylvania College for Women, she developed a lifelong interest in biology and changed her major from English to biology. After graduation she worked as a lab assistant at The Johns Hopkins University and the University of Maryland. She continued her writing, she was creative and, in the midst of the Depression, she also needed money. She wrote articles on fisheries for the *Baltimore Sun* and produced radio broadcasts on marine biology for the Bureau of Fisheries. In 1936 she became a full-time biologist with the bureau, later renamed the Fish and Wildlife Service.

Carson's first book, *Under the Sea-Wind* (1941), was a popular account of marine life. It was science made accessible to a broader audience by a fluent writing style. The book was not, however, a commercial success. By 1949 she was responsible for the publications of the Fish and Wildlife Service, enabling her to combine her interests in science and writing but leaving little time for her own writing. Ten years elapsed before she published *The Sea Around Us*, in 1951. Working on it for three years, often long into the night, she again presented information on marine biology in an accessible style. It was an outstanding success. A reviewer in the *New York Times* noted, "Rarely does the world get a physical scientist with literary genius." The book was a bestseller and eventually translated into 30 languages. The royalties enabled Carson to devote herself full-time to writing. In 1955 she published *The Edge of the Sea*, another critical and commercial success By this point she had a large following of readers, an established reputation and financial security.

As early as 1945 Carson had wanted to write about the effects of DDT, but only in 1958 did she begin work on a manuscript that looked at the deleterious effects of pesticides. She drew upon a wide body of evidence and scientific literature to advance her case. The case was not new. Articles in *Atlantic Monthly* and the *New Yorker* already in 1945 suggested that DDT, invented in 1939, might pose some hazards. After congressional hearings, Congress passed an amendment in 1954 that gave the Food and Drug Administration power to regulate levels of pesticide residue. Carson through her work presented a well-argued case to a broader audience.

*Silent Spring* begins with quotes from Albert Schweitzer, E. B. White and Keats, including, "The sedge is wither'd from the lake, And no birds sing." The image of a birdless spring provides the telling metaphor that runs through the book. The level of pesticide use is destroying the birdlife, she argues, and we will eventually have no birdsong to herald the spring. Carson begins her book with what she called "a fable for tomorrow": the image of a shadow of death, human illness, and destruction of flora and fauna. She seeks to explain what had "silenced the voices of spring in countless towns in America." She chronicles the growing use of chemicals especially DDT, dieldrin, endrin, parathion, and detailed their deleterious effects on humans, plants, and animals. She draws upon a wide body of scientific writing, her list of principal sources running over 50 pages and including the US Department of Agriculture, medical and science journals, official reports, and memos. Carson weaves all this evidence into a compelling narrative that holds the readers' interest and galvanizes their concern. Her image of a small town America shrouded in toxic chemicals is a simple and powerful one. Her message is clear:

> It is not my contention that chemical pesticides should never be used. I do contend that we have put poisonous and biologically potent chemicals indiscriminately into the hands of persons largely or wholly ignorant of their potentials for harm. We have subjected enormous numbers of people to contact with these poisons, without their consent and often without their knowledge.... There is still a very limited awareness of the nature of the threat. This is an era of specialists, each of whom sees his own problem and is unaware of or intolerant of the large frame into which it fits. It is also an era dominated by industry, in which the right to make a dollar at whatever cost is seldom challenged.... The public must decide whether it wishes to continue on the present road, and it can do so only when in full possession of the facts.[4]

Carson not only tolled the bell to warn us of the dangers; she suggested alternatives. She argued the case for biotic controls and for a much more selective use of chemicals.

Today her message seems eminently sensible. At the time, however, there was great controversy. She found it difficult to get portions of the book published in magazines. It eventually appeared in the *New Yorker* in 1962 as a series of three articles. One of the readers, an H. Davidson from San Francisco, wrote to the magazine:

> Miss Rachel Carson's reference to the selfishness of insecticide manufacturers probably reflects her Communist sympathies, like a lot of writers today. We can live without birds and animals, but, as the current market slump shows, we cannot live without business. As for insects, isn't it just like a woman to be scared to death of a few little bugs! As long as we have the H-bomb everything will be OK.[5]

Chemical manufacturers mounted a vicious campaign against her and tried to block publication of the book. In their criticisms, the term *emotional* was often used; a not-so-subtle attack on the fact that she was a woman writing about science. A review in *Time*, for example, used the terms "hysterically overemphatic" and "emotional and inaccurate."[6]

Despite the campaign against her and her arguments, *Silent Spring* was a commercial success. In less than six months half a million copies were sold. In 1963 Carson appeared on a CBS special and before congressional committee hearings. Just as she was reaching a huge audience she succumbed to cancer. She died in 1964 at age 56. Her legacy is monumental. Carson had deepened the American consciousness of the ecological web and the horrendous dangers of toxic pollution from unseen chemicals; she influenced policy and shaped public opinion.

Carson's work marked a new shift in environmental concern. The previous conservation and preservation movements had focused on the wise use of the earth or the need to protect the earth. The danger of overexploitation of resources was replaced by the threat of human and animal extinction, an important stimulus to the US environmental movement. Chemical poisoning was an ever-present threat. Scientific achievements were a double-edged sword: capable of making life easier but also threatening life. Throughout the 1960s toxic pollution of the soil, groundwater, and air was a constant news item. Chemical pollution, oil spills, radiation leaks were regularly reported as endangering human life. There were stories and vivid images. In 1969 the Cuyahoga River was so polluted that it caught fire. Off the Pacific coast, close to Santa Barbara there was a major oil spill. Throughout the 1970s and 1980s events like these showed the constant danger to the environment and to people and reinforced the need for vigilance and some form of monitoring and control. There was a growing ground swell of opinion that the rate of technological progress had yet to match an ecological consciousness. Sometimes, consciousness is raised by specific events.

### Love Canal

In 1892 William T. Love proposed connecting the upper and lower Niagara river in western New York, by digging a six-mile canal. The plan was to generate cheap power from the water flow. The plan floundered after only a part of the canal was dug. In 1920 the land was sold at public auction and became a chemical disposal site. The city of Niagara Falls dumped waste. The Army dumped waste. And the Hooker Chemical Company dumped waste. Between 1942 and 1953 the company dumped 21,800 tons of 82 different chemicals. The carcinogenic cocktail included dioxins, 200 tons of trichlorophenols, 6,900 tons of lindane, 2,000 tons of chlorobenzenes and 2,400 tons of benzyl chlorides. The Hooker Chemical Company did nothing illegal. There was no regulation of chemical dumping, and the local authorities knew of the chemical waste. In 1953 the local board of education purchased part of the canal for one dollar and began to build a school. In 1957 the School Board sold some of the land off to a housing developer. The city constructed a storm sewer through the area in 1960, and eight years later the Department of Transportation built an expressway through the southern end of the canal. As a result of these intrusions and because the steel drums holding the chemicals corroded and leaked, the deadly cocktail of chemical wastes entered into the ground and water. The area was affected by odors from the chemical pit, and chemicals broke through the topsoil, burning pets and children. Toxic sludge seeped into the basements of local houses. By the 1970s people in the area began to complain of unusual health problems. Children who attended the local school were getting sick. Reports of urinary tract infections and seizures, birth defects and miscarriages were abnormally high. In August 1978, after intense agitation by the local community and massive press coverage, New York State declared the area a health hazard, and President Carter named it a national disaster. A local resident, Lois Gibbs, formed the Love Canal Homeowners Association. The cleanup of the area involved state and federal agencies in a program that was to prefigure the Superfund legislation of 1980. This legislation, more correctly known as the Comprehensive Environmental Response, Compensation and Liability Act provided federal authority to clean hazardous sites. The passing of the Act was lubricated by events such as Love Canal with its image of suffering children and distraught households living close to toxic waste sites.

The social scientist Kenneth Boulding has provided an arresting metaphor. He made a distinction between a *cowboy economy* and a *spaceship economy*.[7] In a cowboy economy there is concern with unlimited production and consumption. Growth is not only possible and attainable but desirable. A cowboy economy operates with the assumption of infinite resources, an ever-widening horizon, an ever-extending frontier. In a spaceship economy, in contrast, there is concern with limits. The issues of a spaceship economy are recycling, careful management of finite resources, husbanding precious resources – an economy with limits. The image of the endless horizon was replaced by the picture of a small capsule moving through space. In this simple but provocative metaphor, Boulding captured the essential difference between two environmental discourses competing in postwar USA.

The spaceship concept was telling. By the late 1960s the image of astronauts and spaceships had captured the public imagination. But there was something more tangible from the space probes. For the first time the earth was photographed from outer space. The photos showed a small, fragile planet floating in the inky darkness. It is not accidental that Earth Day was first celebrated in 1970, when people first had a tangible photographic image of the earth as a coherent single unit. Now the earth could be seen as well as envisioned. And this image reinforced the sense of limits, interdependence, and planetary vulnerability.

### Environmental Policies

#### The National Environmental Policy Act

The popular ground swell of opinion for environmental protection was finally given legislative form in 1969, when the National Environmental Policy Act (NEPA) was passed by Congress and signed into law by President Nixon in 1970. The act, which established a national policy to "encourage productive and enjoyable harmony between man and his environment," required environmental impact statements from federal agencies and created the Council on Environmental Quality. Although there had been federal environmental legislation before this – the Oil Pollution Act of 1924, the Clean Air Act of 1955, the Wilderness Act of 1964 and the Clean Water Act of 1960 – NEPA was more than a new legislative measure; it marked the incorporation of environmental concerns into major policy considerations. The act institutionalized environmental awareness into the federal policy process. All federal agencies (except the Environmental Protection Agency) had to file an environmental impact statement

(EIS) for any proposed legislation or program, make this statement public and produce a final report that responded to the results of this public participation. NEPA opened up environmental issues relating to federal policies and programs to a broader public. Issues were raised and debated in public forum. In practice, the act was used in litigation as much as in formal policy making. Environmental groups, citizens and state and local governments used NEPA to take federal agencies to court for not undertaking an environmental impact statement or not doing it thoroughly. From 1974 to 1988, 1,775 cases were filed and 129 injunctions were issued. For example, in July 1983 a number of environmental organizations filed a suit against the Forest Service in the District of Oregon for using herbicides, arguing that the Forest Service had not done enough studies or impact statements "pursuant to their NEPA obligations." The court agreed and an injunction against the use of herbicides was issued and remained in effect until 1988 when, after intense scrutiny and public consultation, the Forest Service had eliminated the use of some herbicides, placed others on the list of last resort, adopted more site-specific techniques and opted to use nonchemical methods where appropriate. NEPA, like many other pieces of environmental legislation, was not only a formal tool of government but also a text used in litigation against federal agencies. Impact statements have become an integral part of governance in the United States at both federal and state levels. Over 30 states now require impact statements for all state policies and programs. The environmental has become part of the discourse of federal and state policy making and implementation.

### The Environmental Protection Agency

While Kirkpatrick Sale suggested 1962 as the beginning of the green movement in the United States, a convincing case could be made for 1970. In that year, on April 22, Earth Day was first celebrated. Aldo Leopold's *Sand County Almanac* was reissued, the League of Conservation Voters and the Natural Resources Defense Council were established, Congress passed the Water Quality Control Act, an important amendment to the Clean Air Act, and the Environmental Protection Agency (EPA) was created. The name of this agency is significant because it designates a very specific and unique charge, protecting the environment. The assumption behind the appellation is revealing: the environment is in danger and it needs and warrants federal protection. The establishment of the EPA heralds an important watershed in US environmental discourse.

The EPA was established by President Nixon to bring coherence and order to the fragmentary nature of federal environmental legislation. Sometimes this agency reinforced differences between federal agencies rather than smoothed them over. For example, the EPA has sought to ban many pesticides whereas the Department of Agriculture has sometimes adopted less stringent standards. The EPA has aimed to reduce the amount of coal burning while the Department of Energy has sometimes fostered coal burning as a way to reduce reliance on foreign energy sources.

The EPA became responsible for establishing national environmental standards, monitoring environmental trends and enforcing environmental legislation. Now the single most important federal authority in environmental politics and policies, the agency was established initially with a budget of $1.2 billion and a staff of approximately 6,700. The budget and staff expanded in the 1970s, shrunk under the Reagan administration and has seen a small expansion in the 1990s. The EPA is headquartered in Washington but has ten regional centers across the country,[8] where much of the work is done, including all federal inspections and enforcement actions and much of the contact and interaction with the states and regulated industries.

While both budget and personnel figures have seen modest growth, the responsibilities and public visibility of the EPA have grown enormously. The agency crafts and enforces regulations. In its first year the EPA was responsible for enforcing the 1970 amendment to the Clean Air Act, establishing national air standards and monitoring states plans for attaining these standards. Under subsequent legislation, the EPA was made responsible for a range of issues, including the enforcement of national water and air standards, the monitoring of dumping in the ocean, the registration and classification of pesticides, the establishment and enforcement of noise and radiation emission standards, the testing and banning of chemicals, the tracking of hazardous wastes, and the cleaning up of hazardous substance sites.

The EPA operates through establishing standards and either enforcing them directly (e.g., hazardous substance site cleanups) or delegating enforcement to state or other federal agencies. EPA enforcement actions (from 1972 to 1989 there were 4,136 undertaken directly by the EPA and by judicial referral) comprise compliance orders, hearings, arbitration, auditing and sanctions, including fines. Judicial referrals involve violations that are turned over to the Justice Department or state and local legal agencies where appropriate. For example, in Texas the owners of a garage were prosecuted for removing catalytic converters from autos. They were found guilty under the antitampering prohibition section of the Clean Air Act and fined $1,750 per vehicle.

Environmental policies and standards, particularly EPA regulations and decisions, have been tested and tried in the courts. The three main actors in most environmental cases are environmental groups, industries, and government agencies. In the earliest years of the EPA, some environmental groups were quick to use the new legislation to enforce environmental regulations. By the 1980s, however, industry responded by forcefully arguing their case. Business interests tried to use the courts to relax regulations whereas environmental groups sought to get tighter rules. Judicial decisions have represented ideology as much as jurisprudence and science. Conservative judges tended to overturn EPA decisions more on the basis of cost and/or exceeding legislative authority than on the basis of public health. The judgments at both the circuit level and the Supreme Court reflect political ideology as much as the specific issues of the case.

The increasing role of the EPA, and federal environmental regulation, is best illustrated through a brief consideration of one policy area. Let us consider air quality, one of the largest programs of the EPA. Air quality control initially lay with states and municipal authoritories. California, Pennsylvania, and New York were the first states to address pollution problems. Air pollution, however, was and is no respecter of state boundaries. It was only in 1963 that a Clean Air Act was passed. Although the Act introduced some small abatement measures, it stated that air pollution control was a state and local problem and did not address the issue of pollution from automobile exhausts. National standards of acceptable levels of air quality were only established by the 1967 Air Quality Act. The most important piece of legislation was the 1970 Clean Air Act which established national standards and in order to achieve these standards set emissions levels from particular sources. For example, motor vehicles were specifically regulated: lead was banned as a fuel additive, and fuel economy measures were mandated. The Act set emission restrictions for specific pollutants including mercury, asbestos, inorganic arsenic, and coke-oven emissions. Later amendments to the Act sought reductions in sulfur dioxide emissions, hazardous air pollutants, and improved air quality in urban areas. The Clean Air Act was a watershed piece of legislation that introduced more federal regulation and control and made provision for citizen suits against polluters and and government officials. The 1990 Clean Air Act extended the 1970 legislation. The 1990 Act identified 189 toxins that had to be regulated, set limits on the emissions of acid rain gases, sulphur dioxide and nitrous dioxide; it also introduced state implementation plans, more public participation and created an allowance trading system for the major polluters and permits for the very large polluters. The 1970 and 1990 Acts set standards of air quality and created specific measures to achieve these standards, including regulating the emission levels for a range of pollutants. The data are clear. The legislation has led to improvements in air quality, especially in urban areas. By any account the Acts have achieved their overall goal of improving the nation's air quality.

Frequently the public feels that the federal government taxes too much, spends too much, and too rarely achieve its objectives. In the United States, in comparison with Europe, the federal government is often portrayed and perceived as meddlesome, inefficient, and bunglesome. One of the rare areas of exception is environmental legislation. In general, there is broad public support for environmental protection, government regulation, and federal controls. There are controversies over education, welfare, and health, but the role of government in environmental issues is generally taken as important and is well received and supported by the public. The success of such measures as the 1970 and 1990 Clean Air Acts have created public and bipartisan support for environmental legislation. Debates may occur over specific policies or particular regulations, but the argument for the need for some kind of environmental regulation or protection has been won. There is a broad consensus that the government has an important and necessary role to play in protecting the environment.

Much has been written about the role and efficacy of the 1970 National Environmental Policy Act, the establishment of EPA and subsequent legislation and judicial processes; much remains to write about. There are many fascinating stories of initial legislation being passed, implemented, challenged, and tested in the courts.[9] In this book, however, we are concerned with the broader picture. The creation of the EPA was a defining moment in US environmental history, for it dramatically changed the dominant environmental discourse. Legislative and judicial action since 1969 has radically transformed the landscape of public policy in the United States. It has introduced an environmental discourse that includes rules and regulations, terms and ideas, standards and performances, data and texts, and has moved the debate beyond a narrow focus to resonate across a wider public.[10] In addition to the actual legislation, the concept of the EPA has helped to create and fashion a bipartisan environmental sensitivity. Environmental issues have entered not only the policy arena, they have entered our language, our culture, our national imagery, and helped define who we are as a people and how we are doing as a society.

## Global Concerns

Environmental issues are no longer just matters of national concern. The issues have become globalized. Ideas about the global predicament regularly assign major importance to environmental issues. National policy-making is now forged and implemented with at least one eye on a growing number of international treaties and standards.

In June 1992 the United Nations sponsored the Conference on Environment and Development (UNCED), otherwise known as the Earth Summit, in Rio de Janeiro, a gathering that included more than 100 heads of state. The key term at the conference was "sustainable development," and a major objective was to research ways to reconcile economic development and environmental quality. The United States along with 156 other countries, signed the *Rio Declaration* and *Agenda 21*, documents affirming a commitment to reconcile economics and the environment. *Agenda 21* proposed to "make trade and the environment mutually supportive" (section I, chapter 2) and called for "environmental concern in decision-making on economic, social, fiscal, energy, agricultural, transportation, trade and other policies" (section I, chapter 8). Environmental policy in the US is now bound up with global concerns. As one of the world's largest economies the US has an important role to play. Sometimes the role is tough as national interest and international requirements can often mesh but sometimes clash. Disputes over levels of acceptable emissions, for example, emerged at the international conference on global climate change in Kyoto, Japan in 1997 attended by Vice-President Al Gore. A compromise was eventually reached.

The Earth Summit was not as a defining a moment as the creation of the EPA; but what it does represent is a recognition that just as the individual states of the union could not solve air pollution by themselves so now there is a clear recognition that today's environmental problems cannot be solved by national policies alone. International policies have yet to move much beyond good intent and long range standard setting. But an important start has been made. National policy-makers, even in such a large and powerful country of the world as the US, now have to recognize global consequences and international obligations. The tension between national sovereignty and international obligations is a theme that we look at in much more detail in chapter 10.

## FURTHER READING

Carson, R. 1962. *Silent Spring*. New York: Houghton Mifflin.
Council on Environmental Quality. 1970–present. *Environmental Quality Annual Report*. Washington, DC: Executive Office of the President.
Ringquist, E. J. 1993. *Environmental Protection at the State Level*. New York: M. E. Sharpe.
Sale, K. 1993. *The Green Revolution: The American Environmental Movement 1962–1992*. New York: Hill and Wang.
Scheffer, V. B. 1991. *The Shaping of Environmentalism in America*. Seattle and London: University of Washington Press.
Shabecoff, P. 1993. *A Fierce Green Fire: The American Environmental Movement*. New York: Hill and Wang.
Vig, N. J., and M. E., Kraft, eds, 1994. *Environmental Policy in the 1990s*, 2nd edn. Washington, DC: Congressional Quarterly.

## NOTES

1  Aldo Leopold, *A Sand County Almanac* (New York: Oxford University Press, 1949), 44–5.
2  Ibid., 138–9.
3  Ibid., 251.
4  Rachel Carson, *Silent Spring* (New York: Houghton Mifflin, 1962), 12–13.
5  The letter was published by the magazine only in the February 1997 issue, p. 18.
6  *Time*, September 28, 1962: 45–8.
7  Kenneth Boulding, "The Economics of the Coming Spaceship Earth," in *The Environment Handbook*, ed. Garrett Debell (New York: Ballantine, 1970), 96–101.
8  Boston, New York, Philadelphia, Atlanta, Chicago, Dallas, Kansas City, Denver, San Francisco, Seattle.
9  Just one example: much has been written about the Comprehensive Environmental Response, Compensation and Liability Act, often referred to as Superfund. See, among other studies, J. A. Hird, *Superfund: The Political Economy of Environmental Risk* (Baltimore and London: The Johns Hopkins University Press, 1994); D. Mazmanian and D. Morell, *Beyond Superfund* (Boulder: Westview Press, 1992).
10  Two examples that show the increase in the amount of "environmental data" and "environmental texts." Under the 1969 act the Council on Environmental Quality had to prepare an annual report, which now is a useful source of data and information about environmental issues. The consistency of reporting from 1970 to the present day provides an opportunity to assess the trajectory of environmental quality. The 1996 EPA publications catalogue contained over 6,000 items, ranging from booklets on radon in the home, lead levels in the atmosphere, the preservation of wetlands, to air quality standards throughout the United States.

# 6

# A Witches' Brew

This is the story of a lake. It is a small lake, only one mile wide and four miles long. It is called Onondaga Lake and is situated in upstate New York beside the city of Syracuse (figures 6.1 and 6.2). Nothing spectacular or fantastically dramatic has occurred here; it is not the site of great revolution, social upheaval or national pride. Its dubious and somewhat shameful claim to fame is its designation as one of America's dirtiest, most polluted freshwater lakes. Newspapers have called this lake a "cesspool," a "backyard septic tank," and "a concoction as vile as found in any witches' brew." By focusing on Onondaga Lake we make no claim to generality. It is a singular story but one that resonates with different myths of progress and competing perceptions of the relationship between people and their environment. The story of Onondaga Lake illuminates many of the themes and ideas we have already discussed. The environmental experience of the United States is embedded in the history and geography of particular places. Here we focus on one particular place.

The story of Onondaga Lake can be characterized as a combination of general themes and historical periods. One general theme weaves in and out of the story. Onondaga Lake is a place where the two environmental metadiscourses, that we identified in the introduction, conflict and compete. Tables 1 and 2 in the introduction describe the characteristics of each. Discourses, we know, are not simple, and they are often contradictory. We know that discourses are never so well defined, but for our purposes here let us agree that in imagining these two we can better understand how it is that Onondaga Lake came to be what it is today. In Ondondaga Lake, New York, as elsewhere in the US, much of its history has been a contest between these two environmental metadiscourses.

**Figure 6.1** Syracuse in context (Syracuse University cartography lab)

We include the story of Onondaga Lake as a way to ground the history of environmental discourses in a particular place over time.

## Gannentaha

The Onondaga Indians knew Gannentaha (Onondaga Lake) as "the Gathering Place." It provided people with an abundance of food and also had greater significance. The Onondaga's relationship with Onondaga Lake is perhaps best characterized by the ecological environmental metadiscourse. Fundamentally, this meant Indian kinship with the earth.[1] They saw Nature as alive, as powerful and present. It was personally and communally significant. Underlying this relationship was a belief that people were neither above nor apart from nature. Historian J. D. Hughes noted that plants, animals, earth, air, and water had an *intrinsic* not *instrumental* value.[2] In general, Indian relationships were not based on utility or economy. The land ethos intertwined with spiritual and religious dimensions. Religion embodied a reciprocal relationship between people and the sacred processes going on in the world.[3] Theirs was a sacred geography. Their relationship to nature was not abstract but localized. These were places they knew and places their ancestors had known.

The environment was the source of life,[4] and life was seen as a process not of subduing nature to human will but of subordinating the human will to natural rhythms that abounded in the landscape.[5] The Native-American discourse stressed interdependence not dominance. We know not to overromanticize Native-American cultures or to believe that Native Americans' perceptions resulted in practices that had little impact on their environment. As we noted in chapter 1, for thousands of years Indians modified their landscapes. Environmental historian William Cronon aptly pointed out, "the choice is not between two landscapes, one with and one without a human influence, it is between two human ways of living, two ways of belonging to an ecosystem."[6] Native-American relationships were not ones of unceasing harmony.

> Indians were uneasy about the paradox of both participating in the world and also exploiting it. Their environmental religions revealed that uneasiness and sought to resolve its tensions, not by denying either the exploitative or participatory dimensions, but rather by affirming them both simultaneously.[7]

Myths and stories formed vital ways of reconciling this paradox. The landscape had the power to shape these myths and stories, which taught children ecological lessons about the reciprocal relationship between humans and other beings. Audrey Shenandoah, Clan Mother of the Onondaga Nation, explained that nature and humans are not separate concepts: "In our language we don't have a word for what everybody calls nature because our ancestors and our tradition are so involved as one with what is called nature, our environment."[8] The concept of *community* was extended to all non-living and living parts of the landscape. Everyone and everything in the landscape was part of an intimate community, a landscape of the collective. (The term *collective* is here defined as something shared or assumed by all members of a group.) Places like Onondaga Lake had significance and meaning. The entire human community felt connected to the landscape. To the Onondaga, the natural world provided a comfort, a source of constant interaction, a reminder of the interconnectedness of life.

The interconnectedness of life extended to the concept of time. Many Native Americans viewed time as a cyclical, not linear, phenomenon. They visualized time as a loop where the future claimed importance in the present and historical continuity influenced the future. Since life was a circle, destined to return and loop around again, any loss of life along the circle diminished the whole. This perspective on time helped to promote more ecologically sound land practices as an integral part of their environmental ethos. A credo of the Onondaga is that every single human being is accountable to the future, the Seventh Generation. Each generation is charged with the moral obligation to protect the environment. Considerations for the well-being of future generations are integrated in the conception of time and place. A Native-American perspective of time and inter-generational equity embraced an ideology that discouraged exploitative prac-tices. The construction of time and sense of place fostered a protective obligation to place.

Onondaga Lake held great significance for the Onondaga and for the larger Iroquois Confederacy. The Iroquois Confederacy, or Five Nations, was com-posed originally of the Onondaga, Oneida, Seneca, Mohawk, and Cayugas and was then later joined by a sixth, the Tuscarora in the eighteenth century. Before the league was established there was constant feuding and fighting between the Iroquois peoples. They were brought together by the Great Peacemaker, Dega-nawida, a Huron, and his spokesperson Hiawatha, an Onondaga later adopted by the Mohawks. They traveled among the tribes promoting peace and advocat-ing harmony. According to the legends, sometime around AD 1400 the Great Peacemaker and Hiawatha, brought together the then-warring tribes. Uprooting a white pine tree on the banks of Onondaga Lake, the Peacemaker buried the weapons of these nations and told the people to live in peace.

The confederation of the five nations became one of the most powerful groups in North America. At the peak of their power in 1600 they dominated the entire northeast. Their alliance with the British blocked the southward advance of the French, and they used their important geopolitical position to broker and ensure their continued dominance. Pressure from the westward expansion, however, was unceasing. The British established a boundary line in 1763 that maintained much of the land of the Iroquois. In the War of Independence, although unwill-ing to get involved, most of the Iroquois sided with the British. The Oneida sided with the Americans. The American victory and the British defeat tolled the beginning of the end of Iroquois dominance in the region.

In 1788 at Fort Stanwix, New York State concluded a treaty with the Onondaga, Oneida, and Cayuga in which the nations did "cede and grant all their lands to the people of the State of New York forever." The Onondaga lost the heart of the land they once had claimed as part of their community.[9] This treaty signified more than just a legal abandonment of claim to land; it also represented an ideological victory by one group of people over another group. The loss of Onondaga Lake was more than the loss of a productive hunting and fishing ground; it was the loss of the spiritual connection with ancestral land, ripping apart the cultural tapestry and causing a spiritual loss of center.

### The Lake as Commodity

In 1654 Father Simon LeMoyne landed upon the shores of Onondaga Lake, stepped from his canoe, and tasted the waters of the salt springs. LeMoyne immediately recognized the commercial value of the salt wells. Within a few years, aspiring settlers, with their eyes on a burgeoning market, arrived to make their fortunes out of the "White Gold." Where the Indian had lived without much use for the salt springs, the Europeans converted the same land to a different purpose. Many European Americans saw their new life as a contest between human will and natural adversity.

In colonial America, the technological environmental metadiscourse evolved under two influences: the existence of physical threats and the environment's symbolic representation of chaos and amorality. The gaze of the settler saw only disorder. One response involved imposing order on the landscape. Clearing the land of trees and underbrush reduced chaos. Time was measured in a linear fashion, not cyclical. More important, the goal of civilizing the new land included a grand vision of progress, an unceasing march forward along a straight path. European settlers no longer lived sustainably but intensely. No longer respectful of nature's laws, Europeans subdued nature to human forms of order, declaring autonomy from the laws of nature and from its influences.

In 1793 commercial salt production signaled the birth of the city of Syracuse; its natural resources provided a particular advantage. For many years, Syracuse was the only place in the United States distant from the seacoast that manufactured salt and shipped it nationwide, earning it the moniker "Salt City." By 1817, the need to find cheaper ways of transporting salt was a major factor spurring the construction of the Erie Canal. European Americans dedicated themselves to the conversion of the wild with an enthusiasm for "improving" the land. Improvement really meant control and subjugation. Environment-as-utility formed the backbone of the new Americans' relationship with nature. Nature existed, but as a commodity to be enjoyed and consumed by humans. For the early settlers, Onondaga Lake was, as with any other natural resources, first and foremost an economic commodity. In Syracuse, the conquest of the landscape occurred most dramatically in 1822, when the physical configuration of the lake was altered to suit the designs of the canal builders. In a notable feat of human engineering, the lake was drained, reducing its surface area by an estimated 20 percent. The result of this technological alteration was increased land available for salt production and human habitation. The lake's disorderly swamps were proudly transformed, dominated, and reconfigured. With the completion of the Erie Canal in 1825, Syracuse sat at the hub of commercial transportation in the state of New York. The lake had become a commodity to be exploited.

In the late 1870s salt production began to decline and the abandoned salt beds made for a particularly easy and inexpensive transition to industry. The Industrial Revolution was in full swing, and late nineteenth-century technology was the bedrock of Syracuse's growth. But this growth was purchased at the expense of the lake, its tributaries and the nearby lands. The industrial order created the arrogance of the industrial mindset. Writer and philosopher Thomas Berry said that "fulfillment meant ever-increasing consumption and every earthly being was reduced from its status as a sacred reality to that of being a "natural resource" available for human use for whatever trivial purposes humans might invent."[10] The natural world stood apart and in contrast to the industrial, progressive life. Unrestrained exploitation of the lake proceeded without question.

In 1881 the Solvay Process Company began producing soda ash near Onondaga Lake, which required the intake of cool water during manufacturing and a location for dumping by-products. The finished product was used in the manufacture of glass, soap, paper, and textiles. Before the decade was over, other major industries such as steel, machinery, and pottery located business on the lake or its tributaries, giving Syracuse a diverse and growing manufacturing base. Continued economic expansion and material wealth was accompanied by an exponential amount of environmental change and degradation. By 1900, the lake had suffered a century of the ills associated with urban growth and technological advancement. The ecological ills that accompanied technological processing remained hidden for many years, slowly and quietly accumulating. But by 1901 pollution of the waters had advanced to such a degree that New York State prohibited the cutting of lake ice for public consumption. In 1920, several companies merged with Solvay Process Company, becoming the Allied Chemical and Dye Corporation, which then became an important national manufacturing power and remained for the next sixty years a key symbol of the industrial order in Syracuse.

Although the primary purpose of the lake was to promote economic growth, this does not mean the lake did not serve other purposes. Both industry and community shared in the use of Onondaga Lake. At the turn of the century lakeshore development boasted a popular summer resort where tourists and locals could fish, swim, and boat; on the other side sat the smoking stacks of industry. Places like Rockaway Beach, Iron Pier, and Long Branch Amusement Park made Onondaga Lake a popular recreation spot. The lake was also a place where people recreated, relaxed, and enjoyed "nature."

Although many Syracusans did not consider Onondaga Lake solely and exclusively an economic commodity, the economic reality of industrialization dominated the city's relationship with the lake. Industrial waste flowed directly into the lake, and as the city grew the lake served as an inexpensive dumping ground for municipal sewerage and refuse. Allied and the city of Syracuse entered into an agreement that allowed the city to pump its sewerage sludge onto beds of industrial waste; it was anticipated that the resulting chemical action would neutralize both wastes.[11] Despite this "solution" the twin problems of industrial and municipal waste further degraded the lake. Although many noticed the environmental degradation of Onondaga Lake, industrial and economic prosperity gave Syracuse its identity and cemented an exploitative relationship. Pollution, though recognized, seemed a small price to pay for progress.

By 1940 the lake had become so odorous and unattractive that it was no longer usable for swimming under New York State public health law. Though some people continued to boat and fish, Syracuse had essentially lost the lake as a community recreational resource.

## Raising the Question

On Thanksgiving Day in 1943, the dike holding back Allied Chemical and Dye Company wastebeds on the western shoreline of Onondaga Lake collapsed. A nasty concoction of sludge and slurry inundated homes and buried the State Fairgrounds. Prompted by this disaster, a trio of local environmental crusaders rallied to the lake's defense. Walter Welch, Crandall Melvin, and William Maloney founded the Onondaga Lake Reclamation Association (OLRA) in 1945. Working together, these activists wrote letters, called community meetings, gathered information, organized press releases, initiated their own surveys of the lake and pressured for state legal action against industrial polluters. They challenged the image and function of the lake as a commodity. In doing so, they contested the way in which many Syracusans had constructed their relationship with the lake.

The OLRA had some successes in fighting lake pollution. In 1945, the local newspaper, the *Syracuse Post-Standard*, featured a series of articles on Onondaga Lake pollution, stimulating public interest in the possibility of reclaiming the lake. The publicity generated by the many letters to the editor motivated New York State Governor Thomas Dewey, then campaigning for reelection, to tour the lake. Following the visit he committed state funds for improving the shoreline. Publicity also increased OLRA membership. The OLRA thus took small but important steps in defining the problem of pollution.

Urban change often begins at the margins and with the few. In Syracuse growing community awareness resulted in questions about the lake's symbolic importance. The Onondaga Lake Reclamation Association called into question, intentionally or not, the kind of urban development that had given shape to the twentieth-century industrial American landscape. Decades prior to the environmental movement of the 1970s this grassroots group took industry and city and county administrators to task.

The OLRA attempted to redefine the community's relationship to the lake. Contesting the privileges of capital, Walter Welch of the OLRA remarked, "The important thing is that Syracuse, Solvay [Process Company], and the environs on Onondaga Lake belong to all the people; not just to stockholders of Allied Chemical and Dye Corporation."[12]

The process of social change is too complex to reduce to a polarity of citizen versus industry. The OLRA did not call for industry to cease operations; rather they hoped that cleaning up the lake waters would rekindle business interests and investment. Their concern with not only the visual aspects of the lake but the restoration of its "usefulness" to the community was significant and revealed how strongly intertwined economic needs are within the cultural values of an industrial community.

The OLRA's intent was not to overturn the existing economic and political institutions but to protest the abuse of a natural resource by emphasizing the consequences of industrial pollution. That this grassroots group had only a marginal effect on changing public attitudes and on prompting lake cleanup is

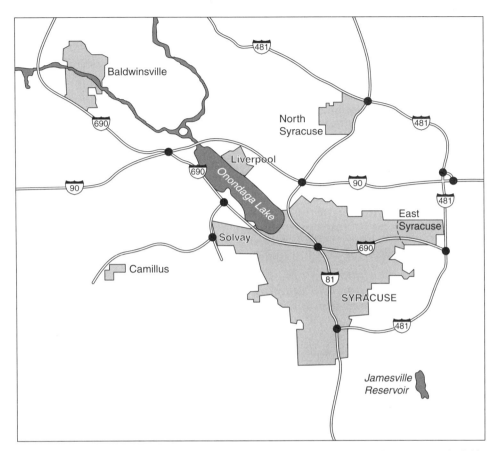

**Figure 6.2** Onondaga Lake in relation to Syracuse (Syracuse University cartography lab)

not surprising given the state of the economy in post-Second World War America. The 1940s and 1950s brought unparalleled growth. Ideologies and the economy complemented each other – growth was good. In 1954, *Fortune* magazine recognized Allied Corporation as a "blue chip" company. Sales that year totaled more than \$150 million, and its assets were worth over \$200 million.[13] In Syracuse, political rhetoric promised cleanup efforts and pollution studies and industry promised cooperation, but ultimately the result was delays and inaction. As the ducking and dodging and delays of the city grew, so too did the frustration of the OLRA. One of the OLRA's leaders, William Maloney, called Onondaga Lake a "seething cesspool of corruption neglected by an administration of incompetence."[14] The powers at city hall and other business elites carefully orchestrated a convincing reply: "Does Syracuse want its people employed, or do they want the lake cleaned up?"[15] Certain interests placed cleanup measures in opposition to growth and expansion; consideration of the environment ran counter to the exploitative practices that had been pursued for almost two centuries. There was no way for the OLRA's objectives to be compatible with those of city leaders. There was a backbone of resistance to even questioning the exploitative practices. In July of 1949 "A Disgusted Syracusan" wrote to the *Syracuse Post-Standard* in response to complaints by some people to do something about Solvay Process Company and the pollution of Onondaga Lake:

> There have many years gone by when they haven't been able to use Onondaga Lake and they got along without it. But they did have the work at Solvay Process Co.
> Why bring this question up now when there is so much talk of unemployment? What good would the lake do poor people when they are out of work?
> Of course it might hurt the pocketbook of a few politicians who are fighting to keep Solvay Process from using it. What will these same people do for the men if Solvay moves?
> Does Syracuse want its people employed or do they want the lake cleaned up? What will bring in bread to the workers?

In 1953, ten years after the dramatic Thanksgiving disaster, New York State quietly settled the claims of those affected. Allied's penalties were viewed as a mere slap on the wrist. The secretive dealings between the state and Allied destroyed the morale of the OLRA, and as Welch recalled:

> We felt betrayed and discouraged.... all along we knew we were pushing against some mighty forces. Allied had a large payroll; they were making considerable money out there. They had friends and ability to influence decisions.[16]

Although its momentum was lost after 1953, the OLRA continued the fight to reclaim Onondaga Lake and remained a voice in opposition to the foot-dragging that characterized the 1940s, 1950s, and 1960s. The association attempted to recover the urban meaningfulness of the natural environment and articulated a cultural need to reconnect people to the environment. It took a small (and perhaps unwitting) step toward reconstituting a whole set of cultural, economic, and political ideologies. The organization initiated public discussion, forcing politicians and industry to negotiate and to acknowledge the existence of lake pollution. This was a victory of sorts, because their pressure made pollution an issue. Most important, the OLRA brought into the public arena a debate that called for a rethinking of the value of Onondaga Lake. By the mid-1940s, the notion of collective responsibility was beginning to reappear, a necessary step in developing a sense of guilt and a sense of obligation to the environment. The OLRA was a social movement that initiated a transformation of urban meaning. They sought to reimagine the city-lake relationship.

### The Problem Worsens

In 1968 a federal study classified Onondaga Lake as the most polluted body of water in the Lake Ontario region, and an activist in 1969 likened the lake to an urban renewal project.[17] Between 1965 and 1970 ecology went from the relative obscurity of academic studies to becoming a household word, and pollution moved onto the national political agenda. Concern for the environment was evident everywhere: from local places, to states, regions, and the nation. In Syracuse, however, as in many other industrial communities the rising ecological consciousness had to compete against the entrenched power of industrial interests. Harry Marley, chairman of the Legislative Committee of the Metropolitan Development Association of Syracuse and Onondaga County, illustrated how intertwined the definition of community and company were in this dramatic (if self-serving) vision:

> We believe that the bold silhouette of the Solvay Plant, the fires of Crucible Steel, and the lights of the city itself can be a thrilling sight to the yachtsman on the waters of the lake at night.[18]

Onondaga Lake came with no operators' manual to prescribe cleanup measures. Growing industry and increasing urbanization during the postwar boom strained the lake's ability to absorb, process and biodegrade the increased levels of waste. Ironically, simultaneous with a heightened concern for environmental degradation was escalation of industrial pollution. Onondaga Lake became a classic example of the *unpolitics of pollution* caught in a cycle of inaction and compromise. Unpolitics are characterized by a great deal of public discussion and numerous statements of good intention but ultimately no action, and hence no cleanup. Frustration grew. In 1974, the *Syracuse Post-Standard* condemned the delay in the Onondaga Lake cleanup as "one of the most flagrant examples of governmental blundering and boondoggling of the twentieth century."[19] Although a heightened awareness of ecology opened up public debate, Onondaga Lake was sentenced to a bureaucratic purgatory.

The air and waters surrounding us cannot readily be fenced in, and pollution is one example of what ecologist Garrett Hardin termed "the tragedy of commons."[20] The tragedy of the commons occurs when people have no obligation to maintain the quality of the land and waters. We can imagine the lake as an instance that demonstrates the tragedy of the commons – it is a space unclaimed and unprotected. Intensified capitalism and urbanization generated the conditions of a tragedy of the commons in Onondaga Lake. During the 1970s people became aware of the overexploitation of the lake under private enterprise. A rush of new technological fix-its and legislative band-aids attempted to control the damage. Nevertheless pollution worsened in the lake despite the acknowledgment of the problem. We know that the technological metadiscourse considers the natural environment not as a member of the community but as a utility. Commons only survive if people have a collective sense of responsibility and stewardship.

As the technological solution to the lake's pollution industrial leaders, the city of Syracuse, and Onondaga County promoted the construction of the Syracuse Metropolitan Sewage Treatment Plant. In the 1970s Onondaga County conducted considerable testing and monitoring of the lake under the guidelines of the New York State Clean Waters Act. In addition consultants for industry, the Upstate Freshwater Institute, the Army Corps of Engineers, and the faculty at Syracuse University and the State University of New York Environmental School of Forestry (SUNY-ESF) also conducted numerous studies. Syracuse, like many cities, found itself dependent on technical reports that tended to polarize the debate as environment versus the economy, a dependency that could lead to what Jesse Jackson aptly coined "the Paralysis of Analysis."

Despite the plethora of testing, the health of the lake continued to decline. Plans for improving the environment of Onondaga Lake were thought to exacerbate the local economic problems of the 1970s and 1980s. The twin problems of a sick environment and a sick economy appeared irreconcilable. The city leaders' ambiguous position and their hesitancy to press for accountability can be viewed more as a survival strategy for the city's economic health than as disregard for the ecological state of the lake.

The chartering of the Environmental Protection Agency in 1970 brought renewed energy to the environmentalists in Syracuse. At the same time, however, the new regulations only added to the confusion of plans and delayed implementation of waste removal and cleanup efforts. The lake was caught in a vicious political cycle: the studies done to determine environmental degradation brought increasingly stringent federal and state laws, resulting in more environmental surveys.

By 1980 over 245 studies, dissertations, and articles on Onondaga Lake had been written. The studies were not frivolous attempts to placate a concerned public; the constant reshuffling of environmental standards called for serious study of the problems. Politicians and industry claimed more studies were needed, and government responded by appropriating funds for continued surveys. In response to the delays, another nonprofit grassroots organization reminiscent of the OLRA, the Atlantic States Legal Foundation, brought a $50-million lawsuit against Onondaga County over the sewerage pollution of Onondaga Lake. Their goal was to force the county to spend the millions that would be necessary to make Onondaga Lake free of pollution.

The icon of industrial Syracuse, Allied Corporation, ceased operations in 1986, leaving no heir but over 200 tons of mercury in the lake. It was the last major manufacturer of a bygone era to leave the Syracuse area, departing for greener (and probably cleaner) pastures elsewhere. After a century of intense industrialization, Onondaga Lake was abandoned by industry. Meanwhile, decades of negative images reinforced opinions that the lake was dead (see figure 6.3.

## Reimagining the Lake

In the early 1970s, newly appointed Mayor Lee Alexander organized a design contest to replace the 100-year-old city logo (figure 6.4). Said Alexander:

**Figure 6.3**   Cartoon of Onondaga Lake. Community attitudes closely paralleled this political cartoon, which appeared in the *Syracuse Herald-Journal* in 1990. (Courtesy of Frank Cammuso and the *Syracuse Herald-Journal* newspaper.)

> When one gazes at the seal of the City of Syracuse, one is inescapably struck by the featuring of factory chimneys pouring out smoke, and one recognizes that what was in 1848 intended to symbolize energetic growth of a city on the move now speaks in a different language to the pollution-conscious citizen of the twentieth century.[21]

The old seal portrayed the solar salt fields, the Erie Canal, and most prominently, seven belching smokestacks. The Syracuse city seal, proudly displayed in public areas and used on city stationery and official documents, connoted a dirty environment that was quickly becoming unfashionable as the environmental movement picked up momentum. Alexander perceptively recognized that the city would need to change its image to keep pace with the cultural and economic trends of the country. Surprisingly, there was great community reluctance to accept a new logo. Typical was the response of the president of the Onondaga County Historical Association: "We do not throw out the portraits of our ancestors because their clothes are out of style." Perhaps Syracusans were not ready to jettison their history while the local economy still grew (despite a declining national economy). There appeared no need to disassociate community identity from an industrial landscape. The old city logo remained in use.

**Figure 6.4**  Syracuse City logo, *c.*1848. The solar saltfield, the Erie Canal, and seven belching smokestacks characterize the city's prosperity. (Courtesy the Mayor's Office and City Hall, Syracuse, New York.)

But by the late 1970s outmoded technology and aging industrial plants made Syracuse a target for disinvestment. Onondaga Lake had become both in physical reality and in symbolism a source not of life but of death. From 1964 to 1984 Syracuse saw employment in the industrial sector decline from one-third to one-fifth of total employment with an absolute decline of some 6,000 industrial jobs.[22] Deindustrialization can result in more than just job losses. A community in the midst of deindustrialization confronts a deep sense of insecurity that grows out of the collapse all around them of the traditional economic base of their community.[23] As Rust Belt cities faced the significant economic transitions, the search for a new economy became a search for a new identity.

We can identify at least three ways in which the reconstruction of a post-industrial city takes shape: the physical construction of new buildings and the refurbishing of old ones, the reconstruction of the city's image, and the renegotiation of a "socioeconomic contract" with its environment (in other words, the construction of its humanity–environment relationship). To compete with the advantages advertised by the new informational cities, the postindustrial city must tempt business opportunities to rebuild its economic base. "Industrial cities are refashioning their image, on the one hand, against a wave of deindustrialization and disinvestment, on the other hand, for capital investment seeking the new, the modern, the postmodern, the postindustrial."[24] Part of the process of rewriting a city's image involves public discussion of its relationship with its environment, a relationship historically built on exploitation, domination and degradation. Dealing with the legacy of industrial pollution has forced many cities to confront not only a myriad of economic and physical problems but also, at a fundamental level, the question of their identity.

By the 1980s it was important to prove that former industrial cities were cleaning up their acts. Prevailing cultural (and economic) fashion dictated that the environment appear healthy, integrated and vital, even within the boundaries of a city. Syracuse now confronted the legacy of industrial pollution and a lake abandoned. In 1984, the community organized the Onondaga Lake Symposium to discuss plans and ideas for the future use of Onondaga Lake. By this time it was clear that in Syracuse the trend away from industrial employment and toward the service industries was underway. Since the lake had served industrial manufacturing needs, a change in the economy meant a change in the city's relationship to the lake. It would no longer symbolize a resource for industrial exploitation. The city now wanted the lake to be reinstated as a *shared* recreational and economic resource. The problem remained twofold: first, the lake was extremely polluted and therefore unusable for recreational activities; second, given the lake was a long-time lost cause (and lost social space) how would the city reintegrate it back into the minds of its people?

The answer to the first problem came in the form of waterfront development schemes. Plans for the downtown borrowed from designs used in other cities. "It's sort of the Bostonization of Syracuse," said one panelist. Projects included the renovation of the lakeside Fort St Marie, the building of bicycle paths along the lakeshore and the construction of the multimillion dollar Carousel Mall to anchor an ambitious development project that would stretch from the downtown to the lake.

As a solution to the second problem of changing people's attitudes city officials, citizen groups, and scientists argued forcefully that cleanup efforts had to happen if the lake was to become a symbol of and for the city. Discussions focused on the lake as a unifying element for the city and its suburbs. But accepting a new image requires an attitude adjustment. A planner for the city's Department of Community Development remarked:

With regard to attitude, I think that one of the first things the city has to do is acknowledge the lake is there, and that although the lake is in its current state – not a good condition – it is not a lost cause. *I think we're going to have to begin to see ourselves as somehow physically, visually, and image-wise associated with Onondaga Lake.*[emphasis added].[25]

In 1986 Mayor Tom Young succeeded in resurrecting a design contest for a new city logo. *Post-Standard* headlines proclaimed, "the City of Syracuse is in the market for a new image." In keeping with this theme, the mayor stated, "We are in search of a fresh new identity that will reinforce a renewed sense of pride and feeling of ownership among the people of our city, as well as present a positive image to visitors."[26] The decline of the local economy made a new image necessary to attract as well as retain investment. An advisory council of advertising executives from the Central New York area chose three finalists from over 50 submitted designs. The wining logo, designed by Bob Ripley, art director of a local design firm, was unveiled in conjunction with a new campaign called "Syracuse, the Heart of New York" (See figure 6.5). Ripley acknowledged that the discussions of reclaiming Onondaga Lake for lakeside development had influenced his decision to include the lake as part of the design. In the new logo Syracuse appears streamlined; tall office buildings and the silhouetted lake suggest the transition from industrial to postindustrial, from the polluted to the clean. Notice how the city landscape has been realigned. The lake, previously

© 1986 City of Syracuse NY

**Figure 6.5**   The current Syracuse City logo, designed by the local design firm Paul, John & Lee. (Courtesy the Mayor's Office and City Hall, Syracuse, New York)

considered the city's backyard dumping ground, is reoriented to the frontyard, the city's entry. The message to the community is to picture Onondaga Lake as the heart of the community and the county. The message to outsiders is that Syracuse has a dramatic skyline, a festive waterfront, and a sleek new look. How far does image blur reality? Commented one symposium attendee, "whenever you see that photograph, I think most of us think, where is that, Seattle or someplace?"[27]

Images such as city logos are not merely innocent depictions, but are used to buoy the economy, plan for the future direction of the built form, and give a sense of place to the community.

At one time the lake was indisputably an industrial commodity. This image has been replaced by an equally hegemonic vision of the lake as a shared space, a place of recreation and appeal. Syracuse elites have created an image paradox: the city wishes to be what it pretends it is. At the same time, it must sell to others that Syracuse is no longer what it used to be. Syracuse's new logo carries with it the power to change attitude. It is an initial attempt to get people in the city to rethink their relationship to the lake, indeed, to the entire physical environment of the city. The image is symbolic of the efforts taken on a physical level (waterfront redevelopment) that must precede changes in identity.

A Syracuse Chamber of Commerce brochure that was sent to businesses inquiring about relocation possibilities constructed a new image of the postindustrial city: "A heightened social awareness for protecting the environment emerged as many manufacturers left the Northeast, leaving pollutants in their wake.... Syracuse has become 'the place' to turn to for environmental technology and expertise."[28] Poised in the center of a region where the environment has witnessed a century of industrial pollution, Syracuse now promotes itself as the location for environmental law, technical development, and firms specializing in environmental cleanup. It is a classic display of the irony of the postmodern condition.

Onondaga Lake has been a place of gathering, a place of spirituality, a place of leisure and recreation. It has also been a place to dump wastes and to tap resources. It has brought prosperity to the city and has suffered ecological destruction. Despite the hegemony of the technological metadiscourse, ideas and relationships found in the ecological metadiscourse have resurfaced in the modern environmental movement. The organic understanding of the world has provided a counterpoint to the dominant metadiscourse. We saw many of these ideas expressed by the Onondaga Lake Reclamation Association and later by people concerned about the quality of the environment for future generations.

Environmental metadiscourses persist. The ecological metadiscourse has resurfaced albeit in a new guise after several hundred years. Promoting a clean and green environment now plays a crucial role in reconstructing a postindustrial city's image. Old industrial cities like Pittsburgh, Cleveland, Detroit, and Syracuse have recently advertised improved environmental quality to compete with places like San Francisco, Denver, Miami, and Seattle. Part of constructing a new identity involves restructuring a new humanity–environment discourse, often attempted via images, logos, slogans, and redevelopment schemes. In the effort to reclaim the lake as both a social space and an economic space, Syracuse is beginning to restructure its relationship with its environment.

The story of Onondaga Lake tells us much about the urban landscape, the development of Syracuse, and the way in which broader values about society and economic priorities can influence the relationship of people to their environment. The lake is a place where fundamental beliefs about the relationship between people and their environment have been formed, contested, compromised, and challenged. It is a small lake, but its message is large.

## FURTHER READING

### Worldviews about the Environment

Berry, T. 1988. *The Dream of the Earth*. San Francisco: Sierra Club Books.

Cronon, W. 1983. *Changes in the Land: Indians, Colonists and the Ecology of New England*. New York: Hill and Wang.

Hughes, J. D. 1983. *American Indian Ecology*. El Paso: Texas Western Press.

Nash, R. 1982. *Wilderness and the American Mind*, 3rd edn. New Haven: Yale University Press.

Petulla, J. 1980. *American Environmentalism: Values, Tactics, Priorities*. College Station: Texas A&M University Press.

Tedlock, B. and Tedlock, B. 1975. *Teachings from the American Earth: Indian Religion and Philosophy*. New York: Liveright.

Vescey, C. and Venables, R., eds, 1980. *American Indian Environments: Ecological Issues in Native American History*, Syracuse, NY: Syracuse University Press.

### Economic Development and the City

Bluestone, B. and Harrison, B. 1982. *The Deindustrialization of America*. New York: Basic Books.

Castells, M. 1983. *The City and the Grassroots: A Cross- Cultural Theory of Urban Social Movements*. Berkeley: University of California Press.

Crenson, M. 1971. *The Unpolitics of Pollution: A Study of Non- Decision Making in the Cities*. Baltimore: The Johns Hopkins University Press.

Duncan, J. 1990. *The City as Text: The Politics of Landscape Interpretation in the Kandyan Kingdom*, Cambridge: Cambridge University Press.

Logan, J and Molotch, H. 1987. *Urban Fortunes: The Political Economy of Place*. Berkeley: University of California Press.

### Onondaga Lake

Many of the newspaper articles, letters and pamphlets may be found in the archive box labeled "Onondaga Lake Pollution" at the Onondaga County Historical Association in

Syracuse. Many of the articles were clipped from newspapers without page citation and these are thus not noted in some of the following references. We would like to take this opportunity to thank the tireless staff of the Association for their assistance.

## NOTES

1 It is misleading to speak of "an Indian religion" because there were and are many distinct and complex traditions within each tribe. Despite different ways of life, myths, and traditions among the tribes, scholars believe there are some basic attitudes common to the North American Indian.

2 J. D. Hughes, *American Indian Ecology* (El Paso: Texas Western Press, 1983), 140.

3 B. Toelken, "How Many Sheep Can It Hold?" in *Seeing with a Native Eye: Essays on Native American Religion*, ed. W. H. Capps (New York: Harper and Row, 1976).

4 C. Vescey and R. Venables, eds, *American Indian Environments: Ecological Issues in Native American History* (Syracuse, NY: Syracuse University Press, 1980), 13.

5 Hughes, *American Indian Ecology*, 16.

6 W. Cronon, *Changes in the Land: Indians, Colonists and the Ecology of New England* (New York: Hill and Wang, 1983), 12.

7 Vescey and Venables, *American Indian Environments*, 24.

8 Quoted in R. Nolan, *Syracuse Post-Standard*, January 15, 1990: A-1.

9 The state of New York still pays members of the Onondaga Nation $2,400 a year as compensation for the loss of the salt-rich deposits along Onondaga Lake.

10 T. Berry, *The Dream of the Earth* (San Francisco: Sierra Club Books, 1988), 203.

11 R. Martin and F. Munger, *Decisions in Syracuse* (Bloomington: Indiana University Press, 1961).

12 W. Welch, *Syracuse Herald Journal*, September 8, 1946.

13 R. Comonolli, *Smokestacks Allegro* (New York: Center for Migration Studies, 1990), 137.

14 W. Maloney, "Pure Water Issue in Onondaga Lake First Essential," *Syracuse Post-Standard*, December 23, 1951.

15 "They Want Work, Not the Lake," *Syracuse Post- Standard*, July 24, 1949.

16 R. Andrews, *Syracuse Post-Standard*, October 16, 1985: A6–7.

17 D. Jackson, "Onondaga Lake Renewal Project," *Syracuse Post-Standard*, June 26, 1969.

18 H. Marley, *Hearings of the Natural Resources and Power Subcommittee of the Committee on Government Operations, House of Representatives* (Washington, DC: US Government Printing Office, 1966), 316.

19 *Syracuse Post-Standard*, February 27, 1974.

20 G. Hardin and J. Baden, *Managing the Commons* (San Francisco: WH Freeman, 1977).

21 "Allied Fighting Pollution," *Syracuse Herald Journal*, April 20, 1970.

22 Comments of D. Mankiewicz in *Proceedings of a Community Symposium on Onondaga Lake: The Inside Story*, ed. L. P. Boice (September 15, 1986), 63.

23 B. Bluestone and B. Harrison, *The Deindustrialization of America* (New York: Basic Books, 1982).

24 J. R. Short, L. Benton, B. Luce, and J. Walton, "The Reconstruction of a Postindustrial City," *Annals of the Association of American Geographers* (May 1993): 5.

25  Comments of E. Carter in *Proceedings of a Community Symposium on Onondaga Lake: The Inside Story*, ed. L. P. Boice (September 15, 1986), 64–5.

26  "The City of Syracuse Is in the Market for a New Image," *Syracuse Post-Standard*, June 6, 1986.

27  Comments of R. Hawks in *Proceedings of a Community Symposium on Onondaga Lake: The Inside Story*, ed. L. P. Boice (September 15, 1986), 71.

28  Greater Syracuse Chamber of Commerce, *Quality, Syracuse: 1991 Business Desk Reference* (New York: Greater Syracuse Services Corp., 1991), B-1.

Part II

# Environmental Discourses in Practice

# Introduction

In part I we looked at the broad sweep of environmental discourses in history and documented those defining moments (and people) that reconfigured humanity–environment relations. In part II we look in more detail at particular environmental discourses emerging in contemporary society and the way in which they influence place, policy, and cultural values. Part I used a wide-angle lens to develop a broad and general picture; part II uses a macro lens to construct a higher resolution view.

Each chapter provides a detailed case study that explores in more detail some of the general ideas and propositions outlined in part I. Chapters 7 and 8 consider the ways in which environmental discourses are connected to a broad range of social criticisms. In chapter 7 we look at the ways in which concern for the environment has become legitimized and institutionalized in society. In this chapter, we show that environmentalism is no longer on the "margins," but in many instances has become integrated into mainstream public consciousness. In chapter 8 we look at how broad social concerns have been linked to environmental issues and ideas in what we may term a discourse of social environmental thought and practice. We pay particular attention to radical environmental thought and ecofeminism and conclude with a discussion of postmodern environmental ethics.

In chapter 9 we discuss the changing relationship between nature and culture in the evolution of the national park system. We argue that the national parks are one of the most visible embodiments of the changing relationship between the American people and their environment. An examination of the history of the national parks allows us to discuss the changing attitudes to wilderness, to raise the interesting proposition of the social construction of nature and to note that national parks are places which embody a profound connection between "national" identity and "national" landscapes.

Environmental discourses are also inherently political, and those politics are the central focus of the next two chapters. In chapter 10 we scrutinize the connection between trade and environment and in particular the debate generated by the signing of the NAFTA trade agreement. We will look at how a range of environmental concerns were voiced in the negotiations, the political lobbying, and resultant compromises and outcomes. It becomes clear that environmental discourses now influence and inform policy in other areas, such as trade and economics. In chapter 11 we explore the growth of the largest environmental organizations and consider the paradox of literally selling their message in a consumer society that they profess to criticize. This is not meant as a cheap shot but more as an honest raising of the type of paradoxes and ambiguities that affect all institutions that seek effective radical change through the present system. We conclude with a brief postscript which explores the ambiguity that often accompanies environmentalism in practice.

# 7

# The Greening of the United States

The environmental movement of the past 30 years has become so successful that it is legitimate to speak of the "greening of the United States." What we mean by this is the growing importance of the ecological metadiscourse. The greening of the United States has occurred in a number of ways. In this chapter we will consider the increasing importance of environmental organizations, the rise of environmental awareness in public consciousness and the emergence of a green capitalism. We focus on mainstream environmental discourses; in the next chapter we consider more radical discourses.

## Environmental Organizations and Green Politics

The environmental movement is something of a misnomer. It is more accurate to think of it as a number of different organizations, groups, and movements motivated by differing objectives. What is not in dispute is the increasing size and importance of environmental groups, especially the big ten, which include the Environmental Defense Fund, Environmental Policy Institute, Friends of the Earth, Izaak Walton League of America, National Audubon Society, National Parks and Conservation Association, National Wildlife Federation, Natural Resources Defense Council, Sierra Club, and Wilderness Society. The membership of all these groups, apart from the Izaak Walton League, which remained at approximately 50,000 from 1960 to 1990, has increased dramatically in the past 30 years. In 1962 the Audubon Society had only 41,000 members; by 1991 this had increased to 600,000. The Wilderness Society increased from 27,000 in 1964 to 350,000 in 1991. The big ten had a combined membership of 8 million by the early 1990s and a combined budget of $250 million. Membership in itself is not a sign of power. The membership, compared to the rest of the population, however, is richer, more affluent, more politically involved, and more active in the democratic process.

The environmental groups have differing aims. The Audubon Society focuses more on wildlife; Friends of the Earth on action; the National Parks and Conservation Association on national parks; the Sierra Club on policy. As just one example, let us look at the Sierra Club in some detail. Founded in 1893 under its first president John Muir, the club was a San Francisco–based organization concerned with preserving the redwoods and high peaks of the Sierras. Even as late as 1959 its membership was only 20,000, but by 1970 it had increased to 54,00 and to over 500,000 by 1995. The growth of the Sierra Club reflects and embodies an environmental awareness, savvy marketing, and an aggressive growth policy.

In 1952 David Brower was appointed the first salaried director of the Sierra Club. He was born in Berkeley and grew up in the Bay Area. He was involved with the club at an early age, joining in 1933, and in the immediate postwar period was involved in what was a turning point. A split occurred between the old guard, which clung to the original idea that the club's aim should be to make the mountains more accessible, and the new guard (of which Brower was part), which wanted the focus on preservation not access, arguing that, in an age of mass transport and tourism, increasing access would prove fatal to the mountains. The new guard won and the long-standing bylaw "to render the mountains accessible" was deleted. Brower was influential in shifting the orientation of the club, increasing its membership and getting it involved in wider policy debates. In the early 1960s there were proposals for dam construction in the Grand Canyon. Brower, working with the Wilderness Society and the Audubon Society, took out full-page adverts in the newspapers asking readers to write to Congress, send money and join the Sierra Club. Thousands did. The IRS threatened to question its charitable tax-exempt status. Brower responded with even more adverts, and membership continued to increase. Under the Colorado River Bill of 1968 the dams had been deleted from its contents. *Life* magazine called Brower the country's "No. 1 working conservationist."[1]

In 1969 Brower lost the board election and was forced to resign. He had increased the membership tenfold, created a full- time staff, raised the visibility of the organization, and been successful in influencing legislation. However, he had spent a lot of money, caused a rift in the club between the volunteers and the full-time staff, and irked the older guard. There were some who saw him as successful and others who saw him as too concerned with power. In his thinking Brower predated environmental organizations by about a decade. He shifted the culture from a small membership to mass membership, from small staffs servicing a mass of volunteers to mass members paying for full-time staff, and from little involvement in direct policy-making to high-profile involvement. His emphasis on mass membership, wide circulation of organizational publications, full-time staff, and visible public policy involvement have become the main goals of the big ten since the 1980s. Brower had showed the way. He was brought back onto the board of the Sierra Club by the 1980s. The club, like many other organizations, had moved toward his view. In the meantime he had helped establish the John Muir Institute (1968), Friends of the Earth, the League of Conservation Voters (1969) and the Earth Island Institute (1981). Brower promoted an environmental awareness through organizations that wielded power and influence.

Today the Sierra Club is one of the biggest, richest, and most influential environmental organizations in the United States. It has over 350 groups across the country and has full-time lobbyists in Washington, DC. From an outdoors club catering to rich San Franciscans hiking in the Sierras, the entity has emerged as a national organization seeking to effect change and influence public policy. It is a powerful constituent part of the environmental movement that has a powerful voice and major role in environmental legislation. The Sierra Club, like other environmental groups, files lawsuits, lobbies Congress, and mobilizes its mass membership

The very success of the large organizations like the Sierra Club has created controversy. One school of thought sees co-option as well as success. The big groups have a place at the table but have lost their radical edge. Few of them ever actually had a radical edge. The Sierra Club began as elitist and has since become more radical. However, the corporate sponsorship that some groups now entertain – the Sierra Club receives corporate contributions from Amoco, Chevron, and Dupont, for example – have caused some to question their commitment. We disagree. These organizations and especially the Sierra Club have become more, not less, effective in lobbying. Our criticisms refer less to funding and more to the marketing and consumerism of the organizations, a topic we will explore in some detail in chapter 11.

Environmental groups have become much more involved in formal politics, and this inevitably involves compromises and negotiations. Politics is the art of the possible. To get things done deals have to be made, friends cultivated, power exercised. Environmental groups have achieved success by their involvement in politics. There has been an upward spiral: the rising wave of environmental interest since the 1960s has been expressed in increased membership in environmental groups, which gained more resources to publicize events, educate the public, and influence decision-makers, and these activities, in turn, have increased membership. For the past 30 years environmental groups such as the Sierra Club and Wilderness Society have achieved unparalleled growth in membership, budgets, full-time staff, and political influence.

Below the big ten are a host of medium- and small-sized environmental groups. Differing in size and objective, they cover the country and the range of issues in a web of pressure group politics operating at the state and local levels. For example, the Atlantic States Legal Foundation (ASLF) was founded in 1984 by Samuel Sage, who was a member and board member of the Sierra Club. The ASLF is based in Syracuse, New York but operates around the country. It is small; full-time staff consists of Sage, a staff attorney, an office manager, and a research assistant. They rely on professional volunteers to help with specific research brought to their attention by the citizenry. The goal is to use the legal process to force businesses to abide by environmental legislation. If they find a case of environmental regulations being broken or flouted the ASLF takes the matter to court. In the 1980s and 1990s it was involved with issues in Syracuse, including the cleanup of Onondaga Lake and the forcing of the biochemical company Bristol Myers Squibb to enforce better screening of its air emissions. ASLF has also been active in Indiana ensuring that manufacturing companies follow the Emergency Planning and Right to Know Act that governs notification about hazardous chemical wastes. There are thousands of ASLF-type organizations around the country. There are even more, smaller organizations concerned with very local issues, often ephemeral, formed by local residents complaining about dumping or pollution and hastily organized to achieve specific goals. These place-specific groups often rise and fall as issues wax and wane. But in the past 30 years these groups now have a discourse to attach to, other bigger organizations to alert and a legal purchase on the political process.

Green politics in the United States have been dominated by pressure group politics. Elsewhere in the world formal green politics have played a more important role in policy-making. In political systems with proportional representation green parties have achieved some success – in Australia, New Zealand, West Germany, and now Germany – with a platform based on ecology, grassroots democracy, social justice, decentralization, and postpatriarchal principles. In West Germany the Green Party crystallized wider concerns of nuclear arms and power, the peace movement and gender issues, and achieved parliamentary representation. In 1990 the Green Party delegates lost their seats but eight seats were gained in districts in the former East Germany. In 1992 the Green Party in France obtained 14 percent of the vote. Green party representation is strongest in multiparty systems with proportional representation.

In the United States, in contrast, the dominance of the two-party system and the sheer expense of electioneering rule out an effective role for the Green Party. The US political system, although discouraging formal political representation outside of the two-party system, is receptive to pressure group activity, including lobbying, mobilizing public opinion, and fundraising. The bigger and more powerful the group the more its pressure yields results. While there are many powerful groups, all of the diverse elements of the environmental movement constitute a significant element in the informal politics of pressure group representation in the United States. The political discourse in the United States echoes with environmental issues.

## We Are All Environmentalists Now?

From surveys it is clear that the majority of the US population sees environmental issues as a serious problem, a threat to human well-being and, compared to many other areas, believes that government regulations have "not gone far enough" and that there is "too little government regulation of the environment." When polls were compared over time, from the early 1970s to the early 1990s environmental awareness and concern had increased. And even when environmental protection is contrasted with economic well-being the proenvironment majority stands up.[2] Environmental concern has weathered economic highs and lows; it is not limited to periods of perceived affluence and neither is it solely a concern of the affluent. Over 70 percent of the US public consistently supports the same or more environmental protection and regulation. Favorable attitudes about the federal government may wax and wane, and over the last 30 years it has been waning rather than waxing, but environmental regulation stands as one of the most publicly supported government positions.

The regular reporting of environmental hazards and pollution has convinced the US public that there is potential and actual danger to human life and well-being. People are less convinced of the limits-to-growth argument and more decided that economic growth has hazardous side effects, especially in terms of environmental quality and health. The majority of people believe that unregulated corporations and industries would willingly sacrifice environmental quality to corporate profits. An environmental sensitivity is now a vital ingredient of American public opinion.

The environment has become something to be protected and guarded. As the United States fractures along many lines, and goes through the so-called disuniting or disentangling of a social consensus, there are a few grand ideas that still garner widespread support. The environment is one of those ideas. It has become a sacred space. We are all environmentalists now. The debate has shifted from arguing for or against environmental standards and regulation. The arguments are about the specific form that legislation should take, not about the basic need for legislation. Conflicts arise when we move from the general consensus to the more concrete particular. When we move from grand statement about environmental quality to detailed discussions of specific areas, policy and regulation conflicts are more apparent. Thus when the EPA tried to introduce more stringent air quality standards in the mid-1990s industry responded by saying that the existing standards were adequate, that the research on respiratory diseases prompting the more stringent standards was faulty, and that the industry was already doing a good job.

### Growing impacts

Environmental sensitivity has grown because we are now much more aware of the human impact on the earth, which depends in large measure on the number of people. Small populations, in general, have less impact than large populations. The history of the United States has been one of increasing population. At the time of the first census, taken in 1790, the population was counted as 4 million. By the midpoint of the next century it was 23 million and 76 million by 1900. As we approach the end of the twentieth century the population has increased to approximately 269 million. But there are still a lot of empty spaces in the United States. Alaska's population density is only 1 person per square mile, whereas Idaho, Montana, Nevada, New Mexico, North Dakota, South Dakota, and Wyoming have fewer than 20 persons per square mile. While there are still wide open spaces in the west, even the great cities have areas that have yet to be concreted. Compared to much of Europe the population cover in the United States is light and thinly spread. But it is a population that walks with a heavy tread. In the early years of the Republic, most work was done by the expenditure of human energy. Technology was limited and needs were restricted by the low level of technological power. Two hundred years later the level of technological sophistication has increased, like the population, by staggering amounts. We can, and do, mine mountains, dam rivers, deflect the seas, bring water to the desert, and cover the land in concrete highways. We can, and also do, create radioactive waste and manufacture chemical sludge and materials that will take thousands of years to decompose. We have filled the environment with both the wonders and wastes of a chemical age. We have irrigated the desert, ploughed over the prairie, cut down the forests, taken oil, gas and coal from the bowels of the earth, established whole industrial complexes, built towns and cities. Our technological ability is embodied in the landscape. Our expectations have grown as well. We now expect fresh water every time we turn the faucet and power to connect when we turn on the electric switch; we expect the darkness to be lit, the desert watered, the hot cooled and the cold warmed. We affect the world with our presence, our technological ability and our needs. It is against this background that the environmental movement has grown and has sought to effect change. For some a return to a previous age, a sort of preindustrial, preurban stage is the desired state. This is neither feasible nor desirable. The difficult task for a contemporary environmental discourse is not to decry the human impact but to channel this impact into a shape that demonstrates a good fit with the environment, that provides the basis for a sustainable society and long-term harmony with the environment. This is a huge task made all the more difficult as our environmental impacts grow and our environmental expectations increase. We want expanding job opportunities for ourselves and our children and a healthy environment for ourselves and our children. The satisfactory resolution to these aims is one of the largest challenges facing not only the American people but people everywhere.

### Rewriting the past

The past is continually rewritten in tune with contemporary concerns and future expectations. The past is less an unchanging truth and more an endless opportunity to see our current obsessions in a distant mirror.

An environmental awareness has been reflected and embodied in new historical discourses in which human deeds are set in a wider environmental context. It is legitimate to speak of an environmental history as a flourishing academic discipline as well as a popular portrayal of the past. General texts include such books as Joseph Petulla's *American Environmental History* (1977) and Roderick Nash's classic *Wilderness and the American Mind* (1982). There are also readers in environmental history, such as Nash's *American Environment* (1976) and more detailed studies. William Cronon's *Changes in the Land* (1983) is an excellent survey of the confrontation between native peoples and colonists in New England; a conflict between two differing ways of constructing human–nature relations. The same writer has also written a history of Chicago, *Nature's Metropolis* (1991), in which the expansion of the city is described in terms of the commodification of nature and the transformation of ecosystems.

One of the most persistent themes in a self-conscious historiography of the United States has been the writing of the west and the western experience. The classic work is by Frederick Jackson Turner. In a paper read to the American Historical Association on July 12, 1894, "The Significance of the Frontier in American History," Jackson suggested that the most significant process in American history was the defeat of the wilderness. The expansion of the frontier created an American identity because it reduced dependence on Britain and Europe, provided the context for government legislation and helped in the creation of a rugged individualism and democratic spirit. All of these ideas are debatable. What is interesting, however, is how this triumphalist notion held sway over the public imagination and historical writing. The frontier thesis, as it has been called, has been continually reinterpreted. This is demonstrated in the successive editions of Ray Billington's classic book *Westward Expansion*. In the first edition (1949) Billington followed Turner's basic premise but noted in the third edition (1967) that "no longer do historians blindly accept the frontier as solely responsible for national development." And in the fourth edition (1974) the role of blacks and Hispanics is noted and "Indians" are given a more prominent position as ethnic minorities.[3] Since this fourth edition a new western history has emerged in which the role of previously ignored minorities such as women, African Americans, Hispanics, and Native Americans is more prominent, the model of progressive improvement is jettisoned and the environmental costs and consequences are central stories.[4] Environmental historians, such as Donald Worster, have paid particular attention to the unfolding human–environment relations in the history of the west.[5] In this new interpretation western history has been told less in terms of the rise to civilization and more in terms of unfolding relations and tensions between nature and people. It parallels the contemporary concern with our relationship to the environment. These environmental histories are the stories for an environmental age and represent the greening of our view of the past, our concern with the present, and our expectations and hopes for the future. For some the benign and celebratory reading by Turner is reinterpreted as the story becomes less of a triumph and more the making of an ecological disaster. A popular writer noted:

This, finally, is the punch line of our two hundred years on the Great Plains: we trap out the beaver, subtract the Mandan, infect the Blackfeet and the Hidatsa and the Assiniboin, overdose the Arikara, call the lands a desert and hurry across it to get to

California and Oregon, suck up the buffalo, bones and all; kill off nations of elk and wolves and cranes and prairie chickens and prairie dogs; dig up the gold and rebury it in vaults someplace else; ruin the Sioux and Cheyenne and Arapaho and Crow and Kiowa and Comanche; kill Crazy Horse, kill Sitting Bull; harvest wave after wave of immigrants ' dreams and send the wised-up dreamers on their way; plow the topsoil until it blows into the ocean; ship out the wheat, ship out the cattle; dig up the earth and burn it in power plants and send the power down the line; dismiss the small farmers, empty the little towns; drill the oil and natural gas and pipe it away; dry up the rivers and springs, deep-drill for irrigation water as the aquifer retreats.[6]

### Extending the concern: urban environmentalism

Traditional environmentalism in the United States was concerned almost exclusively with the so-called natural environment. Conservationists and preservationists devoted their energies to scenic monumentalism (the protection of sites of natural beauty and distinction, like Yellowstone and Yosemite, or sites of historic significance like Gettysburg). The overwhelming emphasis of US environmental thought and action was with wilderness preservation, especially in the creation, maintenance, and expansion of the National Park Service. Cities were not seen as an important subject for most conservationists and preservationists. There was and continues to be a strong antiurban bias in social thought in the United States, which sees cities as "unnatural," ugly, and profane. Environmental issues in the cities were raised not by environmentalists but by citizens concerned with urban reform, public health, and safety. The concerns of urban residents and environmentalists rarely intersected. There were a few exceptions; the landscape architecture of Frederick Law Olmsted, for example, introduced the importance of open spaces in US urban planning. The legacy of Central Park bequeathed us what is today one of the most vital spaces of recreation, social interaction, and spiritual restoration.

More recently, however, the concerns of environmentalists and urbanists have come together in what we may term the *new urban environmentalism*, in which a number of trends have intersected. Economic structural changes, such as deindustrialization, have left many cities faced with abandoned warehouses, factories, and toxic waste sites. Many business elites, citizens groups, and civic leaders agree that the solution to these problems is central to the city's recovery. Even in healthy, growing cities questions of environmental quality are part of their attempt to attract more business investment. Issues of urban economic growth and decline are now bound up with issues of environmental quality, and environmental costs are becoming an important ingredient in measuring success and failure. At the same time that these economic changes were occurring in cities across the country, environmentalism in the United States was maturing beyond a narrow focus on the wilderness. More than 70 percent of people in the United States live in large cities. To ignore these issues is to remain silent about the environment of the vast majority of Americans. As an environmental discourse has increased its base of public support it has begun to incorporate urban concerns.

The new urban environmentalism has a number of strands. Let us concentrate on three broad areas. First there is *the greening of the city*. This takes many forms: the creation of urban farms and gardens from derelict sites, tree planting along meridians and in parks to encourage places for wildlife. Civic authorities, developers, and local groups all share concerns with the greening of the city. Greening mandates have been built into zoning ordinances, and the more enlightened developers work closely with civic leaders to plan expanded easements and land set-asides. Some of the more attractive new real estate developments now quote nature as an integral element in their landscape design. Trees, grass, and native plants have become a keystone in contemporary urban planning. Local groups (often neighborhood organizations) and civic authorities around the country have reclaimed small parks and open spaces. Many of the new industrial spaces being created have open spaces, picnic tables, and streams. Grubby old factories are being replaced by industrial business "parks." The construction of parks and public open space in formerly abandoned industrial sites has been a pivotal part of the renaissance of many cities. Pittsburgh is one of the best examples where the legacy of industrial dereliction has been replaced by green parks.

Second there is *the detoxification of the city*, involving both cleaning up and preventing air pollution, soil contamination, and toxic hazards in rivers, streams, and bays. These efforts have been given tremendous publicity through media coverage of the disaster at Love Canal, the striking visual impact of Cleveland's Cuyahoga river engulfed in flames and increasingly publicized EPA standards. The EPA has created a federal yardstick by which the environmental quality of cities can be measured. Cleanup campaigns vary from the nation's new Clean Air Act, a pioneering effort to integrate environment with economics, to the 1992 regional law setting higher car pollution standards in the Los Angeles area, to the local citizens everywhere who gather on Saturday mornings to clean up parks, beaches, and roadsides. Avoidance of pollution and resource waste is now apparent in business, civic, community, and household concern with recycling. In addition businesses have taken voluntary initiatives with regard to energy efficiency, including green computer programs and more energy-efficient lighting. The cleanup of cities is now seen as good economics, good ecology, and good public relations.

Third there is *the reforming of city*. Here urban environmentalism is part and parcel of other social movements covering a range of social issues, including social justice, gender, and racial equality. Environmental questions have increasingly become the rallying point for the marginalized and the oppressed. Protests against incinerators, waste disposal sites and polluting factories have incorporated issues of social justice as well as environmental quality. The juxtaposition of minority groups with generally poor urban environmental quality has created an alliance between civil rights and environmental activists. The fight against "environmental racism" combines issues of racial equality and environmental quality. The feminist movement has now incorporated environmental thought into "ecofeminism," which sees both pollution and patriarchy as indicators of an unjust society. The environment has now become a site of resistance and political struggle. This third form of urban environmentalism is less concerned with preserving the natural world than in reforming the social world.

There are tensions within the new urban environmentalism. It is not a conflict-free, homogeneous movement. Affluent homeowners wanting to preserve property values, developers needing to meet the bottom line, civic authorities hamstrung by a lack of resources, and local groups seeing environmental issues as an avenue for social reform are all examples of groups in conflict over scarce resources. Despite the tensions, ambiguities, and conflict, however, a new political force is emerging in American cities, a force still fragmented but continuing to provoke and define issues that policy makers will be unable to ignore.

The questions at the beginning of the next millennium will be increasingly focused on the more profound issues of the quality of human life and the urban conditions that future generations will inherit. The new environmental questions will be a rephrasing of many of the old urban questions that we have neglected to answer. From instituting environmentally sound business practices, to demanding cleanup of toxic sites, to protesting the location of new polluting industries, to planting urban forests, the new urban environmental movement is an important extension of traditional environmental concerns.

### The backlash

One of Newton's laws postulates that to every action there is a reaction. It seems to apply as much to the social world as in the physical world. The environmental backlash has taken a number of forms. First there was the Reagan era in which environmental protection and regulation were given a more secondary position. When Reagan became president in January 1981 it marked the ascendancy of a right wing Republicanism concerned more with economic growth and defense buildup than with environmental protection. Government regulation in general and environmental regulation in particular were seen as anathema by some of Reagan's more extreme supporters. The main objectives of the administration were obtained by reducing taxes and increasing defense expenditure. The result, however, was a mushrooming deficit and growing national debt. Reagan and his supporters had little time for environmental regulation. The Council on Environmental Quality and the EPA were cut back. People who were resistant to government regulations were appointed to positions of authority. Perhaps the most well-known case was the appointment of James Watt as Secretary of the Interior. Watt wanted greater commercial exploitation of public land by private companies. He represented what has been termed the "Sage brush rebellion," led by western mining and land interests eager to obtain cheap and easy access to federal public lands. Watt had a rare capacity to put his foot in his mouth at almost every conceivable opportunity. In a speech in 1983 he compared environmentalists to both Nazis and Bolsheviks. Watt was forced to resign in 1983 after another offensive speech. Ironically, the legacy of Watt's appointment was the increasing membership of environmental organizations in the United States.

During this period the environmental movement strengthened its position in Washington, partly because it believed it had to counter actively a hostile atmosphere in Washington. Environmental legislation was no longer assured. The big ten organizations increased their visibility and institutional power, and in the second half of the Reagan presidency they recorded more victories, including passage of the Safe Drinking Water Act (1986), and the 1986 amendments to the Superfund legislation that enshrined community right-to-know clauses. Victory in a partisan atmosphere marked a maturing of the environmental lobby. They could get things done even without a friend in residence at 1600 Pennsylvania Avenue.

Much of the success of the environmental movement derives from its dire prediction that unless something is done the world, to put it succinctly, is going to hell in a handbasket. Images of environmental apocalypse are an important and integral part of environmental discourses. Action and attention have been prompted by forecasts of environmental degradation and social collapse. Writers such as Thomas Berry and Bill McKibben write of the decline in environmental quality with an end-of-the-millennium feel of tragedy.[7] A second backlash to the environmental movement has been fundamental disagreement over these predictions. The more extreme predictions have been refuted by a variety of writers. This has become easier as the worst predictions seem to be receding. In *Eco-Scam*, for example, Ronald Bailey argues that things are getting better. The prophets of doom, according to Bailey and others, refuse to see the improvements and instead write of an apocalypse that is never going to happen. The critiques of environmental apocalypse often widen out to include a more general criticism of contemporary environmentalism. In *Environmental Overkill*, Dixie Lee Ray, a former governor of the state of Washington, not only takes the predictions of ecological disaster to task, but the main thrust of the book is to question much of current environmental regulation, which is seen less as a solution and more as a problem. *Eco-Scam* and *Environmental Overkill* are just part of a growing questioning of both the predictions and assumptions of some environmentalists.

In the 1960s and 1970s the environmental movement dominated the popular writings on the environment. By the late 1980s and 1990s there were counter examples. P. J. O'Rourke is a comic writer who lambasts the liberals. His audience is almost entirely composed of centrists and liberals, giving counterfactual proof to the old adage not to bite the hand that feeds you. O'Rourke savages the people who read him. In 1994 he published a book entitled *All the Trouble in the World*. Some idea of the style is contained in the subtitle *The Lighter Side of Overpopulation, Famine, Ecological Disaster, Ethnic Hatred, Plague and Poverty*. In this 340–page book, O'Rourke spends over 200 pages on environmental issues. He takes ecological scaremongers to task and in rare empirical mode criticizes the alleged huge costs and small benefits of more recent legislation. Although much of his writing is wildly general, this section has a careful assessment of recent literature and recent cost estimates. It is as if even O'Rourke needs the solidity of data to base his attack. When O'Rourke attacks you, you know you are in a position of cultural power; when he bases this attack less on his comic style and more on "scientific data" you know the debate has become really serious.

There is much environmental writing that is smugly apocalyptic. The eco-doom writers have been questioned as have many of the assumptions of the movement. In many cases there have been environmental improvements. Air quality in many US cities is better than it was 30 years ago despite the rising number of cars. More stringent regulations, better technology and more enforcement have made many improvements in the quality of the environment. The picture is complicated however. While the air quality in Pittsburgh has improved dramatically in the past 50 years, the lakes in the Adirondacks have become more acid. And the two are connected. Air quality has improved in cities because of the decline of industry and the use of higher smokestacks, which take particulates away from the city and into the atmosphere. Sometimes the result is more acid rain, especially in places like the Adirondacks, where the underlying geology does not provide a buffer against increased acidity. The net result is better air quality in Pittsburgh and dead lakes in the Adirondacks.

This geographically complex picture is ignored in most discourses. The eco-doom picture fails to see any improvement and continually uses the threat of ecological collapse as a rallying cry. The environmental backlash only sees improvement and fails to note that the deleterious consequences have shifted to new places. Both discourses have an ideological basis. The former feels a need for regulation and greater vigilance. The latter sees in environmental legislation just one more example of a liberal conspiracy and the insatiable demand for more government involvement. The debate has become polarized with the environment often acting as a surrogate for broader conceptions of the role of government and federal regulation. The environmentalists have adopted a more pessimistic view whereas the writers of the backlash have a more optimistic perspective. In the past 30 years, the debate has shifted toward a greater role for intervention. Public opinion in the United States is still more positive about environmental laws and legislation than almost any other area of government. But the backlash, while slow to get started and only recently emerging as a consistent critical tone, will seek to shift the terms of the debate.

While some of the backlash can be dismissed as more ideologically driven, there are some writers who cannot be dismissed quite so summarily. In *A Moment on the Earth* (1995), Gregg Easterbrook argues for environmental optimism. He suggests that in the United States many pollution problems have been cleared up, environmental catastrophes are overplayed in the media, and technological developments, rather than leading to more problems, are bringing more harmony between people and the environment. Easterbrook cannot be easily disregarded because his argument is not based on an aggressive free marketeerism, and he provides convincing evidence of environmental improvement in the United States. Serious writers like Easterbrook raise important questions about many of the common assumptions of environment collapse, highlight areas of improvement and demand a more integrated role for humans in a balanced ecological harmony. They resist the antipeople view that permeates much environmental thinking. This backlash raises the debate beyond the simple slogans of ecological doom and collapse and forces us to look at the difficult questions of the costs of environmental regulation in relation to the risks involved. It is much easier to decry the modern industrial age than to sit down and make decisions about balancing the cost of environmental regulations with the benefits and calculating the attendant risks. However, the environmental movement in the United States has not reached a level of maturity to undertake such a task. We are all environmentalists now, but the precise scope and details are still under construction.

A third form of backlash has been the explicit intervention of right-wing think tanks and foundations in the environmental debate. Through the 1960s and 1970s the debates outside of government were dominated by the big ten environmental organizations. Although they differed in detail there was a common belief in the need for more government regulation. Through the 1980s and 1990s an alternative voice has been heard from the political right that argued for less government regulation, believed existing environmental standards were sufficient and pointed attention to the increasing costs of present and future compliance with regulation. Right wing think tanks such as the Heritage Foundation and the Cato Institute have published a variety of books and reports. In 1993, for example, the Cato Institute published *Apocalypse Not*, which was written by two scientists who questioned the notion of global warming and questioned the harmful effects predicted by many if warming did occur. Organizations such as Free Enterprise Press now produce work that debates the dominant liberal ethos. There is also a flourishing sector of market-oriented environmental writing. *Taking the Environment Seriously* was published in 1993 by the Political Economy Research Center, a think tank based in Bozeman, Montana that combines environmentalism with a concern with property rights, individual liberties, and unregulated markets. This backlash marks the delayed response of the intellectual right and their backers in the business community to the dominance of the environmental concern. The aim is to undermine the perceived liberal bias and to introduce ideas into the general discourse that include the efficacy of free markets to improve environmental quality and the heavy costs and negative consequences of government regulation. These institutions seek to draw the general connection between unregulated markets and improving the environment and more particular relations, such as the argument that less government intervention will produce cleaner air and fresher water. Some environmentalists believe that government regulation is the only answer whereas the right wing backlash maintains the free market as the sacred talisman of environmental salvation.

The backlash does not consist of a critique of environmental protection. Rather the critics argue that current legislation is too costly and too inefficient. The protection and enhancement of environmental quality is still taken as a legitimate and worthy end. Only the means are different. This is not to diminish the differences. Various means in pursuit of the same ends can have radically different outcomes. That there is a shared end, however, is indicative of the enormous power of environmental discourses in the contemporary United States; the basic ideas have the power to transcend major political differences.

### The Greening of the Economy

In the early years of environmentalism in postwar United States, the debate was often polarized between environmental quality and job creation. Well into the 1970s and 1980s the critics of environmentalism used the threat of job loss as a major point of criticism. To change environmental regulation and to impose higher standards of compliance would, argued many business interests, reduce employment opportunities. There was a kind of *idée fixe* that the job generation machine could and should not be regulated, especially for rather dubious notions of environmental quality. Environmental quality was posed against jobs. There has been a thorough critique of this position. In 1958, for example, John Kenneth Galbraith drew attention, in his book *The Affluent Society*, to the difference between private affluence and public squalor. He painted a word picture of the affluent commuter leaving a comfortable home yet driving on cracking roads through polluted neighborhoods and over decrepit bridges. Galbraith argued that to ensure the good life, we need to promote a broader public concern and a wider environmental sensitivity. In *The Costs of Economic Growth* (1967) E. J. Mishan pointed to the negative consequences of unrestrained growth, drawing attention to the social costs and negative externalities not picked up by such crude measures as increasing income or gross domestic product. While the latter may rise in the short term they can lead to an impoverished environment in the long term.

There has been the development of an environmental economics.[8] Traditional economics was simply concerned with the production and consumption of goods and services and how markets operate to allocate scarce resources. It was a very partial view of the world that had the advantages of simplicity, elegance, and a steady belief that, in the long run, the market knew best. This view lacked an ability to see longer-term consequences outside of market calculations and had little conception of resource depletion, externalities, or environmental degradation. An environmental economics has emerged in the past three decades that looks at externalities (a factory may produce jobs but may also create air pollution for the surrounding neighborhood), social costs (e.g., the effect of increased respiratory illness on local children) and a wider net of cost-benefit analyses to evaluate projects (such as factoring in increased individual health costs as well as increased profits to the company opening a new factory).

There has also been a more thorough critique of economics; we can think of it as an alternative economics more in tune with Boulding's notion of a spaceship economy. This alternative position argues that growth is used as a panacea that pays little attention to the quality of growth or redistribution. In this view growth does not lessen inequality, it promotes it. This position is regularly summarized in the annual series *State of the World*. Under such titles as "Picturing a Sustainable Society" and "The New World Order" writers in this series propose an economy based on alternative energy sources (solar, wind, tidal, and geothermal); more efficient energy use (e.g., greater use of bicycles), greater recycling, biological diversity, and the construction of a new set of attitudes toward economic growth and environmental management. This economics constitutes not a new set of tools but an alternative way of looking at the world.[9]

Although this alternative environmental discourse has received little formal recognition from mainstream politicians, we feel that there has been a substantial shift in popular culture. Recycling, for example, has become an integral part of collective and individual behavior in large sections of the public. In the mid-1990s there was renewal of interest in leading a simpler life. After the material excesses of the 1980s, the last decade of the millennium introduced new attitudes. Elaine St James's 1994 book, *Simplify Your Life*, became a national best-seller. The small book offered such advice as moving to a smaller house, getting out of debt, changing the way you shop, and buying a secondhand car. In a world of downsizing, economic uncertainty, and declining incomes the book spoke to material concerns as much as environmental sensitivities. A best-seller does not mark a shift in national consciousness, but neither can it be ignored. The declining incomes of middle-class households and the increased workload has led to a questioning of the traditional material goals. There is a change, small but perceptible, to those with their nose to the prevailing wind, and it indicates a disenchantment with crude materialism and a yearning for a simpler, less hectic life. To what extent it fits in with an alternative economics is something that will unfold at the beginning of the next millennium.

### Green capitalism

Capitalism in the United States is a robust, adaptable system. Yet the business interests that attacked environmental critiques in the 1960s and 1970s showed little confidence in their own system. They assumed that it was so fragile that increased government regulation would knock it over. American capitalism is a more rugged institution that can adapt and change. Business has responded to the wave of environmental concern in a number of ways. First there has been a change in production processes. American industry is now more energy efficient and less polluting than it was in the 1960s. Government regulation, rising costs, and community pressure have made industry cleaner and greener. This is a notable achievement. It is all the more notable if you travel to poorer countries where industrial pollutants continue to clog the air and foul the water. American industry is not perfect and neither has the profit motive been overturned. Rather business has adapted many of its production processes to keep in line with rising standards of environmental regulation and public pressure. In some cases government regulation has actually reduced costs. The compliance with antipollution measures in chemical plants in the US since the mid-1980s has resulted in substantial savings of over 2 million dollars. For every one dollar spent on complying with regulations there has been a saving of almost three and a half dollars as the more productive use of previously waste resources occurred.[10] Environmental regulations have also spurred innovation. Automobile companies have sought to produce cheaper, more fuel-efficient and less polluting cars in part as a response to the environmental regulation. The improvements in overall environmental quality are partly due to this greening of American industry. There are still problems – pollutants continue to find their way into delicate ecosystems – but compared to the 1950s and 1960s there has been a marked change.

A second change has been in the marketing of products. The public surveys that reveal a majority of Americans have a concern with the environment also show that almost 90 percent of Americans are concerned about the impact that the products they purchased had upon the environment. This is a hazy definition. Everything has an impact on the environment; nevertheless it reveals an acute public interest and attests to the integration of environmental concern into the wider society. Corporate capitalism has responded to this new form of green consumerism with green marketing. Companies have formulated a variety of strategies, including environmentally friendly products, recyclable packaging and corporate promotional campaigns that state the company's commitment to environmental protection and improvement. Supermarket shelves are filled with labels that proclaim *earth-friendly, biodegradable, degradable, recycled, dolphin-safe*. So many products were appropriating the term *environmental* that in 1992 the Federal Trade Commission issued guidelines to ensure that environmental advertising had a reasonable basis of fact. This came in the wake of a lawsuit filed against Mobil, which had advertised its Hefty trash bag as photodegradable. Since most of these bags end up in landfills the claim seemed irrelevant. The oil company settled out of court. In 1990 the Natural Resources Defense Council also identified over 20 products that contained chlorofluorocarbons (CFCs) yet still claimed to be ozone-friendly!

Some companies have sought to turn around their corporate image. In 1990 MacDonald's sought to change its negative environmental impact image to a more positive one. The company switched from Styrofoam to paper wrappers and highlighted the environmental benefits of this shift in an aggressive public relations campaign. In fact the environmental impacts were traded rather than eliminated. The production of paper requires more energy and produces more wastewater than Styrofoam. Yet in the public mind paper was "better" than Styrofoam.

It is now apparent that if faced with a choice of similarly priced products, consumers will buy the products they consider to have less negative environmental impact. This finding has been quickly incorporated by US businesses who produce and package "greener" products, sometimes merely in the naming rather than in the production, and promote their environmental commitment.

It is legitimate to speak of the greening of capitalism. It is equally plausible to write about the commodification of environmental issues and concerns. We will explore this issue more fully in chapter 11. Environmental themes dominate contemporary culture to such an extent that they are used to sell products and even whole product lines. One of the biggest growth sectors in the clothes line is outdoor gear. Jackets, vests, and parkas produced by such companies as Marmot, Columbia, and North Face are actively promoted and have achieved tremendous success in the young persons' sector of the market. The image presented in the selling of these items includes an outdoors, environmentally oriented approach to life that fits in with the dominant ideologies of the targeted demographic sector. The companies are selling goods that embody the ideas of the consumers. A paradox is that much of the basic material is synthetic material, such as nylon and Gore Tex, whose production and disposal have negative environmental impacts.

One of the biggest growth areas in the automobile sector has been the sports utility sector. The marketing techniques for the Land Rover, Ford Explorer, Chevy Blazer, and Jeep Cherokee, to take a small sample, use the themes of contact with the wilderness and getting in touch with nature. The sports utility combines the perceived need for comfort and security with adventure and the outdoors – safety and adventure, preferably in a leather interior. The demand for utility vehicles has increased from 1 percent of the US market in 1982 to almost 9 percent by 1995. The paradox is that the vehicles are notably low in fuel efficiency. Unlike a modest sedan, which achieves approximately 28 miles per gallon, the typical sports utility vehicle will rarely reach 18 miles per gallon. As one writer noted, "today's yuppies, who generally regard themselves as having greater environmental consciousness than their parents, wind up driving vehicles that are no more fuel efficient than their parents were."[11]

Up until the New Deal environmental issues in the United States were shaped by nature preservationists and resource conservationists. The emphasis was on aesthetics and efficiency. The preservationists saw wilderness as a kind of sacred space worthy of saving from the economic juggernaut. The resource conservationists had a rationalist belief in the efficacy of scientific principles in the creation of wise use of land. They saw both the natural world and the political world as susceptible to rational analysis and argument. During the New Deal these discourses were combined with a pressing concern to lift the economy from the doldrums. New Deal policies were an attempt to combine the stimulation of economic growth with resource conservation and use. To concerns of aesthetics and efficiency were added issues of equity and economic management.

In the postwar phase economic growth seemed assured, and environmental protection became an important issue because the very basis of continued life seemed threatened. After the Second World War, concern with environmental issues blossomed into a social movement that encompassed traditional concerns with preservation and conservation but now included the mission of saving the habitat. It became a movement because the base of support widened from a narrow range of writers, philosophers, and scientists to a broader public and was embodied in specific government agencies, pieces of legislation, and powerful pressure groups. The discourse of environmentalism extended beyond narrow ecological issues; it became one of the grand narratives incorporating old ideas and new themes. The environment has become associated with everything from the rights of indigenous people, racism, and feminism to major advertising campaigns. Commodities now embody environmental values, movies glorify the wilderness, and our public intellectuals, and our most popular fictional characters all agree that the environment should be protected. The protection of the environment has become a shared assumption with a broad consensus as there has been a greening of business, politics, and the popular culture of the United States.

## FURTHER READING

Bailey, R. 1993. *Eco-Scam: The False Prophets of Ecological Apocalypse.* New York: St. Martin's Press.
Berry, T. 1988. *The Dream of the Earth.* San Francisco: Sierra Club.
Easterbrook. G. 1995. *A Moment on the Earth.* New York: Viking.
Goldfarb, T. D., ed. 1993. *Taking Sides: Clashing Views on Controversial Environmental Issues.* Guilford, Conn.: Dushkin.
Hawken, P. 1993. *The Ecology of Commerce.* New York: Harper.
Kempton, W. , Boster, J. S. and J. A. Hartley. 1995. *Environmental Values in American Culture.* Cambridge, Mass.: MIT Press.
Meiners, R. E. and B. Yandle, eds, 1993. *Taking the Environment Seriously* Lanham, Md.: Rowman and Littlefield.
Reilly, W., ed., 1994. *Environment Strategy America.* London: Campden.
O'Rourke, P. J. 1994. *All the Trouble in the World.* New York: Atlantic Monthly.
Worster, D. 1993. *The Wealth of Nature: Environmental History and the Ecological Imagination.* New York: Oxford University Press.

## NOTES

1   *Life*, May 27, 1966: 37.
2   The supporting data can be found in R. E. Dunlap and R. Scarce, "Environmental Problems and Protection," *Public Opinion Quarterly Journal* 55 (1991): 651–72.
3   Ray Allen Billington, *Westward Expansion: A History of the American Frontier*, 4th edn. (New York: Macmillan, 1974).
4   The following is just a sample of the new western history: W. Cronon, G. Miles, and J. Gitlin, eds, *Under an Open Sky: Rethinking America's Western Past* (New York: Norton, 1992); P. N. Limerick, C. A. Milner II, and C. E. Rankin, eds, *Trails: Toward a New Western History* (Lawrence: University Press of Kansas, 1991); C. A. Milner II, ed., *A New Significance: Re-envisioning the History of the American West* (New York: Oxford University Press, 1996); C. A. Milner II, C. A. O'Connor, and M. A. Sandweiss, eds, *The Oxford History of the American West* (New York: Oxford University Press, 1994); R. White, *"It's Your Misfortune and None of My Own." A History of the American West* (Norman and London: University of Oklahoma Press, 1991).

5   A small sample of Worster's work includes *Rivers of Empire: Water, Aridity, and the Growth of the American West* (New York: Pantheon, 1985); *Under Western Skies: Nature and History in the American West* (New York: Oxford University Press, 1992); *The Wealth of Nature: Environmental History and the Ecological Imagination* (New York: Oxford University Press, 1993).

6   Ian Frazier, *Great Plains* (New York: Farrar Straus Giroux, 1989), 209–10.

7   Thomas Berry, *The Dream of the Earth* (San Francisco: Sierra Club, 1988); Bill McKibben, *The End of Nature* (New York: Random House, 1989).

8   R. Constanza, ed., *Ecological Economics* (New York: Columbia University Press, 1992).

9   See L. R. Brown, C. Flavin, and S. Postel, "Picturing a Sustainable Society," *State of the World 1990* (1990), 173–90; L. R. Brown, "The New World Order," *State of The World 1991 (1991)*, 209.

10  M. E. Porter and C. van der Linde, "Green and Competitive: Ending The Stalemate," *Harvard Business Review*, (1995) Sept.–Oct.: 120–34.

11  J. Bennet, "Four Wheeling No Longer Just a Fad," *New York Times*, February 9, 1995: 10.

# 8

# A Chorus of Voices:
# Situating Radical
# Environmental Discourses

The environment has become a point of intersection for a variety of discourses, hopes, fears, and political action. It is not a singular voice, but a chorus. Indeed, a range of radical environmental discourses have permeated our culture, some of which have been recently constructed, born out of the influence of other social movements. Others trace their roots back to the earliest modern environmental writers and philosophers. They all seek to change and shape cultural values and practices. They also articulate alternative discourses to the technological meta-discourse in the US.

In this chapter we look first at the emergence of radical environmentalism and in particular deep ecology, social ecology, ecofeminism, and postmodern critiques of the environmental crisis. These environmental discourses have differences and similarities, but at the core of their ideological framework is a concern for the environment and for transforming the ways in which people interact with and value the environment. They all promote to varying degrees social, economic, political, and personal change to protect and preserve the environment.

## Deep Ecology

The term *deep ecology* was first used by a Norwegian philosopher Arne Naess in a paper published in 1972 entitled "The Shallow and the Deep, Long Range Ecology Movement." Naess distinguished between two kinds of ecology: the shallow and the deep. Shallow ecology could be found in the dominant technological metadiscourse of western culture and was the overriding ideology of reformists. It emphasized the fight against pollution and resource depletion. Deep ecology, on the other hand, promised transformation and radical changes to society and adopted a different perspective on the environmental crisis. One of the most important discursive tenets of deep ecology is biocentrism or ecocentrism, which contrasts with the anthropocentric (or human-centered) perspective dominating in our society today. A biocentric perspective of the world suggests that humans are only part of the "web of life" – not at the top of a hierarchy but equal with many other aspects of creation, including nonhuman nature. Naess argued that in an anthropocentric perspective, every action is undertaken to protect present and future generations of human beings, which he claimed, jeopardized the long-term integrity of all living beings, including rivers and animals and plants. The only solution was the adoption of a biocentric view.

Since Naess first coined the term, it has been used to refer to a variety of ecophilosophies, including radical green political thought, Earth First! philosophy, academic deep ecology, and animal liberation.[1] The label "deep ecology" was put forward to provide both a critique of reformist or shallow environmentalism and a critique of industrial society.[2] Deep ecologists challenged not only the methods but the underlying philosophy of reformist environmentalism, which they charged had become dependent on their budgets rather than on their visions. They had become too centralized, too reformist, too "shallow" in their ideology. The shallowness of mainstream organizations, deep ecologists argued, was clearly exposed by their willingness to settle for reforms in government policy *without challenging society's basic assumptions or metadiscourse.* Radicals believed that they, not reformist organizations, would foster the sweeping changes that society needed in order to survive.[3]

Bill Devall and George Sessions are two US academics who have helped formulate the deep ecophilosophy. They have argued that the ecological crisis is partly a crisis of consciousness and that the real solution lies in making deep changes to our personal consciousness and our basic conceptions of our relationships to each other and to the nonhuman world. In their book *Deep Ecology*, Devall and Sessions expanded upon Naess's work and formulated a platform statement of deep ecology that included the fundamental principles identified in table 8.1.[4] Table 8.2 notes the main arguments of deep ecology and contrasts them with what we have termed the technological environmental metadiscourse.

Deep ecologists are quick to note that the principles of deep ecology do not provide a formal ideology for radical environmentalism but rather offer a diverse body of ideas from which a variety of lifestyles and social policies are possible and compatible. This body of ideas includes Gandhi's principles of nonviolence, green consumerism, bioregionalism and cultural practices and ideas based on Native-American and Buddhist traditions.

By the mid-1980s a number of books began to appear with the title *Deep Ecology* and the phrase achieved wider circulation. During the same time Aldo Leopold's book, *A Sand County Almanac*, achieved popularity in the United

**Table 8.1**  Deep ecology principles

1   The well-being and flourishing of human and nonhuman life on Earth have value in themselves (synonyms: intrinsic value, inherent value). These values are independent of the usefulness of the nonhuman world for human purposes.
2   Richness and diversity of life forms contribute to the realization of these values and are also values in themselves.
3   Humans have no right to reduce this richness and diversity except to meet human needs.
4   The flourishing of human life and cultures is compatible with a substantial decrease of the human population. The flourishing of nonhuman life requires such a decrease.
5   Present human interference with the nonhuman world is excessive, and the situation is rapidly worsening.
6   Policies must therefore be changed. The changes in policies affect basic economic, technological and ideological structures.
7   Ideological change consists mainly of appreciating quality of life rather than adhering to an increasingly higher standard of living.
8   Those who subscribe to the foregoing points have an obligation directly or indirectly to participate in the attempt to implement the necessary changes.

**Table 8.2**  Dominant environmental discourse vs. deep ecology

| Dominant Discourse | Deep Ecology |
| --- | --- |
| dominance over nature | harmony with nature |
| biosphere as resource | biocentric equality |
| belief in ample reserves | limits to growth |
| high-technology solutions | appropriate technology |
| consumerism | doing with enough/recycling |
| centralized community | bioregion |

*Source*: based on figure 5.1 in *Deep Ecology* by Devall and Sessions (1985)

States and was going through several printings. The land ethic and deep ecology were percolating through the scientific and environmental community to become part of several environmental discourses.

The land ethic and deep ecology discourses argue forcefully that the environment is not a resource for humans but has its own intrinsic value and worth. They call for the defense of the wilderness, and some have acted on this invitation. One of the best-known activists is Dave Foreman, who worked first for the Wilderness Society in Washington. Disenchanted with what he saw as the moderation of conservationists in operating through the lobbies of power, he returned to his job as regional representative in New Mexico. Appalled by the inability to do anything about overgrazing on public lands, the corporate connections of the society, and the growing gulf between volunteers and the full-time workers, he resigned in June 1980. Along with four others he established Earth First!, an organization dedicated to biocentrism (an emphasis on maintaining biodiversity) and biocentric equality (the belief that all species are equal).

The title of the new organization summed up the philosophy of the group. The group was influenced by Edward Abbey, whose 1975 novel *The Monkey Wrench Gang* described acts of environmental sabotage. In 1981 the group staged a protest at the Glen Canyon Dam in the Colorado River and unfurled a 300–foot length of black plastic to create the impression of a giant crack. The caper attracted a lot of media attention, which increased membership to over 1,000. The group also called for the creation of a 716–million-acre wilderness. By the mid-1980s the group had emerged as one of the most visible environment action groups. In their 1987 book *Ecodefense*, authors Foreman and Haywood devote nine chapters to describing activities as varied as tree spiking, road spiking, disabling heavy equipment, trap lines, fence cutting, billboard destruction, spray painting, smoke bombs, sling shots, and computer sabotage.[5] Tree spiking, for example, is used as direct action against loggers and involves the hammering of a 14-inch spike into a tree. The tree may be cut down but the spike will destroy the saw blades used at the mill. Groups would spike trees and then alert the press, thus saving the trees.

As with any radical group that garners publicity, Earth First! was infiltrated by the FBI. And like many other small radical groups internal factions caused a breakup. In the fall of 1990 two factions split; the strict biocentrists left to pursue their agenda through other organizations while the remaining members of Earth First! focused on social justice as well as ecology.

Earth First! is one of the more radical organizations. At this end of the continuum of environmental discourse and politics the concern is with saving the earth through direct action and an unswerving commitment to biocentric equality. Perhaps because of the very success of the bigger organizations, such as the Wilderness Society and the Sierra Club – and by success we mean influence in Washington as well as membership size and sheer economic power – some activists have felt that environmental issues have been incorporated into the power elite and the mass consumerism of US society. In response to this perceived sell-out and the continuing damage to the environment, the more radical environmental organizations will continue to exercise what power they can mobilize.

## Social Ecology

Social ecology is another radical ecophilosophy and was developed primarily by Murray Bookchin, who has written extensively about our ecological crisis and the social and political sources of ecology destruction. In addition to his numerous publications advancing social ecology theory, Bookchin established the Institute of Social Ecology in Vermont to help promote the development of social ecology thinking, a perspective that links domination and hierarchy in human society with the degradation of nature. Social ecology's guiding precept is that we cannot rid ourselves of the ideology of dominating nature until we rid ourselves of hierarchy and class structures in human society. These structures include not only classism, sexism, and racism but also economic exploitation, capitalism, and numerous other social oppressions. For example, the inherent structure of market capitalism, says Bookchin, places no limits to growth because its maxim is "grow or die!" This inevitably leads to a perspective that encourages the domination of nature. Social ecologists want to overturn hierarchies but do not subscribe to the ecocentric perspective of deep ecology. Rather their attention is first to rid human society of hierarchies and exploitation and to address issues of poverty, justice, and political access.

Bookchin has argued that our society has created an ecological crisis because of the power of our hierarchical and authoritarian social, economic, and political structures,[6] which permit some humans to dominate others and nature; however, this domination through hierarchy is not inevitable in human society. Bookchin concluded that we cannot solve the environmental crisis in free-market and bureaucratic capitalist societies. Instead, we must decentralize our social and economic relationships, move away from large-scale, centralized political and social systems, create new forms of democratic community, new forms of economic production and rethink our relationship to technology.[7] We can describe social ecology as an antihierarchical, somewhat anarchist and democratic discourse that emphasizes the interest of humans beings as a whole.

Deep ecologists and social ecologists have engaged in an interesting and ongoing debate. Bookchin has been a vocal critic of deep ecology, arguing that deep ecology is often antihumanist, as it promotes wilderness preservation at the expense of people. Deep ecologists have countered with arguments stating that unless we reject anthropocentrism the underlying cause of the environmental crisis will not be solved. And so the complex debate continues. While these radical environmentalists agree that reformist environmentalism will not solve the environmental crisis, the debate *within* radical environmentalist discourse demonstrates numerous ideological positions, a mosaic of contested positions.[8]

## Ecology and Feminism

The women's movement and the environmental movement are among the most powerful social movements of the late twentieth century, yet for many years they remained unallied. More recently, feminism(s) and environmentalism(s) have found some common ground, making connections in important, although often contentious, ways.[9] For example, one common element to both is their struggle to free themselves from the cultural and economic constraints that have kept women and nature susceptible to exploitation in American society.[10] While some have seen the environment as "genderless," feminist writers have recently argued for a feminist voice in the environmental analytical chorus. They believe that women hold the key to rethinking environmentalism. As one feminist writer explained, "the real story of the environmental crisis is a story of power and profit and political wrangling; it is a study of the institutional arrangements and settings. . . . and cultural conventions that create conditions of environmental destruction."[11]

In this section, we explore the ways in which feminism(s) has contributed to the study of environmental discourse and practices, concentrating on two forms of feminist critique: (1) a broad feminist perspective, and (2) one type of feminist theory of humanity–environment relationships, ecofeminism. We begin by looking at Carolyn Merchant's book, *The Death of Nature*, as an outstanding example of a feminist perspective that explores the historical context of environmental philosophy and the modern construction of humanity–environment relationships. Merchant's book has been widely read and is often cited as an influential contribution to both the study of scientific history and women's studies. Next, we consider Joni Seager's *Earth Follies*, an articulate and accessible work aimed at a general audience, as a template for understanding the contemporary connection between feminism and environmentalism. We then turn to a brief exploration of ecofeminism as an example of how a feminist perspective can contribute to the debates about environmental history and philosophy and provide a critique of its limitations.

### A feminist critique of the Scientific Revolution

One of the earliest and best-known works that takes a feminist perspective in assessing environmental history is Carolyn Merchant's *The Death of Nature*.[12] She argued that many of our contemporary environmental problems have their roots in the revolution in values and knowledge that began centuries ago during the Scientific Revolution and the Age of Enlightenment. In investigating those roots, she noted "we must reexamine the formation of a world view and a science that, by reconceptualizing reality as a machine rather than a living organism, sanctioned the domination of both nature and women."[13]

Merchant detailed the Scientific Revolution as a crucial epoch in which the technological environmental metadiscourse evolved as a complex synthesis of the transformation of new ideas and the redefinition of knowledge.[14] In the sixteenth and seventeenth centuries the philosophies of the technological metadiscourse replaced the then-dominant ecological metadiscourse. In cultures with a premodern or ecological environmental metadiscourse, nature was frequently personified as a woman ("Mother Nature"), and the whole world was considered alive. Nature could be personified as calm or wild, but respect for its existence and force was central. The project of the Scientific Revolution, led by male scientists and philosophers such as Bacon, Hobbes, and Descartes, focused on the search for order and power. In so doing, they redefined class, authority, property, and the social order.[15] In this search for order and power, nature became an object of study: something to be probed, dissembled, evaluated, and observed in order to arrive at immutable truths. Bacon, in particular, encouraged technological progress through the mastery of nature.[16] The rise of the scientific mindset and the project of modernity marked the death of nature – the end of human belief that the world was living and organic.

Nature, no longer seen as a living organism, was perceived through the metaphor of machine. The landscape was mechanized through tools, such as plows and tractors, water wheels, the microscope, street grids, tractors, and oil derricks. (In the twentieth century, the nature-as-machine metaphor was perhaps best epitomized when the modernist architect Le Corbousier declared that a house was nothing more than "a machine for living in.") The search for truth and order was easier when looking at parts, so natural systems became no more than a collection of parts, the planet became something to be engineered and technologically conquered, progress and time were measured in linear segments.

In the newly evolving technological metadiscourse, the world was easier to understand if reduced to categories of opposites. The establishment of dualisms (or opposites) was critical and included nature/culture, is/ought, fact/value, black/white, science/ethics, men/women. Concepts such as nature and culture came to be defined in direct opposition to each other. In other words, dualisms were reliant on each other for their meaning. Nature was defined as all that was not a part of the human world. Culture came to be seen as a product of societies. The idea of hierarchy replaced the notion of holism and interconnectedness. Hierarchy came to be used to justify both social and natural domination.

In addition to its transformation of the way people looked at the world around them, the technological metadiscourse had powerful sexual overtones, since nature had been characterized as female. Domination over nature, according to Merchant, coincided with domination over women. Neither the exploitation of resources nor the exploitation and domination of women was unique; rather they were both the outcome of the practices of a new discourse.

### A feminist critique of the contemporary environmental crisis

In addition to a general feminist perspective applied to a broader historical analysis of humanity–environment relationships, there has been considerable attention given toward applying a feminist perspective to an analysis of modern environmental issues and policy. Unfortunately many of these works rely on theoretical arguments that use weighty jargon and opaque terminology. We have chosen to consider Joni Seager's *Earth Follies* because it is well written and therefore accessible to a general audience. Although we scrutinize Seager's work as representative of a feminist perspective on the environment we caution that it is by no means "the" only argument that can be developed through a feminist perspective. Rather, her work allows us entry into the complex and often exclusive debate now occurring within feminist circles.

Seager's *Earth Follies* explores the contemporary environmental state of the planet from a feminist perspective. The author begins by exploring four "masculinist" institutions as conspirators in environmental degradation: the military, the government, industry, and the "eco-establishment." These institutions are led by men and have embedded masculinist presumptions that are complicit in environmental and human oppression.[17]

Militaries, Seager argued, are major environmental abusers. They are typically beyond the reach of civil law and public scrutiny and often hide behind the rhetoric of "national security" as justification for their activities and abuses.[18] National security can exempt militaries from the restrictions of domestic environmental laws and international treaties. Militaries embrace the rationalist or mechanistic impulse for nature-conquering, translating these impulses into a war strategy[19] and have inflicted damage on the environment in several ways. Chemical herbicides (such as Agent Orange used by the United States in Vietnam), defoliants, napalm, gasoline, and other fuel leaks and toxic waste disposal are but a few examples of environmental abuse by the military. In the 1991 Gulf War, for example, US military action destroyed water systems, fuel supplies, sewage systems, and public health delivery systems and spilled millions of gallons of oil into the gulf and onto the fragile desert ecosystem.[20] All of these examples reflect the destructive consequences of the *active* side of military operations.

The *passive* side of military activity has focused on the development of bigger and better weapons.[21] Research and development has had enormous but silent impact. Daily operations involve the use of a wide variety of chemicals, oils, solvents, paints, gases, and weapons. Nuclear weapons research in places like Hanford or Los Alamos and general weaponry development on most bases around the United States have environmental implications. Radioactivity is only the first on a long list of chemicals and compounds that are potentially lethal to people and the environment. Seager argued that "bases and other military installations were the sleepy environmental hotspots in the late 1980s, and will be the source of some of the biggest environmental catastrophes around the world" into the twenty-first century.[22] The military, however, does not act alone. There exists a gentlemen's agreement between the military and the government; this collusion is held together with the glue of male bonding during which relationships among men are formed and reinforced through informal relations on the golf course and in corporation boardrooms.[23]

Seager asserted, "in patriarchal societies, the power of men as men derives in part from their control of wealth and from the seamless web of relationships among men in government, military and commercial elites."[24] Government officials often have full knowledge of ongoing environmental violations and do little to stop such practices. Militaries argue they are in the business of protecting the country not the environment. And governments, it seems, often agree. Seager's feminist perspective calls for us to look critically at our most basic and unquestioned institutions. Her challenge: if one believes sovereignty, nationalism, territoriality are particularly male constructs, then the entire global system itself, defined by dividing the globe into states that then need to be protected, is somehow reflective of the masculinist need to conquer and control.

Governments and the military are not the only institutions complicit in environmental degradation. Industry contributes to environmental degradation as well, partly by legally or illegally dumping toxic byproducts from industrial processing into rivers, lakes, and the soil. Management creates and then markets environmentally harmful products (like aerosol sprays or pesticides) but when confronted with this responsibility shifts the blame from themselves to "consumer demand" for products. Industrial elites often blatantly and intentionally disregard environmental common sense. Multinational corporations that shift the production of pesticides banned in the United States to locations in the Third World are not aberrations from the norm, their lack of environmental integrity *is* the norm.[25] Executives are removed from the reality of their decision-making and distant from the injuries they inflict on an abstract population.

The fourth institution implicated in the environmental crisis is the "eco-establishment." The eco-establishment is made up of reformist environmental organizations, such as the Sierra Club, World Wildlife Fund, and Environmental Defense Fund. Seager commented, "even the existing power structure of the environmental establishment in North America and Europe is ubiquitously male, and mostly white. The socio-economic complexion of these organizations means they pay little attention to issues which profoundly affect women and children and instead focus on cooperating with government and industry to establish regulations. "The eco-establishment believes in free enterprise and in enlisting business as partners in environmental protection. This is a direct reflection of the environmental movement being increasingly male led and has specific, identifiable consequences in terms of environmental priorities, practices and policies."[26]

*Earth Follies* is an evocative, challenging, and contentious work providing an important illustration of the way a feminist critique examines the environmental crisis and can shape a feminist environmental discourse.

### *Ecofeminism*

Just as there is no single feminism, there is no one ecofeminist theory.[27] Ecofeminism comprises a range of views – from liberal ecofeminism to radical ecofeminism to social ecofeminism – in part because ecofeminism evolved from various fields of feminist inquiry and activism. Some individuals joined ecofeminist groups or began developing ecofeminist theory based on their experiences in the peace, environmental, women's and animal rights movements. They brought with them differing experiences and ideologies, but they shared a frustration with limited opportunities within the environmental movement (as dominated by men) and sought to create a movement based on "women-identified" terms.[28]

The term *ecofeminism* was first introduced in 1984 by the French feminist writer Françoise d'Eaubonne. Simply defined, ecofeminism argues that the connections between the oppression of people and the domination of nature must be recognized in order to accurately understand both oppressions.[29] Although ecofeminists may differ in their short-term practices and philosophies, they concur that there is a critical link between the domination of women and the domination of nature. Ecofeminism sees both pollution and patriarchy as indicators of an unjust society. They also share the common goal of restoring integrity to human relationships and the natural environment. The ecofeminist movement has emerged as a social movement dedicated to both social and environmental reform through personal enlightenment and resistance.

Ecofeminism derives primarily from a feminist analysis that seeks to *empower* and *celebrate* the connection between women and nature. Ecofeminists believe that the subjugation of women and nature is a social construction, not a biologically determined fact, and thus can be changed. They promote sociocultural change and argue for a revaluing of people's biological connections with nature. Ecofeminist projects include the creation of new images and stories to replace those of controlling and dominating nature and women. Ecofeminists want to re-create the nurturing image of women and nature as an alternative to the old images of mastery.[30] Some ecofeminists assert that ecofeminist theories represent a "third wave of feminism" because it demonstrates the need for an environmental perspective for feminism and a feminist perspective for the environment.[31]

Some of the early works to inspire the development of ecofeminism include Rosemary Radford Reuther's *New Woman/New Earth* (1975), Elizabeth Dodson Gray's *Green Paradise Lost* (1979) and Leonie Caldecott and Stephanie Leland's *Reclaim the Earth: Women Speak Out for Life on Earth* (1983). In the past decade, there has been an explosion of both popular and academic works expanding on these earlier works to explore and more clearly articulate ecofeminist theory, which is being advanced by poets, novelists, scholars, activists, spiritual teachers, and artists; they claim to represent a diverse range of women's efforts to save the earth and to transform relationships. There have been books of poems, music, and art exploring the relationship of women and the environment. We include this poem as one illustration of the power and emotion that is evoked in many of these works.

## JUDITH MCCOMBS "THE MAN,"[32]

See, a small space in the woods,
green overgrown with green,
shadows tree brush entangled
At the edge of the clearing a man
a white man, middle-aged, aging
just his face stands out in the dimness
"dominion over every living thing"
a hunter's jacket, hunter's cap
He lifts the spear of his rifle barrel
aims
with cold, hard, arthritic hands
16 years on the line, finally made foreman,
finally inspector, finally retired
The cold, square aging jaws of the man
are barely flushed, a tingle of fear
or pleasure as he aims

diagonally across the clearing
into the black furry mass of the bear
She sits on her haunches, back to a stump,
an ancient, massive, dog-nosed brute
pawing the dogs
who yap & skitter away
(My mother's mother, huge in her dress,
sits in the creek, swatting the water & laughing)
She is warm, stupid; she smells of bear
an abundance of flesh, stumpy limbs,
stone of a head & little pig eyes
teats where she rears, in the black close fur
She smells like my mother/my mother's mother
she does not understand
she won't go away

The man with the rifle aiming
confers with other shadowy men
ranging the edge of the clearing
Each in position: they have agreed
which one will have her/whose turn it is
One of them covers the kill

My mother does not understand
rears, paws, shakes her head & its wattles of fur
thinking she's won

Afterward the body is hoisted
"a sack full of lard" on inaccurate scales
is hung, dressed, weighed on accurate scales
The skull (unshattered, unhurt) is found eligible
for Boone & Crockett official measuring
The head is stuffed & mounted
                              safe on the walls
where every evening he enters, approaches
fires recoils fires into the small stupid eyes
"the thrill of a lifetime" my mother

Indeed, ecofeminism has inspired a growing collection of books about women's spirituality and relationship with nature (sometimes found in the New Age section). For example, Lorraine Anderson's collected works of nature writing by women, *Sisters of the Earth: Women's Prose and Poetry about Nature*, is emblematic of the ecofeminist attempt to define and celebrate a women's view of nature. Anderson believed that "traditional gender socialization in our society helps women relate well to nature by encouraging caring, nurturing, receptivity, empathy, emotional responsiveness, appreciation of beauty and a feeling of kinship with animals."[33] She concluded that "there is a feminine way of being in relationship to nature: this way is caring rather than controlling; it seeks harmony rather than mastery; it is characterized by humility rather than arrogance, by appreciation rather than acquisitiveness."[34]

Another of the leading thinkers on ecofeminism, Judith Plant, has argued that women have long been associated with nature. Metaphorically, women have been seen as "Mother Earth." She explained, "It is no accident that the minister of forests is a man, that the logging company is owned by a man, that the logging truck driver is a man. The rape of the earth becomes a metaphor for the rape of a woman."[35] Environmental destruction is seen as another form of male violence directed against woman-as-earth.

Physically women's work has centered around eating, sex, cleaning, and the care of children.[36] This, argue some ecofeminists, make women more innately connected to nature. Women's lives are involved in sustaining and conserving water, land and forests; this intimacy leaves them with a more immediate understanding of the consequences of environmental degradation. They are often the first to notice environmental degradation in the surrounding environment.

Most ecofeminists celebrate the innate connection between women and nature and argue women have a more caring and nurturing and peaceful way of being than men. Some embrace nontraditional views and practices, such as goddess worship; others embrace religion and poetry and legends and myths as ways to replace existing harmful practices toward women and nature. Several radical ecofeminists believe that the process of re-creating myths, stories and rituals, part of "reweaving new stories," is a means of political change.[37]

### Critiquing the feminist critique

The contribution of feminism(s) to discussions about environmental history and philosophy have been important and will continue to provide new insights. There have been a number of criticisms (or perhaps more appropriately cautions), however, about feminist critiques of environmental history and philosophy that reflect concerns about relying on *only* a feminist analysis to understand the environmental problem.

Radical ecofeminist ideas, in particular, have generated much debate within feminist circles. The radical ecofeminist discourse holds that the primary dynamic behind the domination of women and nature is patriarchy and that this is the only way to comprehend every other expression of patriarchal culture – from hierarchies, to industries, to technologies. For many ecofeminists, patriarchy precedes all other forms of oppression and lays the foundation for exploitation. Just as deep ecology believes the fundamental cause of environmental crisis to be the anthropocentric (or human-centered) perspective, ecofeminists argue it is androcentrism (or men and the masculinist-centered) perspective that deserves primary blame. This position is criticized by those who are wary of attributing a single root cause to multiple problems.

In addition, some of the writings of ecofeminists imply that the people who do not agree with patriarchy as the single, underlying cause of all problems are unenlightened, brainwashed victims (that is, resistance to embracing ecofeminism is easily "dismissed"; nonbelievers work to perpetuate the masculinist perspective). Women who are uncritical and do not accept patriarchy as the root cause of oppression are not "feminist" and represent a danger to a "genuinely feminist perspective."[38] One ecofeminist wrote that those who remain uncritical of patriarchy are doomed to remain outside the *real* work of saving the earth.[39] We, however, resist the self-righteous tone found in some ecofeminist writings and believe, as many other feminists do, that all the problems of the world cannot be reduced to a single cause of "original oppression."

Any narrow feminist analysis that only briefly discusses economics and the environment oversimplifies economic structures and situates them merely as tools of the patriarchy. For example, even Seager (who rejects ecofeminism) stated, "it is clear that industry-generated environmental destruction is seldom, if ever, an inevitability [of capitalism] it is *not* a necessary side effect of industrial progress."[40] We would argue that environmental destruction is most certainly a side effect of an economic system operating *in combination with* an environmental metadiscourse that seeks control over nature. For example, in China, it has been the pursuit of economic development that has accelerated environmental exploitation, despite both a reverence for nature and a cultural history with a distinctly different gender relationship.[41] Many ecofeminist and feminist perspectives struggling to articulate a new environmental discourse unsatisfactorily address class, ethnicity, and age – not as independent agencies/structures but as "subcontractors" of patriarchy. Thus although many ecofeminists would agree that governments and industry are often composed of people from the wealthy elite, few offer little discussion of class as distinct from patriarchy. We would agree that there is a behavioral dimension of morality and socialization, but we find the cursory examination of economic institutions and/or class as a signal that many feminists and ecofeminists are reluctant to explore anything other than patriarchy as the *sole* cause for environmental destruction.

We believe that feminist arguments relying on a single agency (patriarchy) as the lynchpin in the whole system of environmental degradation are problematic. We would counter that human attempts to control nature can be traced back to such technological inventions as fire, the wheel, tools – all of which predate patriarchal societies. Patriarchy is not the original explanation of environmental change and degradation; rather we would agree with the deep ecologists that the anthropocentric view rests at the heart of environmental exploitation. In relying on "gender" as the primary factor, ecofeminists actually construct a new metanarrative in the same tradition as modernists or Marxists. For example, it is highly probable that a rich/white/female/elite member, driving a convertible sports car does not have the same concern for or affinity to nature as a poor/Latina/female/single mother who labors in the strawberry fields in the Central Valley of California. Feminists who see patriarchy as *the* structure responsible for creating environmental degradation dangerously assume that the domination of women and nature is a cross-cultural phenomenon. Woman-as-victim becomes the dominant concept, overlooking the fact that women have collaborated in their own subordination and in the oppression of other women.[42] We must assign women some culpability: after all some women continue to purchase toxic household cleaners, they adorn themselves in fur, they choose to drive gas-guzzling cars (such as sports utility vehicles) and enjoy jet-setting across the globe, thus contributing to the release of tons of carbon dioxide.

Another problem many have with ecofeminism is its suggestion that women and nature have a special affinity, a privileged intimacy. This privilege is celebrated as a source of inspiration and empowerment. But the darker side of this viewpoint is its exclusion of men's important or intimate connection to nature. Some ecofeminists believe and argue that women's voices are more authentic in articulating a new ecological consciousness. As one ecofeminist arrogantly asserted:

> You guys [in the radical or deep ecology movement] are trying to newly articulate a consciousness that women have always articulated. . . . women have always thought like mountains, to allude to Aldo Leopold's paradigm for ecological thinking.[43]

Critics respond that this type of mindset is, ironically, a "sexist ploy." It is inaccurate and problematic to define women as closer to nature than men. This type of privileging, some feminists argue, merely continues the male-defined dichotomy of women/men, nature/culture. In other words, the ecofeminist position that privileges women as closer to nature establishes yet another hierarchy that disenfranchises men. The earth is neither male nor female. Men and women may have different connections to the earth, but one is neither more innate or intimate than the other. Ecofeminism that emphasizes the differences of men and women by reinforcing the idea of women having a closer, more intimate connection to nature runs the risk of perpetuating the very hierarchies it seeks to overthrow,[44] thwarting the possibility of liberation – the very essence of political action against patriarchal culture.

One critic, Janet Biehl, is concerned about the "disquieting tendency" of ecofeminism. She argues that ecofeminism has become so blatantly self-contradictory and problematic that it is incoherent.[45] And because theory should enlighten rather than confuse, the legitimacy of ecofeminists' claim to an alternate "theory" is challenged. Biehl claims that ecofeminism often ignores or rejects important intellectual legacies, such as social theory or the best of western culture and democracy, and instead reinforces irrationalism (through its embrace of goddess worship and prehistoric rituals). Some ecofeminists trace the subjugation of women and the domination of nature to the Scientific Revolution; others connect it to the Judeo-Christian tradition; still others associate it with the Indo-European invasions of nomadic tribes in Eurasia in 4500 BC. These variations are significant and have yet to be resolved. Biehl has criticized ecofeminism for being primarily defined by a plethora of short, often self-contradictory essays on the subject (indeed, much of the ecofeminist literature is found in anthologies and edited collections that neither attempt to resolve the inherent contradictions or engage in debate).[46] Still others have resisted ecofeminist theory because it has for the most part been articulated largely from a white feminist viewpoint. Although women of color are contributing to the development of ecofeminist theory to a greater degree now, some believe that its roots are irreconcilable with their own lives and experiences.

Thus one problem in attempting to come to feminist terms with the environment is, ironically, that it can often be *ecologically* unsound. Ecological principles rely on the construction of the interdependence of many complex systems. There is no one single strand that can be removed from the web. Ecofeminists can fall prey to the temptation to simplify explanations down to the polarization of sex/gender difference, a temptation, however, that continues the reductionist imperative of the modernistic, mechanistic paradigm to which many feminists and ecofeminists are in opposition. The writings of many feminists and ecofeminists do not reflect a perception of the whole (environmental destruction as the result of a complex political, economic, social, and even religious construct) for the sum of the parts (the parts in this case being patriarchal military, government, eco-establishment). The complexity of human experience and interaction and the links between various structures is thus reduced to a single dimension: gender domination. Such a view is based on a linear, cause-and-effect paradigm that cannot elucidate the complexity of the worldwide environmental problem.[47] When every analysis leads to gender and patriarchy as the casual agent, it is essentialist. Gender makes *a* difference but perhaps not *the* difference.

Ecofeminism is often contradictory, often exclusive and often reliant on opaque terminology and language. Ironically much ecofeminist literature does not "liberate" because it remains inaccessible due to obtuse jargon and abstract metaphysics, preventing many women and men from joining in the debate.

Although there are some critical shortcomings with feminist arguments and with ecofeminism, one thing is true: environmental problems are the result of social practices and must be seen *social* problems (as much as physical ones). Feminist perspectives, such as those of Seager, Plant, Anderson, and Merchant, shed valuable light on the parallels between the oppression of women and the exploitation of nature. They elucidate the implications of patriarchal institutions and the masculinization of science in Western culture. They alert us to the numerous dualisms that have permeated the Western intellectual tradition and attempt to articulate a language that moves beyond a simplistic view. Feminist contributions deepen our understanding of the interconnectedness of oppression. The many feminisms – from a feminist critique to ecofeminists – create various "sites" of confrontation that force a dynamic interaction of ideas. The contributions of feminisms to environmental history and philosophy are emerging in other explorations of humanity–environment relationships. For example, Carolyn Merchant's work is a valuable asset in an exploration of our inherited Enlightenment principles of scientific knowledge. Indeed, more recent works, such as Max Oelschlaeger's sweeping history, *The Idea of Wilderness*, are indebted to work by Merchant and other historians of science for their examination of the Scientific Revolution and the values that came to dominance. As many search for a way of moving beyond the dualistic impasses imposed by the technological environmental metadiscourse and toward some conscious reconciliation, some will turn to the feminist perspective. The value of the feminist perspective is to enlarge the set of variables identified in exploring humanity–environment relationships.

## Postmodern Environmental Ethics

In recent years, it has become a cliché to speak of "postmodernism" and the influence of postmodern critiques. The postmodern label seems to have permeated into many aspects of culture: from architecture, to art, to the academy. A postmodern perspective has also been applied to ideas about nature and the environment. In this section we consider the emerging postmodern literature that looks at nature from a critical social and cultural perspective rather than a scientific one.

A postmodern perspective has introduced critiques about ideology, discourse, representation, knowledge, and power that overturn many of our assumptions about the world. It enjoys a playful criticism of unquestioned relationships – humanity–environment relationships or the social domination of certain groups of people, for example. Much of the work considers the historical context in which nature, knowledge and language were defined. Thus a postmodern critique can open up a wider discussion of science, knowledge, language, power, and ideology, all important considerations when analyzing environmental discourses, humanity–environment relationships, and environmental issues and policy.

Under the technological environmental metadiscourse that the modern world has evolved, nature has been categorized as separate from human culture. Some writers have begun to explore the idea that there was a time in which our societies had no dualism and nature had no opposite.[48] That nature had an opposite is an *intellectual* creation, not an immutable "truth." In the Western world, for example, it was Plato who introduced the idea that there is truth beyond nature. Christianity refined this further: God was seen as the creator of nature; nature was somehow distinct from God and hence from human beings.[49] As Carolyn Merchant has illustrated, the Scientific Revolution and the Age of Reason took this even further. Nature came to mean that which is not human. It became a conceptual container, a container that has since become a literal object.[50] Nature was an object to be studied, probed and analyzed in the search for truth (whether or not it would prove to be of God's handiwork is another story). That nature was an object "out there" was rarely questioned.

Environmentalists have begun to incorporate this type of perspective and critical analysis of language and knowledge into discussions about wider economic and political structures. For example, *Postmodern Environmental Ethics* attempts to situate social theory and the postmodern perspective in the inquiry of environmental ethics.[51] Admittedly, defining postmodern environmental ethics remains an unfinished project,[52] because postmodernism itself is difficult to define. Many of the writings in this collection, however, challenge us to explore the role of language and science in the creation of humanity–environment discourses.

Postmodern social theory has also looked at the construction of scientific knowledge. This scrutinizes many of the modernistic ideals of progress, truth, growth, and intrinsic value to show that science is a product of culture and that scientific models are not removed from moral tendencies.[53] This has intellectual implications for those who believe science is value-neutral and that it cannot be held responsible for the environmental problems it creates. It also has implications for those environmental groups that rely on scientific rigor and assessment to convince others of the need for reform. This emerging discourse of social theory suggests that no conceptual issue, such as the knowledge of nature or what is acceptable "risk," can be divorced from its concomitant dimensions of political and institutional legitimations.[54] In our modern society, knowledge and truth have been understood to belong to the domain of science. As a result "our culture has virtually identified the achievement of knowledge with the procedures of science ."[55] As we have seen earlier, however, radical environmentalists, especially deep ecologists (whose early contingency came from philosophy or literature), seek to overturn our society based on science = truth = progress.

One new area of thought to emerge from that of the postmodern perspective is "the social construction of nature." For many years, the study of the environment has been dominated by physical scientists or policy analysts. We have often taken for granted that nature is an objective reality rather than in part a social creation.[56] The postmodern perspective challenges the assumption that nature is a physical entity to be studied and understood only by natural scientists.

Neil Everden's *The Social Creation of Nature*, for example, is a work that effectively explores the social construction of nature. His main argument is that the "environmental crisis" is as much a *social* phenomenon as a *physical* one.[57] For example, for there to be a concept of "pollution," there must first be an understanding of the system or environment in order. Pollution is basically the system out of order. Thus, we must first explore the system of "knowing" or knowledge. Recently there has been an explosion of social science writers examining environmental history, environmental discourses, humanity–environment relationships, and the role that nature and the environment have in cultural value systems.

Another contributor is sociologist Will Wright, who in his 1992 book *Wild Knowledge* argued that the emerging discourse of social theory suggests that the "knowledge of nature" cannot be divorced from its concomitant dimensions of political and institutional legitimations.[58] Nature is our own creation; it is not simply what is "out there," because we keep changing the meaning of what we know to be "out there." "Every act of control, however well-intentioned, continues the amplification of the process that has been unfolding since the Renaissance – the objectification of nature."[59]

To acknowledge the existence of a social construction of nature, we must also admit something fundamental about the nature of knowledge. Knowledge itself (and how it is defined) is power. The concept of nature is thus embedded in our very structure of knowledge. Looking at nature as a social construction allows us to examine various forms of control – economic, social and political – and how certain constructions are institutionalized in our culture.

Wright also argued that science has become ecologically irrational, losing a commitment to sustainability and interdependence. In the age of Enlightenment, physics was recognized as inherently social and political, as an effort to define new ideas of truth and reality.[60] At its very inception, the scientific idea of nature was blatantly political; this new knowledge of nature was part of a political strategy redefining the social, political, and religious order. At some point, modern society lost sight of this fact. Scientific knowledge has become absolute and authoritative; science has been presented as objective, morally neutral and detached from social concerns. But ironically, scientific knowledge held to be objective and neutral is a social theory that denies social concerns.[61] The result is environmental damage and human oppression. In modern society, knowledge and truth are understood to belong to the domain of science, but the increased attention to technological impacts on the environment have helped us recognize that a restructuring of our social and economic priorities necessitates new ways of thinking about nature, knowledge and language.

There has been a backlash to a "deconstructionist" postmodern critique (for every reaction, there is an equal and opposite reaction). Responses include books like *Reinventing Nature? Responses to Postmodern Deconstruction* and *Sacred Interconnections: Postmodern Spirituality, Political Economy and Art*. These works take as their premise that deconstruction eliminates the ingredients necessary for constructing a new environmental metadiscourse, such as God, self, purpose, and meaning.[62]

Some observers contend that deconstructive postmodernism is tempted toward relativism or even nihilism (for example, a relativistic argument about the value of preserving forests might go something like this: hierarchies need to be removed; therefore nothing is better than anything else; therefore plastic trees are just as good as real trees; therefore why spend a lot of money to conserve forests when we can manufacture plastic ones?). Deconstructionism, say some, cannot solve the problem of the environmental crisis because it is not concerned with constructing a new consciousness or discourse.

"Constructive postmodernists", as they call themselves, opt for a critical analysis of cultural practices and paradigms, as well as pose alternatives that might help transcend anthropocentrism, patriarchy, consumerism, and mechanization. They believe there can be a constructive postmodernism that supports ecology and environmental integrity. Constructive postmodernists find meaning in nature and in human connections with nature; they assert the importance of nature-as-sacred, something beyond the reach of nihilistic deconstruction. This perspective is newly emerging (and not well defined or articulated), but it suggests an array of possibilities for transformation and promises to be an important part of the ideological continuum in the future.

The postmodern perspective is concerned with language and how language has directed meanings and values in our society. A view of nature and knowledge as socially constructed offers a variety of ways to challenge assumptions about economic, political, and intellectual institutions that shape our society. The concept that nature is socially constructed is a valuable and essential tool of analysis, but it can fall short of providing a methodology for action. It becomes too easy to criticize nearly all environmentalists: mainstream and conservative environmentalists continue to accept the nature-as-object; deep ecologists or radical environmentalists accept a notion of nature-as-self. But, both extremes share the assumption that nature is a thing, an object; the recipe for a reunification of dualisms, and that of culture/nature, remains elusive. But by considering nature as a social construction, we have another useful tool for unearthing the complex forces that shape our humanity–environment relations. In the following chapter, we build upon these interesting constructive postmodern ideas and look at a specific case study of the social construction of nature by examining the national parks.

## Conclusions

In this chapter we have looked at a variety of radical environmental discourses. Some of them share common points of view – for example that we have erected false and dangerous hierarchies. They often differ in significant ways as well. None offer the "only solution" to many of our most pressing environmental problems and issues. Some even invite individuals to elaborate their own eco-philosophies and to search for new spirituality, new rituals, stories, and legends with which to re-create a different type of environmental discourse. A common thread throughout is a call for rethinking the dualisms (for example, nature/culture, human/nonhuman, value/fact) that permeate our culture. Simply, they challenge many of our held "truths" and assumptions. They are all, in their own ways, valuable because they challenge our assumptions and make us more sensitive to ourselves, to others and to the nonhuman world.

## FURTHER READING

In addition to the books and edited collections suggested here, a wide range of ecophilosophical discussions and debates can be found in numerous issues of *Environmental Ethics*. Past issues contain debates between deep ecologists and social ecologists, and deep ecologists and ecofeminists.

### Radical Ecology

Abbey, Edward. 1975. *The Monkey Wrench Gang*. New York: JB Lippincott.
Devall, Bill. 1988. *Simple in Means, Rich in Ends: Practicing Deep Ecology*. Salt Lake City, Utah: Peregrine Smith.

Devall, Bill and George Sessions. 1985. *Deep Ecology: Living as if Nature Mattered*. Salt Lake City, Utah: Peregrine Smith.

Foreman, David. 1991. *Confessions of an Eco-Warrior*. New York: Harmony Books.

Fox, Warwick. 1990. *Toward a Transpersonal Ecology: Developing New Foundations for Environmentalism*. Boston: Shambhala.

Hunter, Robert. 1979. *Warriors of the Rainbow: A Chronicle of the Greenpeace Movement*. New York: Holt, Rinehart and Winston.

LaChapelle, Dolores. 1978. *Earth Wisdom*. Silverton, Col.: Way of the Mountain Center.

List, P. C. 1993. *Radical Environmentalism; Philosophy and Tactics*. Belmont, Calif.: Wadsworth.

Lee, M. 1995. *Earth First!* Syracuse, NY: Syracuse University Press.

Merchant, C. 1992. *Radical Ecology: The Search for a Livable World*. London: Routledge.

Naess, Arne. 1989. *Community and Lifestyle*. Cambridge: Cambridge University Press.

Nash, Roderick. 1989. *The Rights of Nature: A History of Environmental Ethics*. Madison: University of Wisconsin Press.

Paehlke, Robert. 1989. *Environmentalism and the Future of Progressive Politics*. New Haven, Conn.: Yale University Press.

Pepper, David. 1993. *Eco-Socialism: From Deep Ecology to Social Justice*. London and New York: Routledge.

Scarce, Rik. 1990. *Eco-Warriors: Understanding the Radical Environmental Movement*. Chicago: Noble Press.

Sessions, George, ed. 1995. *Deep Ecology for the 21st Century: Readings on the Philosophy and Practice of the New Environmentalism*. Boston: Shambhala.

Snyder, Gary. 1974. *Turtle Island*. New York: New Directions Books.

*The Trumpeter* (journal of deep ecology and philosophy). LightStar, PO Box 5853, Victoria, BC, Canada V8R 6S8.

## Social Ecology

Bookchin, Murray. 1982. *The Ecology of Freedom: The Emergence and Dissolution of Hierarchy*. Palo Alto: Cheshire Books.

——1990. *The Philosophy of Social Ecology: Essays on Dialectical Naturalism*. Toronto: Black Rose Books.

——1990. *Remaking Society: Pathways to a Green Future*. Boston: South End Press.

Clark, John, ed. 1990. *Renewing the Earth: The Promise of Social Ecology*. London: Green Print.

*Harbinger: The Journal of Social Ecology*. PO Box 89, Plainfield, VT 05667.

## The Feminist Perspective and Ecofeminism

Adams, Carol, ed. 1993. *Ecofeminism and the Sacred*. New York: Continuum.

Anderson, Lorraine, ed. 1991. *Sisters of the Earth: Women's Prose and Poetry about Nature*. New York: Vintage Books.

Biehl, Janet. 1991. *Finding Our Way: Rethinking Ecofeminist Politics*. Montreal and New York: Black Rose Books.

Bradiotti, Rosi, Ewa Charkiewicz, Sabine Hausler, and Saskia Wierigna. 1994. *Women, the Environment and Sustainable Development: Towards a Theoretical Synthesis.* London: Zed Books.

Caldecott, Leoni and Stephanie Leland, eds, 1983. *Reclaim the Earth: Women Speak Out for Life on Earth.* London: The Women's Press.

Diamond, Irene. 1994. *Fertile Ground: Women, Earth and the Limits of Control.* Boston: Beacon Press.

Diamond, Irene and Gloria Feman Orenstein, eds, 1990. *Reweaving the World: The Emergence of Ecofeminism.* San Francisco: Sierra Club Books.

Gaard, Greta, ed. 1993. *Ecofeminism: Women, Animals, Nature.* Philadelphia: Temple University Press.

Griffin, Susan. 1978. *Woman and Nature: The Roaring Inside Her.* New York: Harper and Row.

Kolodny, Annette. 1975. *The Lay of the Land: Metaphor as Experience and History in American Life and Letters.* Chapel Hill, NC: University of North Carolina Press.

Merchant, Carolyn. 1996. *Earthcare: Women and the Environment.* New York: Routledge.

Plant, Judith, ed. 1989. *Healing the Wounds: The Promise of Ecofeminism.* London: Green Print.

Rocheleau, Dianne, Barbara Thomas-Slayter, and Esther Wangari, eds. 1996. *Feminist Political Ecology: Global Issues and Local Experiences.* New York: Routledge.

Seager, Joni. 1993. *Earth Follies: Coming to Feminist Terms with the Global Environmental Crisis.* New York: Routledge.

Shiva, Vandana. 1989. *Staying Alive: Women, Ecology and Development.* London: Zed Books.

Sturgeon, Noël. 1997. *Ecofeminist Natures: Race, Gender, Feminist Theory and Political Action.* New York: Routledge.

Warren, Karen, ed. 1996. *Ecological Feminist Philosophies.* Bloomington: Indiana University Press.

## Critical Theory/Postmodern Approaches

Connor, Steven. 1989 and 1992. *Postmodernist Culture: An Introduction to Theories of the Contemporary.* Oxford: Basil Blackwell.

Everden, Neil. 1992. *The Social Creation of Nature.* Baltimore and London: The Johns Hopkins University Press.

Griffin, David Ray, ed. 1990. *Postmodern Spirituality, Political Economy and Art.* Albany, NY: State University of New York Press.

——, ed. 1993. *Founders of Constructive Postmodern Philosophy: Pierce, James, Bergson, Whitehead and Hartshorne.* Albany, NY: State University of New York Press.

Leiss, William. 1972. *The Domination of Nature.* New York: George Braziller.

Merchant, Carolyn, ed. 1994. *Ecology: Key Concepts in Critical Theory.* New Jersey: Humanities Press.

Oelschlaeger, Max. 1994 *Caring for Creation: An Ecumenical Approach to the Environmental Crisis.* New Haven, Conn.: Yale University Press.

——, ed. 1995. *Postmodern Environmental Ethics.* Albany: State University of New York Press.

Soulé, Michael and Gary Lease, eds, 1995. *Reinventing Nature? Responses to Postmodern Deconstruction*. Washington, DC: Island Press.

Wright, Will. 1992. *Wild Knowledge: Science, Language, and Social Life in a Fragile Environment*. Minneapolis: University of Minnesota Press.

## NOTES

1   Peter List, *Radical Environmentalism: Philosophy and Tactics* (Belmont, Calif.: Wadworth Publishing Company, 1993), ix.

2   Bill Devall, "Deep Ecology and Radical Environmentalism," in *American Environmentalism*, eds, R. Dunlap and A Mertig (1992), 52.

3   Max Oelschlaeger, *After Earth Day: Continuing The Conservation Effort* (New Haven, CT: Yale University Press, 1992).

4   Bill Devall and George Sessions, *Deep Ecology: Living as If Nature Mattered* (Salt Lake City, Utah: Peregrine Smith, 1985), 70.

5   D. Foreman and D. Haywood, *Ecodefense: A Field Guide to Monkeywrenching*, 2nd edn. (Tuscon, AZ: Ned Ludd Books, 1987).

6   List, *Radical Environmentalism*, 11.

7   Ibid., 11–12.

8   Timothy O'Riordan, "The Challenge for Environmentalism," in *New Models in Geography: The Political-Economy Perspective*, eds. R. Peet and N. Thrift (London: Unwin-Hyman, 1989). It is also interesting to note that despite considerable ideological differences, many deep ecologists, social ecologists and even mainstream/reformists environmentalists have incorporated the ideas of the historic founders of environmental thinking in the United States, such as Henry David Thoreau, John Muir and Aldo Leopold.

9   It is commonly accepted in feminist studies that there exist many feminisms, or perspectives, with which a person can approach a problem. We would argue also that there are many environmentalisms and would situate environmental philosophy along a continuum that contains a range of environmental positions: from conservationists to preservationists to deep ecologists to social ecologists to ecofeminists and everywhere in between. That both feminism and environmentalism as movements and as philosophies sit on a continuum thus allows for many points of intersection.

10  Carolyn Merchant, *The Death of Nature: Women, Ecology and the Scientific Revolution* (London: Wildwood House, 1980), xv.

11  Joni Seager, *Earth Follies: Coming to Feminist Terms with the Global Environmental Crisis* (New York: Routledge, 1993), 3.

12  Merchant, *The Death of Nature*.

13  Ibid., xvii.

14  For continuity, we have used the term "technological environmental metadiscourse." Merchant uses the term "Mechanistic worldview" in her book.

15  Will Wright, *Wild Knowledge: Science, Language, and Social Life in a Fragile Environment* (Minneapolis: University of Minnesota Press, 1992), 61.

16  Merchant, *The Death of Nature*.

17  Seager, *Earth Follies*, 7–8. However, Seager never really defines what she means by "masculinist." She loosely refers to it as male-defined objectives, as male culture as the dominant ideology or as a type of cultural hegemony that sustains patriarchal

authority and legitimizes a patriarchal social and political order. Her undeveloped definition of masculinist is ultimately problematic.

18   Ibid., 14.
19   Ibid., 19.
20   Ibid., 19–22.
21   Ibid., 30.
22   Ibid., 30–1.
23   Ibid., 110.
24   Ibid., 118.
25   Ibid., 76.
26   Ibid., 199.
27   For example, there is liberal feminism (which, like reform environmentalism, seeks to alter human relations through the passage of new laws and regulations); there is radical feminism (which analyzes women's oppression via a critique of an overarching system of patriarchy); and there is social feminism (which attempts to synthesize radical and liberal feminism with the Marxist tradition).
28   Seager, *Earth Follies*, 223.
29   Carol Adams, ed., *Ecofeminism and the Sacred* (New York: Continuum, 1993), 1.
30   Judith Plant, ed., *Healing the Wounds: The Promise of Ecofeminism* (London: Green Print, 1989), 215.
31   Adams, *Ecofeminism and the Sacred*, 4.
32   From *Against Nature: Wilderness Poems* (Paradise, CA: Dustbooks, 1979). The publishers have made every effort to obtain permission to reproduce this poem.
33   Lorraine Anderson, ed., *Sisters of the Earth: Women's Prose and Poetry about Nature* (New York: Vintage Books, 1991), xvi.
34   Ibid., xvii.
35   Plant, *Healing the Wounds:* 1–5.
36   Ibid., 213.
37   Irene Diamond and Gloria Feman Orenstein, eds, *Reweaving the World: The Emergence of Ecofeminism* (San Francisco: Sierra Club Books, 1990).
38   Victoria Davion, "Is Ecofeminism Feminist," in *Ecological Feminism*, ed. K. Warren (London and New York: Routledge, 1994), 8.
39   Sharon Doubiago, "Mama Coyote Talks to the Boys," in Plant, *Healing the Wounds*, 40–4.
40   Seager, *Earth Follies*, 72.
41   Huey-li Li, "A Cross-Cultural Critique of Ecofeminism," in *Ecofeminism: Women, Animals, Nature*, ed. G. Gaard (Philadelphia: Temple University Press, 1993), 276.
42   Li, "A Cross-Cultural Critique of Ecofeminism."
43   Doubiago, "Mama Coyote Talks to the Boys," 41–2.
44   Diamond and Orenstein, *Reweaving the World*, 102.
45   Janet Biehl, *Finding Our Way: Rethinking Ecofeminist Politics* (Montreal and New York: Black Rose Books, 1991), 1–2.
46   Biehl, *Finding Our Way*, 1–3.
47   Li, "A Cross-Cultural Critique of Ecofeminism," 273.
48   Neil Everden, *The Social Creation of Nature* (Baltimore and London: The Johns Hopkins University Press, 1992). We agree with this general statement as it relates to Western European culture but take issue with the historical limitations of his argument because this concept exists today in many indigenous cultures. For example, Audrey Shenandoah, Clan Mother from the Onondaga Nation, explained that

nature and humans are not separate concepts: "In our language we don't have a word for what everybody calls nature because our ancestors and our tradition are so involved as one with what is called nature, our environment" (Shenandoah in Nolan, 1990).

49  Everden, *Social Creation of Nature*, 20.
50  Ibid., 96.
51  Max Oelschlaeger, ed., *Postmodern Environmental Ethics* (New York: State University of New York Press, 1995).
52  Ibid., 15.
53  Worster, 1977.
54  Wright, *Wild Knowledge*, xii.
55  Ibid., 21–3.
56  Everden, *Social Creation of Nature*, 102.
57  Ibid., 7. It is important to note that this is an idea shared by many radical environmentalists, not just "postmodernists."
58  Wright, *Wild Knowledge*, vii.
59  Everden, *Social Creation of Nature*, 130.
60  Wright, *Wild Knowledge*, 61, but see also Merchant, *Death of Nature*.
61  Wright, *Wild Knowledge*, 7.
62  For instance, they assert that deconstructionists often deny the reality of history, objectivity, science, the soul, and democracy. This has led critics to claim that deconstructionists are self-defeating. See, for example, David Ray Griffin, ed., *Postmodern Spirituality, Political Economy and Art* (Albany: State University of New York Press, 1990), x.

# 9

# Nature, Culture, and the National Parks

Let us begin with a provoking notion: nature is socially constructed.

In this chapter we explore the notion that the physical environment, often called nature, is not a physical entity "out there," but rather is a social creation.[1] We develop this theme by examining national parks as representations of changing ideas about nature in the United States.

In the dominant technological environmental metadiscourse the term *nature* is often counterposed against *culture*, signaling the difference between the natural and the artificial; the god-given and humanity-constructed. We explore further the idea of the social creation of nature by focusing on the problem of perceiving nature and culture as exclusive and opposite concepts. This problem is well illustrated in the enduring practice of dividing national parks into two categories: nature parks and culture parks. There exists perhaps no better example of the artificiality of the nature/culture dualism than the national parks.

There has been no universally agreed-upon definition of what constitutes a national park – it is not explicitly defined in the original legislation nor has it been clarified in more recent efforts to reconsider the mission of national parks. In fact, this has been a philosophical issue debated throughout the history of the parks and it remains a highly contentious subject. Currently the national park system comprises almost 370 units of more than 80 million acres. These 370 units fall into approximately 16 different categories of parks (table 9.1).

The designation of any national park requires federal legislation, which necessitates a series of steps, including the formation of an effective social and

**Table 9.1**  Units of the national park system

| | |
|---|---|
| 51 | National Parks |
| 23 | National Battlefields/National Military Parks |
| 4 | National Battlefield Parks/National Battlefield Sites |
| 32 | National Historical Parks |
| 71 | National Historical Sites |
| 76 | National Monuments |
| 26 | National Memorials |
| 13 | National Preserves |
| 9 | National Wild and Scenic Rivers and Riverways |
| 7 | National Rivers |
| 18 | National Recreation Areas |
| 14 | National Seashores and National Lakeshores |
| 3 | National Scenic Trails |
| 1 | International Historic Site |
| 4 | National Parkways |
| 11 | "Others" (includes National Capital Parks, the White House) |
| 363 | Total units |

*Note*: A tabulation of park units and designations reveals that there are more culture/historic parks than nature parks, an interesting and perhaps surprising fact.

*Source*: compiled by the authors from National Park Service, *National Parks for the 21st Century: the Vail Agenda*. (Post Mills, Vermont: Chelsea Green Publishing/National Park Service, 1993) and *The National Parks: Index 1989* (Office of Public Affairs and the Division of Publications, National Park Service. GPO:1990 – 262–098/00001. Washington, DC: Government Printing Office, 1990).

political coalition and the process of debate, negotiation, and compromise. National parks, therefore, are created in a politicized context. Each unit in the park system is an expression of our political culture at a particular time in our history.[2] Each reflects a definition (or idealization) of nature.

The history of national parks has been of interest to many scholars and park enthusiasts,[3] who have situated national parks in a broad social context and have explored the parks themselves, the contributions of park creators and administrators, and even the very terms *park* and *wilderness*. They have shown the ways in which Americans attitudes toward the outdoor environment have changed and how these attitudes have influenced both the creation and the meaning of parks. Many forces have shaped national parks; this chapter focuses on two: legislative designations and political conflicts over policy or specific parks. These two concurrent processes defined and redefined the purpose, function, and ideology of national parks.

The first process is the periodic emergence of what we will term "park movements" to reconsider the criteria for parks to be designated as national parks. The primary outcome of these park movements has been federal legislation that amended the criteria for park designation, thus creating new types of national parks. New designations of national parks have also contributed to the expansion of the system itself. Several movements have reflected efforts to shape a meaningful system, to modify the structure of the national parks, and to articulate how Americans view the national parks.

The second process is the eruption of political conflicts over specific proposed or existing parks. Often these struggles have revolved around issues of development rights or management policy, but equally as often they have fundamentally challenged the national park ideal and purpose. These conflicts, both local and national in scope, have arisen because of the publication of Park Service documents, studies, or ecological surveys or because of the initiative of individuals or organizations such as congressional representatives, intellectual elites, park supporters, park opponents, and non-profit environmental organizations (such as the Conservation Foundation or the Sierra Club).

Together these two concurrent forces – park movements and park political struggles – have influenced the meaning of parks. An understanding of these two interdependent historical forces situates the national parks in the broader context of the evolution and change in environmental discourses.

### Movements and the Designation of New Parks

Historically, there have been four broad movements that have shaped the contemporary national park system by creating laws establishing new parks. Each movement arose for a different reason, mirroring the political, intellectual, cultural, and geographical imperatives of the time. Each defined a new type of national park unit, expanding the national park system and the ways people use, visit, and think of national parks. The commonality among the park movements is the attempt to *preserve* and *honor* a place of significance – a canyon, a mountain, a grave, or a beach.

The first movement, we term *preservation of spaces*, began in the late nineteenth century. It has been well documented and described.[4] Out of this movement the first national parks, Yellowstone in 1872 and Yosemite in 1891, were created.[5] The origins of how and why the movement began are complex. Most park historians agree that the pressure to create the first national parks arose as an aggregation of several cultural forces. First, the influence of the Romantic and transcendentalist movements were a major force in shaping the attitudes of educated, upper-class Americans during the late nineteenth century. Second, the rapid settlement of the west along with increasing industrialization and urbanization in the east prompted many intellectual elites to reevaluate their attitudes about "nature" and "culture."[6] The conservation movement gained impetus as other factors arose. The intellectual search for a distinct American identity compelled many to reevaluate the outdoor experience. Many of these same elites had journeyed to Niagara Falls, New York, subsequently voicing concern over its condition. They were convinced that the falls had become overcommercialized and inaccessible and feared that "scenic wonders" such as these could be destroyed if unregulated and unprotected.

Eventually, the movement coalesced into an effective political coalition led by intellectual figures such as John Muir and Gifford Pinchot. They were aided by the endorsement and outdoor enthusiasm of President Theodore Roosevelt. The conservationists called upon Congress to set aside vast areas to be designated national parks. Scholars have argued that the early conservation movement presented the first challenge to the unquestioned environmental metadiscourse of unbridled consumption and exploitation of land in the new nation.

Historian Alfred Runte chronicled the meaning of national parks in American history in his book *National Parks: The American Experience*. His central argument is provocative: the driving force behind the movement to establish national parks arose not solely out of environmentalist or conservationist ideology but also as a reaction to the dearth of recognized cultural achievements in a young nation in the nineteenth century. In comparison with Europe the United States had no castles, no ancient ruins, no Shakespeare, and no Sistine Chapel.[7] To compensate, Americans turned to monumental scenic landmarks as substitutes for man-made achievements and as America's contribution to world culture. Great chasms, thundering waterfalls, and towering peaks became America's secular cathedrals and were considered "national" assets. These natural monuments and the creation of national parks themselves were considered uniquely American and contributed to humanity in the same manner the Swiss Alps, Stonehenge or the Parthenon did in Europe. In fact, national parks have been referred to as America's "crown jewels," a certain reference to the gems of European monarchs. Runte concluded that one major root of the original national park movement was inspired by monumentalism – places of splendor, drama, and other natural wonders. Monumentalism, in mountains, canyons, gorges, and other dramatic geologic and topographical features, thus became the predominant national park ideal. It was in fact linked to quasi-aesthetic romantic notions of the sublime. Dramatic scenery inspired deep emotive qualities and became ingrained in the American imagination. Places such as Yellowstone and Yosemite became the archetypes of "nature" and "wilderness."

Runte's argument is important and intriguing because it places both the ideals behind the national parks and the national parks themselves as a *cultural expression*. National parks are socially constructed – embodiments of the values a society deems important, time capsules that reveals attitudes and perceptions dominant at the time of their creation.[8]

It is important to our argument to see that the creation of any national park is somewhat arbitrary and artificial. There is no national park "out there" waiting to be discovered and marked. The delineation of park boundaries, for example, is often contested, negotiated, and compromised. Hence park boundaries, as products of social construction reflect culture and politics.

National parks, people, and nature exist in an intricate arrangement of political, social, legal, intellectual, and sentimental relationships. Parks are as much about statesmanship, philanthropy and cultural values as they are about ecology.

From their inception, national parks have been enmeshed in debates about the accepted definition of parks. Should they just be isolated wilderness? Some argued that parks were natural environments and should be kept as natural as possible. They were in ideological conflict with those who believed that parks could also be constructed areas and should be as accessible to public use as possible. This division embedded a tension between purpose and ideal in the parks from the earliest years.

On one issue there was little debate: park advocates did not intend for the parks to remain idle. Use of the parks was fundamental to the national park ideal: public access and enjoyment would illustrate (and legitimize) a park's worth to the nation. Over time the concept of use in national parks evolved to include activities such as inspiration, education, and recreation. From the beginning then, public utilization was an important element of park philosophy. Secretary of the Interior Hubert Work reinforced this ideal when he wrote in 1925 that "the public should be afforded every opportunity to enjoy national parks and monuments ... parks and monuments should be kept accessible by any means practicable."[9] Although ideals of pristine wilderness and dramatic scenery remain ingrained in our twentieth-century imagination as founding park ideals, so too have the ideals of public access and use.

### Sacred spaces

As the citizens of the United States began to reconstruct the nation out of the ashes of the Civil War the second park movement, *sacred spaces*, articulated a new spin on the concept of preservation. Amidst the political and social uncertainty of Reconstruction political elites recognized the importance of doing something to heal the nation's war wounds and to commemorate all those who fought. The Civil War was seen as a defining moment in the American story, and many believed that battle sites should be preserved. Thus this park movement provided the earliest efforts to preserve "sacred ground." In 1890, only a few years after the creation of the first national park, Congress passed legislation establishing two national battlefields – Chickamauga (in Georgia) and Chattanooga (in Tennessee) – to stand as lasting memorials to the great armies of the Civil War. They might also be considered the second and third National Parks (although they were not called "parks").

The inclusion of battle sites and military parks as sacred space was a departure from the original national park ideal of monumentalism. The leaders of this movement aimed to designate and protect select places considered profoundly significant in American history. The valuing of cultural significance meant natural features were not the overriding factor in determining whether a space was an important part of American history and identity. Although the Romantic outlook never disappeared completely, this park movement introduced notions of historical significance in identifying places worthy of park status and created an emerging tension: the conflict over whether cultural areas measured up to the national park ideal. This tension between parks as nature and parks as American history and culture would prove to be important and enduring.

### Historical places: the role of "culture" expands

The new century brought accelerated changes to national parks. In 1906 Congress passed the National Monument and Antiquities Act, an achievement that arose out of the third park movement, we term *historical places*, to expand and modify the meaning of national parks. This legislation was designed to articulate more clearly and protect American history by including both natural and human-constructed areas of significance. The Antiquities Act further expanded the agenda of the national park ideal to include historic landmarks, historic and prehistoric structures or archeological sites (notably prehistoric Native American sites). For the first time, Americans recognized pre-Columbian cultures as an important part of US history. Among the new sites designated as national memorials or national historic parks were Chaco Cultural National Historic Park in new Mexico (1906); Gila Cliff Dwellings in New Mexico (1907); Muir Woods in California (1908); Devils Towers in Wyoming (1906); and Abraham Lincoln Birthplace in Kentucky (1916). The interest in preserving and gathering objects or sites of historical significance or antiquity was an important driving force behind the legislation. Without the Antiquities Act it is possible that many areas of significance would have been destroyed before Congress passed legislation to protect them.[10]

The Battle Sites and Military Parks Act and the National Monument and Antiquities Act testify to the important role of parks in preserving, protecting and showcasing American culture. It is evident that the conflict over nature and culture and park ideals remained ingrained even among park advocates. The Park Service itself admits that debates about which emphasis ought to be primary or appropriate have gone in and out of fashion according to political winds.[11]

### Creating the National Park Service

During the first decades of the twentieth century the number of national parks increased, and so had the criteria for designation as a national park. However, the national park ideal would be characterized by rugged, spectacular landforms.[12] The romantic notions of nature and wilderness as sublime and the ideology of monumentalism remained the preeminent forces shaping National Park Service and US perceptions of national park ideals.

Regardless of the new criteria for the newest sites, all parks were without an administrative structure to manage the parks. There was no park system per se. Each unit was separately administered according to location and purpose by the Secretary of the Interior (the nature areas of Yellowstone, Yosemite, etc.), the Secretary of War (historic battlefields and military parks) or the Secretary of Agriculture (historic sites and monuments).

Many park advocates felt that the lack of an institutional administrator left the parks vulnerable to political whims. They worried that politicians were too quick to yield to economic development projects by either deactivating areas of parks or allowing commercial activities on park lands. Finally in 1915 Congress established a National Park Service, and President Woodrow Wilson signed the National Park Service Act into law, bringing more than 36 national parks into the park system. As the culmination of long-standing attempts to integrate and incorporate the variety of units already designated national parks, the act was also seen as the best hope of guarding parks against the inherent uncertainties of the political climate.[13] It attempted to clarify the role of the National Park Service and charged it to

> promote and regulate the use of the Federal areas known as national parks, monuments and reservations hereinafter specified by such means and measures as conform to the fundamental purpose of the said parks, monuments and reservations, which purpose is to conserve the scenery and the natural and historic objects and the wild life therein and to provide for the enjoyment of the same in such manner and by such means as will leave them unimpaired for the enjoyment of future generations (National Park Service Act, title 16, sec. 1)

The legislation creating the National Park Service contained a glaring omission. Culture sites were not included as parks within the purview of the National Park Service. The new system contained only nature parks. Yellowstone, Yosemite and other national parks finally belonged to a system, but at no point could anyone state with any sense of final authority that "this is what a park should be."

### Consolidating the national parks

During much of the 1930s and 1940s, the Park Service expanded its agenda; other changes to the park system were also intricately linked with the socio-economic programs of Roosevelt's New Deal. New Deal programs such as the Civilian Conservation Corps profoundly impacted the parks through public works projects such as road and trail construction and the building of hotels and other park accommodations.[14] The Works Progress Administration also engaged in infrastructure repair and construction at many parks across the country. The programs of the New Deal improved the physical condition of parks and provided an impetus for park expansion.

Roosevelt's New Deal programs did much to improve the condition of the parks, but perhaps his most significant action occurred in 1933 when he transferred national monuments, national battlefields, and national cemeteries into the National Park Service jurisdiction. The move had been prompted by National Park Service director Horace Albright, who saw that the inclusion of these "cultural assets" would make the Park Service a truly national agency and would give it a broadened constituency that would ensure more attention (and money) from Congress.[15] Roosevelt's reorganization thus enlarged the domain of the national park system by 56 parks.[16]

In 1935 Congress passed the Preservation of Historic Sites Act, which recognized the wealth and diversity of places and people who had contributed to

American identity. The legislation broadened the Park Service's sphere of influence in historic preservation, incorporating places such as Mount Vernon (the home of George Washington) and Monticello (the home of Thomas Jefferson) into the National Park System and declaring these sites historically important and therefore nationally significant. Although many new parks were being created for their scenic monumentalism, parks had also become the time capsules of US culture.

In the decades following the Second World War, the Park Service witnessed a rapid expansion of properties and a doubling, even tripling, of visitors to the parks. The postwar years were ones of economic prosperity and were characterized by industrial expansion and urban/suburban development. The increasing affordability of automobiles gave people more mobility and changed the way in which leisure time was spent. It stimulated new attitudes about the out-of-doors. Increased numbers of visitors to the parks raised concerns about access. By the 1950s many park advocates and even Park Service administrators felt the park system had grown beyond its ability to provide adequate staff, facilities, and protection. As a response to growing concerns about the physical conditions of parks and increased visitors, the Park Service proposed to embark on "Mission 66," in 1956, a program designed to rehabilitate the condition of parks through a series of projects, including increasing staff, building and repairing roads, and investing federal funds in scientific surveys and studies.[17] Although the Park Service recognized the inadequate state of many of the parks, it was pressured to continue expanding programs and adding new parks. Much of this pressure came from political elites who realized the political benefits they would derive from creating a national park for their constituencies.

### Parks for the cities: the debate over urban national recreation areas

The fourth movement, *recreation areas*, to expand and modify the park system was a result of executive and congressional concerns about recreation and access to national parks. In late 1950s Congress authorized an Outdoor Recreation Resources Review Commission to study the problem of open space and recreational opportunities for the nation. Congress was responding to the increasing extensions of urban centers, highways, and residential, commercial and industrial development around the nation. In 1962, after three years of research, the commission issued its report, which stated that outdoor opportunities were most urgently needed near metropolitan areas.[18] Further, the commission found that simple activities – walking, hiking, and picnicking – were the outdoor activities in which Americans most participated. The report concluded that few recreation areas were near enough to metropolitan areas for a Sunday outing. Noting that the federal government was in a better financial and leadership position to implement the creation and establishment of recreation areas around the country, the commission recommended that the National Park Service begin planning for national recreation program units. These national recreation areas would be located in or near urban areas and designated primarily for outdoor

**Table 9.2** Public recreation areas, 1965 (in millions of acres)

|            | Urban       | Non-urban  | Total       |
|------------|-------------|------------|-------------|
| Federal    | 35.9        | 410.7      | 446.6       |
| State      | 4.3         | 35.4       | 39.7        |
| County     | .7          | 2.3        | 3.0         |
| Municipal  | 1.4         | .6         | 2.0         |
| TOTAL      | 42.3        | 449.0      | 491.3       |
| Percent    | 9%          | 91.%       | 100%        |
| Population* | 123,813,000 | 68,372,000 | 192,185,000 |
| Percent    | 64.4%       | 35.5%      | 100%        |

*population estimate based on Bureau of Census, "Population Report," 1966.

Source: The Conservation Foundation. *National Parks for the Future*. (Washington, DC: The Conservation Foundation, 1972), 76–7.

recreation use rather than for natural or historic preservation. The recommendation proposed new criteria for parks designed expressly to accommodate high use.

The fourth and most recent national park additions thus were the national recreation areas (NRAs): seashores, lakeshores, and urban recreation areas. It was a response to the perceived problem that wilderness in Park Service terms was neither available nor accessible to most of the urban population (table 9.2). The additions reveal the political influence of major metropolitan areas and the eagerness of the politically ambitious to harness this influence, the increasing concern for open space and environmental quality, and the increasing acceptability of federal support in matters of local concern.[19]

The first recreation-oriented park was the Cape Cod National Seashore. The creation of Cape Cod set an important precedent for the creation of what would be referred to as "nontraditional" parks – these included seashores, lakeshores and urban recreation areas. Both policy and ideological issues emerged from congressional debates about the creation of a national seashore. The Park Service was challenged to learn new ways of accommodating the concerns of nearby communities, something it had not had to do often in the more remote and isolated parks. Perhaps most important, the creation of Cape Cod National Seashore, located within a day's drive for nearly one-third of the US population, sparked a major philosophical debate about national park criteria, and implicitly about the national park ideal.

Not long after the creation of Cape Cod National Seashore, other seashores and lakeshores were designated. In 1972 Congress authorized the Golden Gate National Recreation Area in and around San Francisco and the Gateway National Recreation Area in the New York and New Jersey metropolitan area. The profile of the national park system was further broadened with the addition of these two urban NRAs.

Urban NRAs were significant because they reflected new criteria, and they redefined national significance to include areas not only unspoiled by development, but also accessible to the public. Thus the establishment of subsequent recreation areas was justified on a three-part basis: public access, historical significance and natural preservation.

The NRAs stirred debate both inside and outside of the Park Service. The opponents of NRAs felt these new parks would destroy national park values and jeopardize the national parks of the traditional sort (nature parks). Underlying the debate was a vague perception that concepts and ideals had swayed away from the original park ideology. No longer did a park need to be monumental or even green to be included, or so it seemed. Opponents argued that the criteria for selection were different from (and thus inferior) to those used to designate traditional parks, because man-made features such as parkways, reservoirs, and parklands were included. Such features were not sublime.[20] In the opinion of many Americans (and members of Congress) commonplace topography did not inspire nature worship, and thus it did not belong in the park system.

The opponents also argued that urban NRAs possessed only local and not national significance. Previously the issue of scale (local or national value) had not been debated with any vigor. With the addition of urban NRAs, however, conflict about geographical scale and about what constituted national or local significance ensued. Opponents questioned whether a city could have a park of national significance. Recreation areas thus challenged the national park ideal and purpose by challenging the definition of significant as well as national.

The concept of national significance has been a guiding principle for national parks, but it is an ambiguous and changing concept throughout park history. Just as the creation of any national park is a reflection of social and political influences at a given point in time, so too is the concept of national significance. Whether an area deserves the appellation of national significance depends on the eye of the beholder.[21] For many, it would seem that urban spaces were unlikely to possess attributes of national significance. However, judging a park's merit based on its location is problematic.

> Yosemite is an acknowledged nationally significant area.... well over half of Yosemite's visitors are Californians, and a majority of those come from the San Francisco metropolitan areas. Does that fact make Yosemite merely a regionally significant site? Golden Gate NRA, located entirely within the San Francisco metropolitan area, contains attractions that appeal primarily to people from outside the region – Alcatraz Island, for example, whose visitation is estimated to be over 90 percent non-Californians.[22]

Debate over the inclusion of national recreation areas introduced one of the first instances in which nonprofit environmental organizations opposed rather than supported the designation of new parks. One of the more vocal opponents was the Conservation Foundation, which voiced concerns about recreation areas in its 1972 report on national parks.[23] The task force claimed that national park programs had lost their focus and were responding to too broad an array of stimuli. "They have tended to fill vacuums, and they desperately need to rediscover a unifying ethic." The report suggested that the efforts to make the Park Service more inclusive had only diluted the mission of environmental preservation, and recommended that parks designated as NRAs be eliminated from the jurisdiction of the Park Service because they de-emphasized preservation and focused too much on recreation. The Conservation Foundation considered the Golden Gate NRA and the Gateway in New York to be "anomalies," and while it noted that these lands possessed park like values,

> nevertheless these projects, as conceived, are not *intrinsically* National Parks and would require services and facilities which are quite different from those found in traditional resource-based park units. We recommend that the Gateways be transferred as soon as possible to appropriate state or regional agencies for administration.[24]

On the one hand we applaud the Conservation Foundation's concern that the Park Service agenda had broadened beyond its ability to provide efficient and effective management. On the other hand, we are critical of its narrow and somewhat elitist view of what a park should be. After all Thoreau's Walden, just outside of Concord, Massachusetts, was relatively close to an urbanized, industrialized part of the United States. Thoreau did not value Walden for its millions of acres (the pond was in the midst of about 61 acres) or for its vast scenic wonder, but as a setting or environment that transported him into a different way of being.

The position of the Conservation Foundation and the recommendations of its report are significant in highlighting the conflicts within and outside the Park Service with regard to national park ideals. This foreshadowed what would become decades of "second-class" status for many nontraditional parks.

## The Crown Jewel Syndrome

Despite more than a century of evolution and additions to the park system, Yellowstone and Yosemite continue to epitomize the national park idea. Douglas Rettie discusses the crown jewel syndrome and notes that the label *crown jewels* is reserved for only a select number of national parks – Yellowstone, Yosemite, Grand Canyon – places with a special mystique.[25] Not surprisingly these are the nature parks (indeed, the label "crown jewel" would not be applied to even the most renowned and revered historic sites, such as the Statue of Liberty or Independence Hall). The crown jewel distinction has several repercussions. First, it establishes a hierarchy of national parks. Crown jewels are the *crème de la crème;* all others are situated somewhere below them in the hierarchy. Second, the distinction implies and often is used politically to argue that some parks are more entitled to the Park Service budget than others.[26] Third, casting parks in a hierarchy makes it easier to disregard the lowest-ranked parks. Historically, various national park supporters have advocated that the national park system be limited to the crown jewels and that everything else in the system be transferred to another agency. When Park Service professionals themselves cast doubts about the worthiness of a park's existence or about its cost this goes beyond merely assigning a hierarchy. It jeopardizes the park system's diversity.[27] The crown jewel syndrome can go beyond derogatory aspersions and may result in disproportionate allocations of personnel, money, and sentiment.

The concept of a hierarchy of national parks implies a well-defined set of categories, but the actual composition of a hierarchy has never been described, perhaps because not all Park Service professionals subscribe to the notion of a park hierarchy, nor has such a hierarchy ever been articulated as "official" park policy. It is likely, then, that a national park hierarchy may take many forms. We present one possibility in figure 9.1.

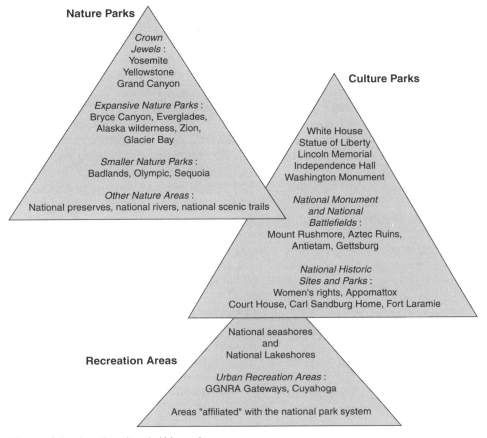

**Figure 9.1**  A national parks' hierarchy

The hierarchy depicted in figure 9.1 might best be described as a quasi-trichotomy. It shows two dominant categories of parks: nature and culture. Recreation areas, however, are neither yet both. They remain outside either of the two park ideals. Herein lies the complexity and contradictory nature of urban recreation areas. These and many other parks cannot be placed in rigid categories, but often contain elements of both park ideals. This reveals the limitations inherent in the social construction of nature/culture dualism.

Shown the hierarchy depicted in figure 9.1, many Americans probably would agree that Yellowstone and Yosemite are more significant or important than the Appomattox Court House or the Gila Cliff Dwellings. It is also probable that many would rank a renowned historic site such as the Washington Monument (culture park) as more significant to the park system than Hot Springs (Arkansas) (a nature park). However, few would list any culture park as more significant than the crown jewels or many of the "second-tier" nature parks.

Of course, any interpretation of a hierarchy depends on one's knowledge of national parks, perspective on the national park ideal and interest. For example, an avid Civil War historian would undoubtedly rank national military parks and battlefields as significant, but a naturalist might consider the expansive wilderness areas to be of most significance. There is a multiplicity of readings of national parks.

Although the concept of hierarchy remains both unofficial and difficult to confirm, it remains a potent and effective subtext that can be employed by both Park Service administrators and others (like Congress) as a measure of opposition to those that are not considered to be the crown jewels.

The very first parks fixed an image of grandeur, pristine wilderness, and incomparable wonders that subsequent national parks were measured against. Opponents have labeled recreational areas "playgrounds," implying these parks are not historically, culturally or naturally significant. Images of physical grandeur and remote wilderness still resonate deeply within US culture, and so it is not surprising that many still devalue recreation areas. American's continued preoccupation with scenic monumentalism has obscured the value of other park units, including historical sites, but most notably the recreation areas.

Advocates of the early national recreation areas argued that these new inclusions did not represent a dilution of park ideals. They reasoned instead that the original legislation for national parks had mandated that public use was a crucial element in national park purpose. Because they were located near urban areas, NRAs promoted public use through more convenient (and less expensive) access. Recreation areas were therefore a solution to concerns about access and recreation for the US public as well as protection against commercial, industrial, or residential development. They further argued that for nearly a century parks had functioned as federal subsidies for middle-class Americans who could afford the vacation time to visit and use the parks.[28] They pointed out that there had been no federally supported recreational opportunity available to the urban poor and emphasized that the original legislation mandated parks for *all* the people, not just the affluent. Thus recreation areas helped the national park system expand its role in a democracy by increasing access. They also challenged the metadiscourse that assumes nature does not exist in the most humanized of landscapes, the city. And yet soon after the establishment of NRAs, these sites were widely regarded as areas of less merit than nature sites. The word *recreation* has become a pejorative for many Park Service professionals.[29]

Despite the controversial nature of the NRAs, there was significant political support for them. This political support led to the establishment of additional parks and recreation areas. In 1977 California Congressman Philip Burton pushed through Congress the largest single legislative package in national park history.[30] The National Parks and Recreation Act added 15 new units to the national park system, marking the apex of that system's expansion.

## Political Battles over Specific Parks and Park Policy

Park movements have been only one force in an evolutionary process within the national park system. The meaning of national parks has also been defined by a series of political battles over specific parks or policy. Often these struggles set precedents or defined new ideals. Some of these political struggles were incidental but nevertheless influential on the national parks. The history of the parks is filled with numerous battles; we intend here to introduce only a few examples to demonstrate that a political battle over a specific park often has an impact on the entire system. In turn, these impacts can influence environmental discourses.

One of the more influential struggles and one that environmentalists still lament today was the battle over Hetch Hetchy in California's Yosemite National Park. In 1901 San Francisco city developers petitioned the Department of the Interior to use Hetch Hetchy Valley for a dam and reservoir, thereby providing a permanent supply of fresh water for a growing city of more than 500,000 people. This proposed development project threatened to set a new precedent for the entire park system. Earlier schemes to exclude lands from national parks had been limited to the outside edges of the reserves. Hetch Hetchy Valley, however, was not on the fringe of Yosemite National Park but was centrally located. The political struggle over Hetch Hetchy was a struggle over the integrity of the Park Service: if the inner sanctum of Yosemite could not be protected in perpetuity, no national park could be considered safe.[31] Park preservationists, led most vocally by John Muir, argued that the valley rivaled the splendor of Yosemite and thus should remain protected from development. Their fervent arguments, however, did not sway Congress. In 1913 it voted to permit San Francisco to begin construction on the dam and to flood the valley floor. Today, Hetch Hetchy Valley lies under water. The loss of Hetch Hetchy had a profound impact on conservation and environmental organizations. Many organizations established permanent lobbying groups to fight similar threats; these groups proved to be important players in future struggles.

The creation of Everglades National Park in 1934 also greatly influenced national park principles. This park was devoid of monumentalism; its topography hardly suggested drama or splendor. The battle for this new park propelled conservationists to articulate the importance of the new science called ecology. The Park Service and park advocates argued that the Everglades was worthy of inclusion in the system because of its unique and fragile ecology. The successful battle to secure congressional authorization thus confirmed a new commitment to protect and preserve an ecological system. Everglades National Park became the first national park to be based on a biological perspective and conservationist ideology. Support for the new park indicated that Romanticism, although not entirely dead, had made way for an emerging scientific rationale of conservation ecology. The creation of this new park, at the time considered an anomaly, symbolized the emergence of new ideals for national parks and had lasting and profound implications. It marked a new direction in park management policy, and, since its inclusion, the Park Service has elevated conservation ecology ideas as guiding principles in park management policy.

Since their inception, many parks have been under threat – from hunting, logging, or mining interests and, more recently, from the strain of massive tourism and pollution. Development projects have periodically threatened the integrity of parks and generated heated public debate, resulting in numerous legislative controversies. One of the most notable involved the proposal to deactivate or decommission Jackson Hole National Monument in Wyoming. In 1943 Congress was persuaded that opportunities for economic development in timber, mining, and grazing outweighed the value of the national monument as preserved for the US public and voted to abolish the park, which eventually was vetoed by President Franklin Roosevelt. This struggle highlights two important points: first, political elites have not always acted to protect and preserve the parks; second, attempts to decommission national park property have occurred. Although the permanence of the national park system has been taken for granted, in its history more than 60 areas were decommissioned; some were transferred to state or local government, others returned to private ownership.

In addition to overt political contests over specific national parks, the results of broader national political debates have impacted on the parks. For example, in some instances federal legislation not intended to change or modify the park system *per se* has affected park service philosophy and policy. The Wilderness Act of 1964 and the National Environmental Policy Act of 1970 set new requirements for environmental protection and mandated that all federal agencies (including the Park Service) implement the new policies. The flurry of environmental legislation during the 1970s – the Clean Air Act, the Clean Water Act, the Endangered Species Act – also redefined the role of the Park Service in protection and preservation. Much of this legislation asserted that the guiding principle for the national parks should be preservation and interpretation of natural landscapes and ecosystems, directly affecting Park Service management policy.[32]

Public debates about the condition of parks and the direction of park policy have also generated political struggles. Often these debates are results of Park Service reports or agendas for the future. In 1980 the National Park Service responded to a congressional request for a report on the state of the parks to identify and describe threats endangering them and to discuss the broad spectrum of problems facing the parks. Importantly, the Park Service was charged to discover which threats and problems would damage park resources or seriously degrade "important park values."[33] The report was disheartening. The parks, it concluded, suffered from a wide variety of threats: internal ones such as overcrowding and overbuilding; external ones such as urban encroachment and air and water pollution. The Park Service estimated that the 1990s would require significant action and an infusion of federal funds in order to protect and preserve all the parks but above all the nation's "crown jewels."

Between 1960 and 1990, the Park Service tripled its acreage, and the number of visitors to the park increased from 80 million to 257 million.[34] Many observers felt the National Park Service stood at a crossroads. In 1991 it celebrated its seventy-fifth anniversary by holding a symposium at Vail, Colorado, bringing together hundreds of experts, Park Service employees, and other interested parties. The symposium was designed to address issues of critical importance to the Park Service and to review and reconcile challenges, strategies and missions for the twenty-first century. It proved to be an unprecedented display of bureaucratic introspection. The result of the symposium was a 137–page document referred to as the *Vail Agenda*. While acknowledging that the Park Service's purposes had evolved significantly in the first 75 years, the document reaffirmed that the national parks were places that symbolized a defining time in US history.

The symposium outlined new objectives and introduced many suggestions. Of note was the suggestion that the Park Service establish an office dedicated to policy, which was in part a reflection that it has no central office to handle national politics and that each park battle was fought as a separate issue rather than as part of a broader park policy. The suggestion to create a policy office was a recognition of an inescapable conclusion. Since the National Park Service falls under congressional jurisdiction, national parks are created and redefined in an *inherently* political process – the political process unfolds on the national political stage. National parks are and will continue to be subject to the political climate (and a national political agenda) as long as Congress retains its jurisdiction.

## The Social Construction of National Parks: Some Conclusions

The history of US national parks is inevitably an outcome of America's long and complex history, one full of debate, diversity, and contradictions. The national parks and the national park system constitute a dynamic mosaic, crafted anew by each successive generation or park movement, yet reflecting the array of political, social, economic, and technological forces that have shaped US history and environmental discourses. For all its history, though, the national park system has been an improvisation.[35] A series of political conflicts and park movements has altered in some way the management, acquisition, and meaning of parks in the United States. Each has introduced or shifted an ideological emphasis, introduced new standards and practices, shown the vulnerability of parks to a broader political process, or set alarming precedents. The absence of an agreed-upon standard by which to measure a park's value or contribution has left an indelible legacy within the Park Service. In the early years many Park Service professionals were uncomfortable managing historic sites (many still are); in the later years, many were equally reluctant to take on the responsibility of recreation areas.[36]

National parks have served as a barometer of society's changing attitudes and perceptions.[37] A range of environmental discourses have been challenged or modified; ideals have become less Romantic and more ecologically oriented; preservation now exists, albeit in conflict with a heightened commitment to recreation; and finally criteria for new parks have been broadened to allow for an appreciation of the many ways in which people can experience and appreciate the out-of-doors. Our ideas about national parks and about the Park Service itself have been subject to periodic adjustments.

There have always been conflicts about the purpose and ideals of national parks, there have always been worries about inadequate funding, there have always been threats to the integrity of the system itself. The history of the Park Service has been characterized by the growing complexity in its mission, changing agendas, new policies and the shifting of park ideals. This evolution can be seen as a dilution of the original concept of national parks or as a broader effort to articulate a more inclusive discourse which embraces alternative humanity–environment relationships.

There are two ways to perceive the present-day park system. The first is the view of the system as an "uneven" collection of sites that unevenly represent America's natural and cultural heritage, which leads to the conclusion that the system exists as a hierarchy in which some parks are more equal than others and that the national park ideal has been compromised.[38] The second viewpoint suggests that the national park system is more than merely the sum of its parts, which inclines toward the conclusion that no park is better than or inferior to others, only different. Simply by being included in the system each park unit has achieved a measure of national significance. The latter view also recognizes that each park is an expression of its time, a statement by one generation for those to come later; thus efforts to devalue or divest the system of a given park is a reflection only of temporal changes in social values, economic cycles or changing perspectives.[39]

The overriding mission of the National Park Service is not only to protect resources of significance to the nation, but also to convey the meanings of those resources to the public in a continuing process of building national identity.[40] Our understanding of national parks is as preservers of "the historical, cultural and natural foundations of the Nation." After a century of change and expansion, one thing seems clear: there can be no single overriding ideal, no single criterion that illustrates natural or historic significance in a system defined by incredible diversity and complexity. Parks are not just places of recreation and entertainment, they are not just scenic wonders, they are not just merely memorable; they are *places of meaning*.

In contemporary US society, national parks are more than just beautiful places, more than history and heritage. They reflect our discourses about nature, the wilderness, and the city, and they embody part of the national identity.

## FURTHER READING

There are many books about the national parks available. We have listed several here:

Albright, Horace M., as told to Robert Cahn 1985. *The Birth of the National Park Service: The Founding Years, 1913–33*. Salt Lake City: Howe Brothers.

Chase, Alston 1987. *Playing God in Yellowstone: The Destruction of America's First National Park*. San Diego: Harcourt Brace Jovanovich.

Everhart, William. C. 1983. *The National Park Service*. Boulder, Col.: Westview Press.

Foresta, Ronald 1985. *America's National Parks and Their Keepers*. Washington, DC: Resources for the Future.

Garrison, Lemuel A. 1983. *The Making of a Ranger: Forty Years with the National Parks*. Salt Lake City: Howe Brothers.

Hartzog, George, Jr. 1988. *Battling for the National Parks*. Mt Kisco, NY: Moyer Bell.

Hummel, Don. 1987. *Stealing the National Parks: The Destruction of Concessions and Park Access*. Bellevue, Wash.: Free Enterprise Press.

Linenthal, Edward Tabor. 1993. *Sacred Ground: Americans and Their Battlefields*. 2nd edn. Urbana: University of Illinois Press.

Lowry, William 1994. *The Capacity for Wonder: Preserving National Parks*. Washington, DC: Brookings Institution.

*National Parks for a New Generation: Visions, Realities, Prospects* 1985. Washington, DC: Conservation Foundation.

*National Parks for the Future* 1972. Washington, DC: Conservation Foundation.

Rettie, Dwight. 1995. *Our National Park System: Caring for America's Greatest Natural and Historic Treasures*. Urbana: University of Illinois Press.

Ridenour, James. 1994. *The National Parks Compromised: Pork Barrel Politics and America's Treasures*. Merriville, Ind.: ICS Books, Inc.

Rothman, Hal. 1989. *Preserving Different Pasts: The American National Monuments*. Urbana: University of Illinois Press.

Runte, Alfred. 1987. *National Parks: The American Experience*, 2nd edn. Lincoln: University of Nebraska Press.

Sax, Joseph. 1980. *Mountains without Handrails: Reflections on the National Parks*. Ann Arbor: University of Michigan Press.

Udall, Stewart L. 1988. *The Quiet Crisis and the Next Generation*. Layton, Utah: Gibbs-Smith.

Wirth, Conrad. 1980. *Parks, Politics and the People*. Norman: University of Oklahoma Press.

## NOTES

1  For example, N. Everden, *The Social Creation of Nature*. (Baltimore: Johns Hopkins University Press, 1992); C. Harrison and J. Burgess, "Social constructions of nature: a case study of conflicts over the development of Rainham Marshes," *Transactions of British Geographers*, (19), 1994, 291–310. D. Harraway, *Simians, Cyborgs and Women: the Reinvention of Nature*. (New York: Routledge, 1991); M. Oelschlaeger, *The Idea of Wilderness: From Prehistory to the Age of Ecology*. (New Haven: Yale University Press, 1991); K. Thomas, *Man and the Natural World*. (London: Allen Lane, 1983); W. Wright, *Wild Knowledge: Science, Language and Social Life in a Fragile Enviornment*. (Minneapolis: University of Minneapolis Press, 1992).

2  D. Rettie, *Our National Park System: Caring for America's Greatest Natural and Historic Treasures* (Urbana: University of Illinois Press, 1995).

3  H. Albright, *Origins of National Park Service Administration of Historic Sites*. (Philadelphia: Eastern National Park and Monument Association, 1971); A. Chase, *Playing God in Yellowstone: The Destruction of America's First National Park* (San Diego: Harcourt Brace Jovanovich, 1987); L. Dilsaver (ed.), *America's National Park System: The Critical Documents*. (Lanham, MD: Rowman and Littlefield, 1994); R. Foresta, *America's National Parks and Their Keepers*. (Washington, DC: Resources for the Future, 1985); G. Hartzog, Jr, *Battling for the National Parks* (Mt Kisco, NY: Moyer Bell, 1988); H. Huth, *Nature and the American: Three Centuries of Changing Attitudes*. (Berkeley: University of California Press, 1957); H. Rothman, *Preserving Different Pasts: The American National Monuments* (Urbana: University of Illinois Press, 1989); A. Runte, *National Parks: The American Experience*. (Lincoln: University of Nebraska Press, 1987); C. Wirth, *Parks, Politics and the People* (Norman: University of Oklahoma Press, 1980).

4  Huth, *Nature and the American*; R. Nash, *Wilderness and the American Mind* (New Haven: Yale University Press, 1982); J. Petulla, *American Environmental History: the exploitation and conservation of natural resources*. (San Francisco: Boyd & Fraser, 1977).

5  Some argue that Yosemite was the first national park. In 1864 Congress created Yosemite by transferring the land to the state of California as a protected reserve; however, it was not designated as a "national park" until 1891.

6  Nash has described early US attitudes toward the wilderness and concluded that in the early years of settlement Americans feared the wilderness. They associated the wilderness with the fear of the unknown, chaos, amorality. At the close of the nineteenth century, however, Americans possessed a growing confidence in the ability to "conquer" or control nature. Confidence replaced fear and was part of the reason intellectual elites could reconstruct their perceptions of the wilderness, and by extension, the city (Nash, *Wilderness and the American Mind*).

7  Runte, *National Parks*, 11.

8  T. Cox, "From Hot Springs to Gateway: the Evolving Concept of Public Parks, 1832–1976" *Environment Review* (1980), 5(1): 20.

9  H. Work, "Statement of National Park Policy, March 11, 1925" in L. Dilsaver *America's National Park System*, 63. Runte, *National Parks*, argued that early concerns about national parks focused on ways to increase and ensure tourism in the parks. It was common acceptance, even by many park supporters, that tourism and

increased public use was the best defense of park resources against development projects such as mining, timber and grazing. As the park system evolved, the ideal of use and access would result in efforts to pursue increased visitors to the parks by expanding railroads, building roads for automobiles, and providing infrastructure such as hotels and concessionaires. In the early years of the parks, few were concerned about the impact of visitors on the parks, and the promotion of public use was not a real issue among park advocates because most parks were located in isolated, hard-to-reach areas.

10  Rothman, *Preserving Different Pasts*, xi.
11  National Park Service, *National Parks for the 21st Century: the Vail Agenda*. (Post Mills, Vt: Chelsea Green Publishing/National Park Service, 1993), 74.
12  Runte, *National Parks*, 55.
13  Ibid., 104.
14  Dilsaver, *America's National Park System: The Critical Documents*, 65.
15  Rettie, *Our National Park System*, 5.
16  However, many Park Service professionals were not happy about the cultural inclusions. See, for example, Rettie, *Our National Park System*.
17  Dilsaver, *America's National Park System: The Critical Documents*, 193–5.
18  Statement of L. Rockefeller, "A Report to the President and to Congress by the Outdoor Recreation Resources Review Commmission, Laurance S. Rockefeller, Chairman, January 1962" in Dilsaver, *America's Naional Park System*, 224.
19  Cox, "From Hot Springs to Gateway," 20.
20  The tension between ideals of sublime and picturesque is nicely illustrated in this example. A picturesque place or area does not inspire the stronger emotions associated with the sublime. Rather, picturesque can be places of decay, rough but "charming" rather than distinguished. For example, old barns can be picturesque; the Grand Canyon is sublime. Consider this example from the autobiography of Lemuel Garrison, a Park Service ranger:

> I ride on horseback to the very top of the trail through Donahue Pass on the eastern boundary of Yosemite National Park and stop abruptly. Suddenly, I see to the far edge of the world in the eastern distance, across an endless jumble of wild mountain tops. Standing as tall as I can before the Lord, I am humbled and bareheaded and silent. I have met Creation. (L. Garrison, *The Making of a Ranger: Forty Years with the National Parks*. (Salt Lake City: Howe Brothers, 1983), 300–1.

21  Rettie, *Our National Park System*, 6.
22  Ibid., 32.
23  The Conservation Foundation has been one of the Park Service's most consistent support groups. It is a resource-oriented think tank that has a reputation for political neutrality.
24  Conservation Foundation, *National Parks for the Future: An appriasal of the National Parks as they begin their second century in a changing America*. (Washington, DC: Conservation Foundation, 1972), 15.
25  Rettie, *Our National Park System*, 73.
26  Ibid., 74.
27  Ibid.
28  The issue of entrance fees at parks is of little consequence here. They have been either nonexistent or very affordable. Rather the issue was that the working class

had neither the time to travel great distances nor necessarily the money to purchase transportation to the parks.

29   Rettie, *Our National Park System*, 50.
30   Park historians have noted that the National Park Service has rarely reacted negatively to any proposed park or recreation area that has strong congressional support. The custom of the National Park Service is to respond favorably to proposals from influential Congressmen like Burton.
31   Runte, *National Parks*, 79.
32   The recommendations of the Conservation Foundation in its 1972 report testified to the influence environmental organizations had on shaping or refocusing national park ideals. As previously mentioned, the Conservation Foundation felt that the Park Service needed to return to the original mission of conservation (however inappropriate that may be given the historic diversity of the parks).
33   Dilsaver, *America's Naional Park System:*, 406 (emphasis added).
34   The 1978 addition of 40 million acres of Alaskan wilderness contributed greatly to this figure.
35   Rettie, *Our National Park System*, 14.
36   Ibid., 2.
37   Cox, "From Hot Springs to Gateway," 14.
38   Rettie, *Our National Park System*, 25.
39   Ibid., 27.
40   National Park Service, *National Parks for the 21st Century*, 14.

# 10

# The Politics of the Environment: A Case Study

Environmental discourses have spilled over from traditional domestic policy concerns to other areas. In this chapter, we concentrate now on the growing connection between environmental discourses and trade policy with particular attention to the debates around the North American Free Trade Agreement (hereafter NAFTA), signed in 1992 and approved by Congress in 1993. This case study illustrates the growing importance of environmental themes in federal policy-making.

### Trade and Environment: Global Concerns

Two of the most important issues facing the global community in recent years, if not for longer, have been environmental concerns, and trade and economic growth. On the one hand, environmental issues of ecosystem integrity and livability of the planet have emerged as primary concerns. On the other hand, issues of trade and economic growth have remained important, especially the belief that full and equitable participation in the world trading system is one of the most important ways to increase living standards. For much of the postwar world these two debates remained separate. Indeed they appeared to be antagonistic. Economic growth was often seen as detrimental to environmental quality. Even the words used in the two debates lay opposite each other. Environmental *protection* contrasted with the notion of economic *deregulation*. *Managed* ecosystems were seen to be at odds with the ideas and practice of *free* trade. The debates and words differed so sharply because of the two distinctly polarized communities: traders and environmentalists. On the one side of the barricade were the free trade proponents who were convinced that strong measures to protect the environment would hinder business competition and would cause disruption to commerce. On the other side were environmentalists, who worried that free trade undercuts existing environmental protection laws. Between these two communities lay a chasm of language, background, cultures and goals. Each worked and lived within different environmental discourses.

The trade policies of the post-1945 world, as embodied in GATT (General Agreement on Trade and Tariffs, although the length of the debates has caused some journalists to comment that the more accurate acronym is the "General Agreement to Talk and Talk") enshrined free trade as the desired state of affairs. GATT, introduced in 1947, is the major international agreement on trade rules, a framework for international trade policy, and a forum for dispute resolution. Government regulation that inhibited such free trade was seen as a block to the smooth operation of the global trading system. Under the GATT system, trading partners can appeal to an international panel if they believe conditions exist that promote an unfair advantage; a member nation can challenge a domestic law of another member as a barrier to trade.

The "dolphin-safe tuna" issue, promoted by environmentalists to help protect the dolphin population, is a good example. In August 1991 an international panel of GATT trade arbitrators ruled that the United States violated trade rules when it banned tuna imports from Mexico because Mexican fishing crews used purse seine nets, which kill a high number of dolphins. According to the GATT panel, the United States violated GATT articles by imposing a unilateral trade measure that discriminated against Mexico's method of production. US legislation protecting a species (the dolphin) outside its national jurisdiction had been successfully challenged. Environmentalists, who had initiated the movement for the US ban on this type of tuna, felt the GATT ruling failed to distinguish between issues of national concern and those designed to protect the global commons. Environmentalists in the United States have cited this ruling as a harbinger of what could happen with NAFTA.

In the last two decades environmentalists, at both the international and national levels, have sought to influence trade policies. Mainstream environmentalists do not believe that trade is inherently bad for the environment, and argue that increased trade can exist with sufficient environmental protection. The Sierra Club, although opposed to NAFTA, is not opposed to expanded trade and stated, "We believe that if governments build clearly defined, binding obligations for environmental protection into trade agreements, increased trade can help improve environmental quality."[1]

The concept of *sustainable development* is one of the intellectual links forged between environmental protection and economic growth. Sustainable development is a vague term without a clear consensus on how to implement "sustainability." It gained international currency in 1987 through the publication of the United Nations Brundtland Report, *Our Common Future*, which defined the term as "meeting the needs of the present without compromising the ability of future generations to meet their own needs." This is a fairly loose definition, and not surprisingly may invite multiple meanings. There are many dimensions to sustainability – environmental, social, ethical, and economic.

In June 1992 the United Nations sponsored the Conference on Environment and Development (UNCED), otherwise known as the Earth Summit, in Rio de Janeiro, a gathering that included more than 100 heads of state. The key concept at the conference was sustainable development, and a major objective was to research ways to reconcile economic development and environmental quality. The United States along with 156 other countries, signed the *Rio Declaration* and *Agenda 21*, documents affirming a commitment to reconcile economics and the environment. *Agenda 21* proposed to "make trade and the environment mutually supportive" (section I, chapter 2) and called for "environmental concern in decision-making on economic, social, fiscal, energy, agricultural, transportation, trade and other policies" (section I, chapter 8). In the months following the Earth Summit many environmentalists saw the NAFTA negotiations as the United States' first test of *Agenda 21* and the Rio principles.

### Trade and Environment: National Concerns

Until very recently environmentalists in the United States did not have much of a role in trade policy-making. Environmental concerns were issues of domestic policy whereas trade agreements were issues of economic foreign policy. In most conflicting cases, foreign policy interests superseded domestic environmental goals. In recent years, however, the two policy areas have intersected. Environmental quality is linked to economic activity, not only at home but abroad, and many environmental problems are no longer limited to the domestic sphere but are international in scope. As a consequence, the issues that environmentalists confront and debate have broadened to include trade. The negotiations surrounding NAFTA were caught up in the widening shadow cast by environmental concerns in US politics. NAFTA marks the first time in the history of trade negotiations that environmentalists were part of the negotiation process.

### *NAFTA: a brief history*

In 1990 President Salinas of Mexico approached the United States proposing a free trade treaty. President Bush responded and negotiations began. Throughout 1991 and 1992 NAFTA was discussed inside the environmental and labor movements; it also was given a wider airing because it became part of US presidential election debates. In December 1992 NAFTA was signed by President Bush, President Salinas and Prime Minister Mulroney and was then amended by a new US administration and discussed in Congress before final approval. In November 1993, the US Congress approved the North American Free Trade Agreement, a text of some 2,000 pages. NAFTA now binds more than 370 million people together in a $6-trillion economy, connecting the US, Canadian, and Mexican economies into a unified regional market stretching from the Yukon to the Yucatan.

### The shaping of NAFTA by environmental concerns

During NAFTA negotiations, environmental nongovernment groups were excluded from the formal negotiations process. They did, however, monitor the process closely. As early as spring 1992, prior to public release of the NAFTA text, negotiations had proceeded far enough for environmentalists (as well as labor groups) to develop a list of conditions for their support of NAFTA.[2] US trade negotiators initially attempted to dismiss environmental concerns as peripheral or as a barrier to competition but reluctantly found themselves addressing these issues and contending with an extremely complex and diverse community.[3] In June 1992 the Natural Resources Defense Council published *Environmental Safeguards for the NAFTA*. And in that same month, one newspaper opined that the "environment is a key trade-pact issue."

Environmental organizations mobilized quickly and their concerns were articulated and publicized months before Bush, Salinas, and Mulroney signed NAFTA. Because of this mobilization trade negotiators, Congress, business elites, and even President Bush addressed environmental issues. Although Bush administration officials insisted they would address environmental issues only outside of NAFTA, political pressure compelled them to include language in the text of the agreement itself.[4] Bush's EPA administrator, William K. Reilly, confirmed that the Bush administration made significant compromises to secure active support for NAFTA.[5] Among the more notable efforts, Reilly commented that the US trade representatives office worked closely with the EPA during negotiations. Reilly also co-chaired two of the negotiating team's subgroups during negotiations, and he participated in all other NAFTA discussions involving the environment. It was the first time an environmental leader was appointed to the trade representatives' standing advisory committee. In addition, the Bush negotiating team formulated an "action plan" that included the "green provisions" in both the NAFTA text and several bilateral agreements (table 10.1).

Many environmental groups saw these NAFTA environmental provisions as having significantly "greened" the trade agreement. Trade ambassador Carla Hills claimed that NAFTA was the "greenest" trade agreement ever negotiated. It would appear that some environmental organizations agreed; following the establishment of the North American Environmental Commission, the National Wildlife Federation was one of the first major environmental groups to endorse NAFTA; others followed. Still other groups felt NAFTA provisions were not strong or detailed enough. Many environmental groups wanted NAFTA to state explicitly that lax environmental regulations or enforcement should constitute "unfair trade practices"; others demanded that more money be invested in the Border Plan.[6] Thus despite the Bush administration's efforts, the green provisions in NAFTA fell behind the *rising* curve of environmental expectations.

**Table 10.1**   "Green provisions" in NAFTA as negotiated by the Bush administration

- The NAFTA preamble explicitly noted that the signatories resolved to "promote sustainable development" and "strengthen the development and enforcement of environmental regulations."
- NAFTA resolved to protect subnational (or subfederal) units of government to set higher standards on environmental regulations, provided there existed scientific grounds. This compromise arose out of environmentalist concerns that a state's stricter environmental standards, such as many of those in California, could be undercut to avoid the charge of "barrier to free trade." Indeed the NAFTA text called for the signatories to agree to work toward *upwards* harmonization of environmental regulations (Chapter 7b, Article 905.3). (Despite this provision, some groups such as the Sierra Club continued to argue that US environmental sovereignty was threatened by NAFTA.)
- The NAFTA treaty (Chapter 1, Article 104) explicitly recognized and enforced already existing international environmental treaties, such as (1) the 1987 Montreal Protocol, which limited CFC, ozone-depleting substances; (2) the 1973 CITES or Convention on International Trade in Endangered Species of Wild Fauna and Flora, and (3) the 1989 Basel Convention on the Control of Transboundary Movement of Hazardous Wastes and Their Disposal.
- NAFTA called for "the parties [to] recognize that it is inappropriate to encourage investment by relaxing domestic health, safety or environmental laws" (chapter 11, article 1114.2) in an effort to address concerns about the establishment of "pollution havens" in Mexico.
- Under Bush's initiative, NAFTA established the Integrated Environmental Plan for Mexican–US border areas (the "Border Plan"), committing the United States and Mexico to strengthen enforcement of environmental laws, reduce pollution through joint programs and improve environmental conditions along the border. To this end, the Mexican government pledged $460 million for the Border Plan and the Bush administration promised $379 million for the first five years after NAFTA's passage (subject, of course, to congressional appropriations).
- Finally, in response to other environmentalists' concerns, in September 1992, the three governments agreed to establish a North American Environmental Commission to promote long-term cooperation toward improving the environment.

In a December 1992 press conference, President-elect Clinton stated that although he endorsed NAFTA he believed environmental issues had not been adequately addressed. Shortly after his inauguration in January 1993 Clinton chose not to open the basic text to renegotiation but opted instead to negotiate a side agreement to address the enforcement of environmental laws to satisfy complaints about NAFTA's inadequate treatment of environment issues. That agreement, known as the North American Agreement on Environmental Cooperation (NAAEC), was seen as the mechanism to monitor, assess, and publicize the environmental performance of all three countries. The NAAEC preamble reconfirmed "the importance of the environmental goals and objectives of the NAFTA," emphasized "the importance of public participation in conserving, protecting and enhancing the environment" and reiterated the goal of "achieving sustainable development for the well-being of present and future generations."

(Table 10.2 details the "green improvements" included in the agreement.) During the 1993 negotiations on NAAEC the leaders of seven environmental groups pledged their support for NAFTA, provided the agreement increased money for border cleanup and enhanced enforcement powers for the border authority.[7] The final result of negotiations was the establishment of the Commission for Environmental Cooperation, a "bigger and better version" of the North American Environmental Commission proposed by President Bush in September 1992.[8] Clinton's trade negotiators increased the funds to several programs and gave more enforcement power to the commission for environmental regulation and protection.

Both the NAFTA environmental provisions negotiated by the Bush administration and Clinton's subsequent negotiations of NAAEC represent two significant developments with regard to trade and the environment. First, the

**Table 10.2**    "Green Improvements" to NAFTA as negotiated by the Clinton administration in 1993

- Under Article 14 of the NAAEC, any individual or nongovernmental group can make a complaint alleging a government's failure to enforce its national environmental or labor laws. This provision also gave the commission's arbitration panel the power to level fines (up to $20 million in the first year) or even impose trade sanctions for "failure to effectively enforce its environmental laws with respect to traded goods."
- US farmers are protected through strict application of US pesticide requirements on food imports.
- The Border Plan was expanded to include the creation of a permanent border authority institution to plan, coordinate, build, and manage environmental projects along the border. Clinton also increased the US investment in this program to $5 billion over five years, starting in 1994, in an effort to ensure environmental cleanup and infrastructure investments.
- The Commission Council, comprised of cabinet-level representatives, are required to hold public meetings in the course of all regular sessions, thereby creating a public forum to hear complaints. It committed the three countries to make information publicly available in line with US "community right-to-know" principles. This provision also gave US citizens the right to challenge objectionable environmental practices in Mexico or Canada.
- The Audubon Society was successful in lobbying Clinton's negotiating team to add to Article 104 (the enforcement of existing environmental treaties) the Migratory Bird Treaty. With this inclusion the Audubon Society announced its support of NAFTA.
- In response to concerns about sovereignty and domestic environmental regulation discussed earlier, the NAAEC recognized "the right of each [signatory to the NAFTA] to establish its own levels of domestic environmental protection and environmental development policies." Each country would thus retain its sovereignty over environmental regulations while working towards "upwards harmonization." The question of sovereignty, however, remains ambiguous. Although the provision explicitly reinforces sovereignty of environmental regulation, by allowing citizens and nongovernmental groups to monitor the other two parties to ensure that they are living up to their own *domestic* standards (Part Two, Article 3), some environmentalists continued to feel the provision did not sufficiently detail the problem.

provisions illustrate the influence of environmental concerns on policy negotiations and, second, the creation of common ground between trade and environmental interests, evidenced through the process of negotiation, expectation, and compromise. Indeed, many of the major environmental groups made their views known on advisory committees, in reports and correspondence, in comments on draft documents and through formal and informal consultations. Because of their involvement and influence in the debate and negotiations to include "green provisions" in NAFTA many environmental groups, such as Conservation International, the National Audubon Society, Environmental Defense Fund, and World Wildlife Fund, endorsed NAFTA.

NAFTA's inclusion of environmental protection and regulation is the result of compromise among traders, politicians, and environmentalists. And while many environmental groups such as the Sierra Club and Greenpeace felt that negotiation efforts did not meet their criteria for endorsement, NAFTA became a trade agreement that many traders and environmentalists could and did endorse. The negotiations of traders, politicians, and environmentalists achieved some measure of common ground, a common ground that addressed the needs of both expanding free trade and environmental protection. As a World Wildlife Fund (WWF) position paper noted, "NAFTA creates a precedent for linking economic forces with environmental protection . . . helping to foster integration of economics and ecological protection throughout the globe."[9]

Following congressional approval of NAFTA in November 1993, Clinton invited three former Bush administration officials to attend the signing ceremony – Carla Hills, former trade representative, William Reilly and Colin Powell – because, as Reilly relates, "we had helped make NAFTA a green treaty." NAFTA's green provisions were a response to environmental concerns and a result of a bipartisan efforts.

### NAFTA: the debates

The debates about NAFTA embodied and reflected wider social concerns about the quality of life and definitions of progress, growth, and sustainable development. The NAFTA debate was as complex and divisive as any in recent memory, revolving around multiple issues: the impact of NAFTA on US job losses or gains, public health and safety issues, and implications for environmental quality.[10] Of the many debates contained within the larger one, however, environmental and labor concerns dominated US participation. From the beginning of negotiations the media gave an unprecedented degree of attention to environmental considerations, helping to accentuate public interest in environmental concerns. The environmental debate became one of the more conspicuous debates as Congress faced the impending vote in the fall of 1993. NAFTA would be "good" for the environment by providing border cleanup programs and cooperative agencies and by improving the environmental status quo in Mexico through economic growth, argued both the current Environmental Protection Agency administrator, Carol Browner, and her predecessor, William

K. Reilly. NAFTA would accelerate environmental degradation and threaten US environmental laws, claimed NAFTA opponents such as Greenpeace and the Sierra Club. One economist wryly noted that in the NAFTA debate, "Everyone is wrapping themselves in the green flag."[11]

## NAFTA and sustainable development

If, as some environmentalists believed, NAFTA was a test of *Agenda 21* principles to fully (re)integrate economics and the environment, then NAFTA must be considered noteworthy as an international agreement for its *explicit* inclusion of environmental protection. In the NAFTA preamble the signatories resolved to "promote sustainable development," an objective unprecedented in US international policy. It was the mention of sustainable development as a NAFTA goal that gave the environmental community a legitimate entry into the NAFTA debate. Gordon Binder, a Senior Fellow at WWF, argued that economic growth with NAFTA would generate new resources to support environmental protection efforts in all three countries, especially in Mexico.[12] Binder's NAFTA analysis for WWF also cited a Princeton University study that found rising incomes to correlate directly with reduced emission levels. These examples show that one of the many definitions of sustainable development appears to focus upon economic growth as a means to increased social wealth and stricter environmental protection.

To other environmentalists, however, sustainable development requires radical political and economic transformation, such as the eradication of private property or a restructuring of local governments and a rethinking of the basic elements involved in humanity–environment relationships.[13] Ironically, although NAFTA frowned on most federal subsidies, including environmentally oriented ones, it supported subsidies for oil and gas exploration. The nongovernmental environmental organization Greenpeace concluded that although the NAFTA preamble encouraged "sustainable development" it failed to promote this concept in actual provisions. Greenpeace criticized the NAFTA chapter on energy deregulation, which encouraged investment in new petroleum sources and gave US and Canadian petroleum firms access to a once-protected Mexican market. This, argued Greenpeace, promoted even greater fossil fuel consumption and would continue "extravagant and destructive patterns of energy consumption."[14] According to Greenpeace, rather than encouraging sustainable development, NAFTA embodied the principles of economic development based on the Western model of resource exploitation. NAFTA promoted an economy characterized by long-distance distribution of goods and services, as well as decision-making removed from those who bear the impact – attributes these environmentalists considered unsustainable economic development. Greenpeace contended that a sustainable economy would be characterized by shorter lines of distribution and locally owned production units where decision-making is local, thus enhancing self-reliance and democracy. NAFTA's formula for economic development would continue in the business-as-usual style, and "no amount of green paint . . . will fix a trade deal that would enshrine an unsustainable model of development."[15]

Free trade, as conceptualized by many radical environmental groups, limits the ability of government to control corporate activity; this means weaker environmental and food safety laws, unsustainable exploitation of resources and undemocratic decision-making. Not only free trade but also the economic values and institutions encouraging this kind of development were unsustainable. Environmental groups such as Friends of the Earth, Earth First! and Greenpeace criticized free trade as *inherently* incompatible with sustainable development. As scholar and environmental writer Michael Redclift wrote, "sustainable development, if it is to be an alternative to unsustainable development, should imply a break with the linear model of growth and accumulation that ultimately serves to undermine the planet's life support systems."[16] This interpretation of sustainable development prioritizes environmental, social, and ethical considerations over classical economic measurements of prosperity, such as increased GNP. This interpretation comes from an environmental discourse that calls for a dramatic transformation of humanity–environment relationships. Many radical environmental groups recognized their interpretation of sustainable development was distinctly different from that of the trade negotiators as well as those mainstream environmental organizations supporting NAFTA.

Democracy and public participation are also part and parcel of some models of sustainable development. Nearly all environmental organizations opposed to NAFTA were critical of its behind-the-scenes negotiations. The process of including local decision-making is especially important to direct-action or grassroots groups. To achieve true "sustainable living" decision-making must occur locally, not centrally, and governments must empower local communities.[17] Greenpeace noted that all but three of the 111 advisors invited to participate in the NAFTA negotiations represented large corporations, and it criticized the trade deal for reading like an "international bill of rights for transnational corporations." Environmental groups were concerned about the public's noninclusion in the NAFTA dispute resolution and settlement process because it restricted democracy and public right-to-know laws. They also criticized the negotiation process for devaluing and ignoring the concerns, interests, and experiences of the many poor people in Mexico and the border region. Friends of the Earth opposed NAFTA because nongovernmental organizations could not initiate a process that might eventually lead to formal sanctions against environmental polluters.[18] Such actions, according to NAFTA, can only come at the request of governments and with the support of two- thirds of the parties involved. Friends of the Earth maintained that NAFTA's failure to address the issue of public participation made the preamble's claim of promoting sustainable development spurious.

### NAFTA and sovereignty

Sovereignty, like sustainable development, is a slippery concept. The Oxford Dictionary defines it as 1: the power to govern without external control; 2: the supreme political power; 3: having independent authority. Sovereignty has long presented obstacles to enforcing international treaties and agreements. In the NAFTA debate, the question of sovereignty revolved around environmental laws and international trade policy. The Sierra Club's primary opposition to NAFTA lay in its perception of NAFTA threatening environmental protection because it compromised US environmental standards. This perception lies with the complex relationship between NAFTA and another international agreement, GATT.[19] NAFTA incorporates the jurisprudence of GATT, and under the GATT system, as mentioned earlier, trading partners can appeal to an international panel if they believe conditions exist that promote an unfair trade advantage and can challenge the domestic laws of another member if they are seen as barriers to trade. For many environmental groups, the concern over NAFTA and environmental sovereignty is the result of the GATT panel's previous international decision on the US–Mexico dispute over the tuna–dolphin imbroglio. The ruling was taken to mean that NAFTA and free trade could encourage partners to relax their environmental standards in order to compete fairly in the global marketplace. The Sierra Club argued that, should a NAFTA dispute panel find that a US environmental law interferes with trade, the United States would have to either change the law or face sanctions against their exports. The Sierra Club was concerned that environmental laws could be overruled because of trade considerations. NAFTA supporters argued this was flawed legal reasoning and in fact pointed out that NAFTA set environmental standards to "upwards harmonization" (those with less stringent standards would be required to raise them).[20]

Some environmentalists, including former EPA administrator William Reilly, contended that it was unfair to expect NAFTA to resolve all the environmental problems of world trading rules established by GATT. They have a point. Resolving issues of sovereignty and of cultural and technological differences will require extensive negotiation. Expecting NAFTA to definitively delineate "sovereignty" with regard to international environmental and trade concerns is perhaps expecting too much. But it is telling that environmental opponents criticized what they saw as an inherent bias in NAFTA favoring trade over environmental protection, arguing that this bias could threaten sovereignty (in this case defined as the will of the people to protect the environment). The ambiguity of the language of the NAFTA text led some environmentalists to see the agreement as maintaining the "environment versus trade" dualism rather than moving toward reconciliation.

The issue of sovereignty raises difficult questions, and it is not simply a problem of insularity and fear in international forums. Global citizenship and global environmental agreements require a rethinking of identity and authority and also a consciousness that "community" is both local and global. Before any international agency can enforce a mechanism for genuine pollution prevention, nations must surrender some of their closely held independence. This is no small task, and it is not something than can be solved in one trade agreement. Discussions about sovereignty and environmental laws are important in raising the potential conflict arising from international trade with regard to environmental protection.

## NAFTA and the Environmental Movement

Environmental groups were deeply divided over the North American Free Trade Agreement. In 1993 the *Washington Post* noted, "For Environmental Groups, Biggest NAFTA Fight Is Intramural," and the *New York Times* commented, "Environmental Movement Splits Over Support For Free-Trade Pact."[21] NAFTA, more than any issue since the modern environmental movement emerged, revealed the ideological split in the nation's environmental movement.[22] The article in the *Washington Post* reported, "Environmentalists have long battled loggers, dam builders and interior secretaries, but rarely with more heat than they have turned on themselves in the debate over the North American Free Trade Agreement." This internal conflict took place over the trade agreement itself, the political tactics of the debate and perceptions of the dilemmas of free trade.

Environmentalists who supported NAFTA included such mainstream or reformist organizations as the National Wildlife Federation, Natural Resources Defense Council, the Environmental Defense Fund, and World Wildlife Fund (WWF). WWF was hopeful that NAFTA, if enacted, would advance environmental protection in Mexico and would push environmental issues into other trade agreements. These NAFTA supporters, including the Environmental Protection Agency, argued that NAFTA was better than the status quo because it provided an unprecedented opportunity for the United States, Mexico, and Canada to cooperate on cross-border environmental problems. A WWF position paper noted, "with NAFTA the [Mexican] environmental status should change for the better... without NAFTA, the Mexican environmental situation will remain unacceptable to US and Mexican environmental groups."

The Sierra Club was one of the few mainstream groups to oppose the treaty. Mike McCloskey, chairman of the Sierra Club, agreed that the nonassociation of the Sierra Club with the so-called mainstream groups in the NAFTA debate represented a repositioning of the Sierra Club. The Sierra Club's thirty-page analysis of NAFTA asserted there were major flaws in the document, which it suggested could only be resolved by reopening the negotiations. More "radical" or direct-action groups, such as Greenpeace, Friends of the Earth, and Public Citizen also issued position papers opposing NAFTA for its inability to promote sustainable development and to reconcile potential threats to environmental protection.

Each side in the internal debate accused the other of distorting the facts and failing to recognize economic or political reality. The anti-NAFTA environmental organizations claimed the pro-NAFTA environmental groups were creatures of Washington, DC, having been co-opted by the Clinton administration and corporate funders. Some critics noted that the majority of supporters for

NAFTA were mainstream groups seeking the cooperation of business elites for environmental protection. But Jay Hair, president of the National Wildlife Federation, thought those environmental organizations opposed to NAFTA were "putting protectionist polemics ahead of concern for the environment."[23]

For NAFTA supporters, the fracturing of the environmental movement so publicly over NAFTA was distressing. William Reilly, former administrator of the US EPA and NAFTA proponent, summarized his own thoughts on the "family feud":

> We confront in the NAFTA debate two visions of environmentalism, a conflict between environmentalists every bit as important as the conflict between environmentalists and free traders. One is insular, defensive, focused on holding what we have, fearful of international forums, concerned with local control and insensitive to its effects outside our borders, and opening up a chasm between one faction of American environmentalism and the interests of developing countries. The other vision of environmentalism is future oriented, outward-looking, unafraid of harmonization, concerned to make new connections and attuned to the possibilities of a whole new world.[24]

Environmental groups in support of NAFTA seemed to appreciate that the environment was considered at all and argued that NAFTA, despite any perceived flaws, was better than no NAFTA.[25]

Underlying the exchange of rhetoric, however, are tangible environmental issues. The NAFTA debate highlighted the environment–trade dilemmas that can thwart efforts to reconcile expanding trade and the environment. On the one hand NAFTA's promotion of increased mobility of capital through investment and elimination of tariffs could give a poorer country like Mexico greater revenue to invest in cleaner industries; on the other hand such investment could undermine environmental standards by allowing polluting industries to escape the more rigorous US regulations.[26] Contradictions such as these abounded in the NAFTA debate, and the dilemmas posed by the possibility of free trade with Mexico were frequently highlighted. Some environmentalists perceived Mexico as an environmental basket case, a cesspool of toxic waste and corrupt government practice. These environmentalists worried that NAFTA would encourage capital investment in Mexico, a country some saw as having lax environmental enforcement, thereby creating "pollution havens." In particular, many environmental groups worried about the border region between the United States and Mexico, known as the Maquiladores. Investigations had revealed some alarming public health conditions and illegal toxic discharges, portending for some public health officials and environmentalists what free trade might bring. Sierra Club contended that with regard to border cleanup and environmental improvement, "it may be difficult for Mexico to muster the *political will* to create that infrastructure." Other environmental groups worried that NAFTA would make it more difficult to control the exporting of US waste to Mexico because the increased traffic across international borders might overwhelm control efforts.

Yet another dilemma focused on the potential threat of increased trade of endangered species. A 1991 WWF study, for example, argued that NAFTA would bring increased tourism; increased tourism would in turn lead to more trade, both legal and illicit, in furs, exotic leather goods, parrots, sea turtle products, and other valuable and endangered species.[27]

Underlying these discussions about the specific limitations of NAFTA and the dilemmas created by expanding free trade was something more subtle and perhaps more profound: questions about free trade, the environment and national sovereignty – questions that reach into the heart of reconciling international trade and the environment. The debate about NAFTA and the environment was as much a *discursive philosophical dilemma* as it was *economic*.

The environmental debate was more than just an internal conflict among environmental groups as they struggled to define sustainable development, to articulate the environmental problems posed by expanded trade or to protect domestic sovereignty. In the NAFTA debate, traders talked about the environment, and environmentalists engaged in trade policy analysis. The chair of the Sierra Club observed, "environmentalists never really dealt with trade issues, so we are all learning." The NAFTA environmental debate unearthed a set of cultural and political differences in which concerns about the environment played a significant role. The confrontation of these two communities forced each into a dynamic interaction with ideas about economics and the environment, tariffs and subsidies, and the possibilities of increased economic growth bringing increased environmental degradation. This interaction has added to a growing collection of critical inquiries seeking to integrate trade and the environment and to rework humanity–environment relationships. It is precisely this process of confronting differences and negotiating measures of environmental or trade protection that inched the trade and environmental community beyond the chasm and on to common ground, if only briefly.

It may be convenient to dismiss the environmental debate as merely window dressing for business and political elites who hoisted the "green" banner not out of conviction but to sway voters still sitting on the fence. There might be some truth to this, but to evaluate the environmental community as a group of inconsequential actors is to ignore the political victory they achieved by placing these issues on the table. When the Sierra Club released its "Analysis of the NAFTA" in October 1993, major newspapers and wire services covered the story. Additional environmental groups held press conferences to announce their NAFTA position. One commentator warned, "Protection of the environment and our jobs can't be dealt with as afterthoughts. They're at least as important as trade issues themselves and need to be negotiated as an integral part of the treaty."[28] In addition to the press conferences sponsored by environmental organizations, more than 50 articles in major newspapers and magazines addressed NAFTA and the environment in their publications. *The Economist* asked, "Should Trade Go Green?" and headlined, "Trade and the Environment: The Greening of Protectionism." *The Nation* explored "NAFTA – the View From Tijuana." A *Fortune* headline read, "How Zealous Greens Hurt Growth" and the

*National Journal* touted, "The New Eco-nomics" and "The Road from Rio." Even the *Atlantic Monthly* asked, "What Price Economic Growth?" The *National Law Journal* claimed, "Critics Ask If NAFTA Is 'Green' Enough." An issue of *Challenge* criticized "NAFTA as Social Dumping"; *Environment* featured "Prospects for a Green Trade Agreement," and an *Amicus Journal* headline read, "Trading Away the Environment?"[29] Many other headlines pertaining to the NAFTA environmental debate appeared between June and November of 1993.

The NAFTA debate, which appeared to focus initially on the merits of free trade and the removal of tariffs, expanded to include labor and environmental interests so much so that many Americans judged NAFTA not on economic terms but on criteria encompassing a breadth of economic, environmental, social, and labor concerns. In fact, Rhode Island Senator John Chafee, who boasts a strong environmental record, reminded his fellow senators that NAFTA, after all, was not an *environmental* but rather a *trade* treaty.[30] Opening up a public discussion such as this is a victory of sorts. A *Los Angeles Times* article noted, "the mere fact of the discussions is a triumph for the coalition of more than 50 US, Mexican and Canadian environmental and labor groups that have been pushing the subject to the forefront."[31] It was not that the environment was merely an issue; actual compromise was achieved with regard to environmental protection. NAFTA's inclusion of environmental standards was, according to Vice-President Al Gore, "a history-making achievement to have the endorsement of environmental standards written into the language of the trade agreement itself."[32] "This debate has changed for all time the way that future trade deals will be made," noted Carl Pope, executive director of the Sierra Club.[33] The environment is now a prominent element in world trade negotiations as evidenced by environmental provisions incorporated in both NAFTA and the European Union's Maastricht Treaty.

### Greening the New World Order?

The objectives of reconciling economic development and environmental protection, initially set forth under the Bush administration, continued to be important goals in the Clinton administration. In June 1993 President Clinton established the President's Council on Sustainable Development. The council is charged with developing bold new approaches to *integrate* economic and environmental policies. To realize that objective, the council will need to define the term, a process involving the solicitation of opinions from a variety of representatives from industry, government, environmental, labor and civil rights organizations. The NAFTA debate signaled the beginning of this process.

NAFTA is more than just a document. It is emblematic of much of the new momentum in the international economy in which trade negotiations are bound up with concerns over environmental protection and sustainable development. Environmentalists are still divided on how effective NAFTA's environmental provisions have been, but they all agree on one thing: there remains much to be done to integrate environmental concerns into the international trade regime. Growing recognition of the international nature of many environmental problems has led to an increased acknowledgment that international trade mechanisms have not considered the global commons. Whether environmentalists supported or opposed NAFTA, the debate opened up both a domestic and international dialogue on reconciling trade and the environment. NAFTA demonstrates the role that environmental issues can – and will – play in the development of international economic and trade policies. As other nations negotiate for more open economic markets, NAFTA may be the model for addressing environmental issues.

The variety of environmental discourses voiced in the NAFTA debate provides rich alternatives to prevailing ideas and values about trade, development, and environmental protection. Environmental concerns, although not at the center, are no longer on the periphery of national economic policy, and the political implications are making themselves apparent. It is clear from the NAFTA debate that issues of trade, sustainable development, and environmental protection are no longer separate from each other.

## FURTHER READING

The following books have been selected to provide introductions to the debates surrounding international issues of trade, economic development, sustainable development and environmental protection.

Arntzen, J, I. Hemmer, and O. Kuik, eds, 1992. *International Trade and Sustainable Development*. Amsterdam: VU University Press.

Borman, Herbert and Stephen Kellert, eds, 1991. *Ecology, Economics, Ethics: The Broken Circle*. New Haven: Yale University Press.

Daly, Herman. 1977. *Steady-state Economics*. San Francisco: W. H. Freeman.

Daly, Herman and Kenneth Townsend, eds, 1993. *Valuing the Earth: Economics, Ecology and Ethics*. Cambridge, Mass.: MIT Press.

Fisher, Julie. 1993. *The Road from Rio: Sustainable Development and the Non-Governmental Movement in the Third World*. Westport, Conn.: Praeger.

French, Hilary. 1993. *Costly Tradeoffs: Reconciling Trade and the Environment*. Worldwatch Paper 113. Washington, DC: Worldwatch Institute.

Hufbauer, Gary C and Jeffrey J. Schott. 1993. *NAFTA: An Assessment*, rev. edn. Washington, DC: Institute for International Economics.

Hurrell, A. and B. Kingsbury, eds, 1992. *The International Politics of the Environment*. Oxford: Clarendon Press.

Leonard, Jeffrey H. 1988. *Pollution and the Struggle for the World Product*. Cambridge: Cambridge University Press.

National Commission on the Environment. 1993. *Choosing a Sustainable Future: The Report of the National Commission on the Environment*. Washington, DC: Island Press.

Pearce, David and Warford, Jeremy. 1993. *World Without End: Economics, Environment and Sustainable Development*. New York: Oxford University Press.

Pearce, David, Edward Barbier, and Anil Markandya. 1990. *Sustainable Development: Economics and Environment in the Third World.* Brookfield, VT: Gower.

Pepper, David. 1984. *The Roots of Modern Environmentalism.* London: Routledge.

Redclift, Michael. 1987. *Sustainable Development: Exploring the Contradictions.* London and New York: Routledge.

Repetto, Robert. 1985. *The Global Possible: Resources, Development and the New Century.* New Haven, Conn.: Yale University Press.

Robinson, Nicholas. 1993. *Agenda 21: Earth's Action Plan.* New York: Oceana Publications.

Zaelke, D., P. Orbuch, and R. Housman, eds, 1993 *Trade and the Environment: Law, Economics and Policy.* Washington, DC: Island Press.

# NOTES

1   Sierra Club, *Analysis of the North American Free Trade Agreement and the North American Agreement on Environmental Cooperation,* October 6 (Washington, DC: Sierra Club, 1993b).

2   John Audley, "Why Environmentalists Are Angry about the North American Free Trade Agreement," in *Trade and the Environment: Law, Economics and Policy,* eds, D. Zaelke, P. Orbuch, and R. Housman (Washington, DC: Island Press, 1993), 195.

3   Jan C. McAlpine and Pat LeDonne, "The United States Government, Public Participation, and Trade and Environment," in *Trade and the Environment: Law, Economics and Policy,* 205–7.

4   Theodore D. Goldfarb, "Issue 1: Will NAFTA Be Good for the Environment?" in *Taking Sides: Clashing Views on Controversial Environmental Issues,* ed. T. Goldfarb, 6th edn. (Guilford, Conn.: Dushkin Publishing, 1995), 5.

5   We owe a debt of gratitude to Mr William Reilly for giving us access to his archives and granting us time for interviews.

6   Gary C. Hufbauer and Jeffrey J. Schott, *NAFTA: An Assessment,* rev. edn, (Washington, DC: Institute for International Economics, 1993), 91–3.

7   Goldfarb, "Issue 1," 10.

8   Hufbauer and Schott, *NAFTA: An Assessment,* 99.

9   As with the Sierra Club, WWF also issued a NAFTA position paper: *The North American Free Trade Agreement and the Environment,* (Washington, DC: World Wildlife Fund, 1993).

10  There are many personalities who became involved in the NAFTA debate. Ross Perot, for example, became one of the most vocal opponents of NAFTA and captured media attention during his year-long on-then-off-then-on again presidential campaign. He prophesied that NAFTA would bring about massive job losses in the United States (see his *Save Your Job, Save Our Country: Why NAFTA Must Be Stopped – Now* (New York: Hyperion, 1993)). (He became *the* leading opponent of NAFTA, as witnessed in the televised debate between him and Vice-President Al Gore on the eve of the congressional vote in November 1993 (see, for example, Cook Rhodes, "Hill Finds It Cannot Ignore Perot's Lingering Presence," *Congressional Quarterly Weekly Report* 51 (Oct. 2, 1993): 2671–3). Other notable personalities opposed to NAFTA who generated publicity against the treaty include Representative Richard Gephardt; Michigan Representative and House Majority

Whip David E. Bonoir (see his commentary "NAFTA: Exporting US Jobs," *Washington Post*, Friday Sept. 17, 1993, A-21); Jim Hightower, a conservative radio commentator ("NAFTA – We Don't Hafta," reprinted in the *Utne Reader*, July/Aug. 1993, 97–100); Mike McCloskey, the chairman of the Sierra Club (see the numerous press releases from the Sierra Club between 1992 and 1993); Ralph Nader, a long-time consumer advocate who criticized that NAFTA would weaken food, drug, air, water, automobile, and industrial safety laws (see his article in the *Los Angeles Times*, "A Deal That's Hazardous to Health," Aug. 6, 1992, and the *Public Citizen Report*, 1992); Greenpeace also published two reports on trade and the environment. ("UNCED Undermined: Why Free Trade Won't Save the Planet," March 1992, and Carol Alexander and Ken Stump's "The NAFTA and Energy Trade," 1992 are both published and available from Greenpeace.)

A range of economists were engaged: from conservatives like James M. Buchanan and Milton Friedman to liberals like Paul Samuelson and James Tobin (see Sylvia Nasar, "A Primer: Why Economists Favor Free-Trade Agreement," *New York Times*, September 17, 1993, A-1; and "Businessmen for NAFTA," *The Economist* 329: Oct. 16, 1993); William K. Reilly, former administrator of the EPA made numerous public appearances on behalf of the environmental community support-ing NAFTA; Jay Hair, president of National Wildlife Federation (one of the first national environmental organizations to commit itself to trade policy analysis); Representative Max Baucus of Montana and Senator John Chafee, a Republican from Rhode Island (see "Should Congress Approve the North American Free Trade Agreement? Pro," *Congressional Digest* 72 (Nov. 1993): 278.

For a good overview of the NAFTA debate in general, see Gary Hufbauer, Jeffrey J. Schott, and Ellen Meade, *North American Free Trade Issues and Recommenda-tions* (Washington, DC: Institute for International Economics, 1992) Several issues of *The Economist* between December 1992 and November 1993 also provide good summaries of the various debates. The rest of the paper will focus on the environ-mental debate, although debates on labor and job wages, for example, were equally prominent during this time.

11   Bruce Stokes, "The Road From Rio," *National Journal*, May 30, 1992, 1286–7.
12   Gordon Binder, *NAFTA and the Environment: Questions and Answers about the North American Free Trade Agreement*. World Wildlife Fund White Paper (Washington, DC: World Wildlife Fund, October 1993).
13   David Pepper, *Eco-socialism: From Deep Ecology to Social Justice* (New York: Routledge, 1993).
14   Greenpeace, *NAFTA: Trading Away Tomorrow* (Washington, DC: Greenpeace, 1993).
15   David Morris, "How About a Fair Trade Agreement?" *Utne Reader*, July/Aug. 1993, 100–13.
16   Michael Redclift, *Sustainable Development: Exploring the Contradictions* (London and New York: Routledge, 1987), 4.
17   Bill Devall, and George Sessions, *Deep Ecology: Living as If Nature Mattered* (Salt Lake City, Utah: Peregrine Smith Books, 1985).
18   Friends of the Earth, "Testimony of Friends of the Earth before the Subcommittee on Energy and Power Committee on Energy and Commerce," September 22, 1993 (Washington, DC).
19   GATT, introduced in 1947, has been criticized by environmentalists for its lack of environmental awareness. (Indeed the word *environment* appears nowhere in the

GATT.) Environmentalists are fairly unanimous in agreeing there is much reform needed in the GATT. For thoughts on environmental reform in the GATT, see Peter Uimonen and John Whalley, "Trade and Environment: Setting the Rules" (Washington, DC: Institute for International Economics, 1992); Charles Arden-Clarke, *International Trade, GATT, and the Environment*. Gland, Switzerland: World Wildlife Fund, May, 1992).

20  There is not room in this chapter to detail the legal arguments (they are vast and intricately complex). Rather, the point is to raise the arguments about sovereignty and sustainable development as a way to introduce the struggles facing the environmental community as it confronts new policy terrain. For sound analysis of this topic, see Nicholas Kublicki, "The Greening of Free Trade: NAFTA, Mexican Environmental Law, and Debt Exchanges for Mexican Environmental Infrastructure Development," *Columbia Journal of Environmental Law*, 19, no. 1 (1994): 59–140.

21  Sources for these newspaper citations are: Peter Behr, "For Environmental Groups, Biggest NAFTA Fight Is Intramural," *Washington Post*, September 16, 1993, D-10 and Keith Schneider, "Environmental Movement Splits over Big Group's Support for Trade Pact," *New York Times*, September 16, 1993, A-1.

22  We have long recognized the diversity within "a" social movement (such as the civil rights or the women's movement). The internal diversity of the environmental movement, although well chronicled by scholars (such as Hurrell and Kinsburgy, *The International Politics of the Environment*; David Pepper, *The Roots of Modern Environmentalism* (London: Routledge, 1984); J. Petulla, *American Environmental History: The Exploitation and Conservation of Natural Resources* (San Francisco: Boyd and Fraser, 1977); T. O'Riordan, *Environmentalism* (London: Pion, 1981); and R. White, *North, South, the Environmental Crisis* (Toronto: University of Toronto Press, 1993)), is perhaps less understood and acknowledged among the general public. We would argue that the reaction of surprise by the media over the "family feud" in the NAFTA debate and the attention given to this issue illustrate that many people believed the environmental movement to be homogenous.

23  Behr, "For Environmental Groups, Biggest NAFTA Fight Is Intramural," D-10.

24  William K. Reilly, "Free Traders and Environmentalists: Differing Goals, Conflicting Cultures," lecture at Stanford University, October 13, 1993 (copy from the Institute for International Studies, Room 200, Encina Hall, Stanford University, Stanford, CA 94305).

25  Reilly, "Free Traders and Environmentalists"; William K. Reilly, "The Greening of NAFTA: Implications for Continental Environmental Cooperation in North America," *Journal of Environment & Development* 2, no. 1 (Winter 1993).

26  Hilary French, *Costly Tradeoffs: Reconciling Trade and the Environment*. Worldwatch Paper 113 (Washington, DC: Worldwatch Institute, 1993), 5.

27  Debra Rose, "A North American Free Trade Agreement: The Impacts on Wildlife," World Wildlife Paper (Washington, DC: World Wildlife Fund, 1991).

28  Jim Hightower, "NAFTA – We Don't Hafta."

29  References for these newspaper headlines are "Should Trade Go Green? How to Stop Protection for the Environment Becoming Protectionsim in Trade," *The Economist* 318 (Jan. 26, 1991): 12–14; "Trade and the Environment: The Greening of Protectionism," *The Economist*, 326 (Feb. 27. 1993): 25–6; Joel Simon, "NAFTA – The View from Tijuana," *The Nation*, Nov. 30, 1992; Louis S. Richman, "How Zealous Greens Hurt Growth," *Fortune*, March 23, 1992, 26; Margaret E. Kriz, "The New Eco-nomics," *The National Journal*, May 30, 1992; Bruce Stokes, "The

Road from Rio," *The National Journal*, May 30, 1992; Jonathan Schlefer, "What Price Economic Growth?" *Atlantic Monthly*, December 1992, 113–18; Robert Heckarts and Tira Harpaz, "Critics Ask If NAFTA Is 'Green' Enough," *The National Law Journal*, Dec. 21, 1992, 17; Sheldon Friedman, "NAFTA as Social Dumping," *Challenge*, 35, no. 5 (Sept./Oct. 1992): 27–32; Justin Ward and Glenn T. Prickett, "Prospects for a Green Trade Agreement," *Environment*, May 1992; Justin Ward and Kathrin Day Lassila, "Trading Away the Environment," *Amicus Journal*, June 1993: 9–10.

30  Reilly, "The Greening of NAFTA."
31  Juanita Darling, "Environmental, Labor Groups Make Voices Heard," *Los Angeles Times*, August 7, 1992, B-5.
32  Jerry Roberts, "Gore Says Sierra Club Is 'Simply Wrong' about Trade Pact," *San Francisco Chronicle*, September 27, 1993.
33  Sierra Club, "Press Release: House of Representatives Trades Away Environment with Pro-NAFTA Vote," November 17, 1993 (Washington, DC).

# 11

# Selling the Environment or Selling Out?

In one of the "Peanuts" cartoon classics, *A Charlie Brown Christmas*, the hero laments the commercialization of Christmas. Although Charlie Brown believes some things should remain sacred and spiritual, he is aware that everything and anything can be consumed by consumerism. His worry echoes the fear of many: can everything, including criticisms of the status quo, be reduced to commodities?

The modern-day environmental movement was nurtured in the antimaterialist climate of the 1970s.[1] But by the end of the 1990s many environmental organizations offer an array of products, such as Sierra Club tote bags and Greenpeace coffee mugs, through catalogs and magazines. Some organizations now manage stores and outlets as environmental commodities take up even more "cultural space." Instead of generating action, the distraction of producing and consuming merchandise threatens to push the ideological goals of these groups into the background. Has environmentalism, too, become commercialized?

The juxtaposition between environmental ideological rhetoric and material ambition makes us uneasy. It should: the messages are contradictory. On the one hand environmentalists critique many of the fundamental tenets of modernism: technology, growth, mass production, and mass consumption. On the other hand environmental organizations are situated within our culture and therefore partake in the reproduction of precisely the cultural values they criticize. Environmental organizations operate in this consumer culture, yet they call for excesses of consumption to cease. They themselves desire or require "growth" in the form of increased membership and contributions, yet they promote sustainable development for others and support antigrowth measures. These organizations must reach a larger public without succumbing to a relentless "growth syndrome" mentality. The paradox: efforts to promote environmental organizations and their ideologies, even those of radical environmentalists, often unwittingly reproduce the modern impulse to produce and consume.

In looking at how the commodification of environmentalism evolved from the 1970s to the 1990s[2] we trace the evolution of environmental merchandising as a response to the need to reach a wider audience through magazines, catalogs, television, newspapers, and other means of communication. The promotional efforts of the Sierra Club illustrate this evolution well. As a member of the Group of 10 – the large, powerful mainstream organizations – the Sierra Club's "commercial evolution" reflects changes that many established environmental organizations have experienced.

To make sense of the commercialization of environmentalism, we must understand that environmentalism and merchandising are connected in a larger system of images and signs.

## Selling the Environment

Proponents of the environmental movement have two objectives: to convert the public to its cause by increasing awareness and to motivate the public to improve the problematic conditions in the environment through institutional and value changes. It is the first objective that has created the tension between ideological rhetoric and conspicuous consumption. Environmental organizations have relied on increasingly sophisticated promotional efforts to introduce environmental issues and capture public support.

### The 1970s: selling the environmental message

The late 1960s and early 1970s were characterized by optimism and enthusiasm, spurring a rush of environmental concern, legislation, and lawsuits. Leaders of mainstream organizations, intent on reducing pollution and environmental degradation, focused their efforts on lobbying the government and changing the rules of the game. Established groups, such as the Sierra Club and the Environmental Defense Fund, led this new wave of action. Members of mainstream groups did not believe that entire political and economic systems needed to be transformed or overthrown. They were confident that environmental protection could be successfully managed within the existing framework of institutions.[3] Theirs was a pragmatic reform.

Swept up in the force of the environmental awareness revolution many environmental organizations caught the current of changing political and public consciousness, and some sought to sell a new ideology, and to shift the emphasis from *local* volunteerism and activism to *national* involvement. Changing times called for more sophisticated organizations, and this resulted in increased professionalism in the organizational structure and in efforts to appeal to a wider public audience. Professionals who were highly skilled in marketing and sales brought this knowledge and experience into various environmental organizations.

The Sierra Club is a good example. It entered a new stage of political and promotional activity in the 1960s. One debate centered on the battle over the proposed Southwest Water Plan to dam the Colorado River in two locations in the Grand Canyon. The Grand Canyon plan paralleled that of the Glen Canyon, a battle the Sierra Club had fought but lost. In 1960, borrowing on material assembled during the earlier battle over Glen Canyon, the Sierra Club toured a traveling slide show and published a book, *Time and the River Flowing*, which dramatically documented the loss of Glen Canyon. David Brower, then executive director of the Sierra Club, also launched an innovative publicity campaign that included a full-page ad in the *New York Times*, asking, "Should we also flood the Sistine Chapel so tourists can get nearer to the ceiling?" The newspaper ads, spaced over ten months, exerted tremendous public pressure on politicians. In this battle Sierra Club leaders mobilized the dispersed forces of wilderness preservation, and, in a persuasive display of political force, they defeated the proposed dams.

The newspaper ads contained "coupons" of protest for readers to send to members of Congress. Within 24 hours of starting the ads, the Internal Revenue Service concluded the ad was *legislative*, not *educational*, and somewhat irritated at the organization anyway, they revoked the coveted tax status. No longer could contributions be tax deductible. According to Brower, this cost the Sierra Club about a half a million dollars in deductible contributions.[4] In effect, the IRS fined the Sierra Club for its environmental activism. The IRS action, however, actually helped the defense of Grand Canyon. The club lost its tax status but gained in membership as people rallied in support. The leaders of the Sierra Club recognized the power of the mass media to sway public opinion.

In 1970 Sierra Club officers responded to the earlier IRS decision by establishing the Sierra Club Legal Defense Fund as a separate and tax-deductible organization to carry out the club's legal efforts. But more than structural changes occurred. It also offered new international and national Sierra Club outings and considered ways to merchandise Sierra Club products to generate revenue and support. The savvy new professionals worked closely with the media in an effort to connect people with the environmental message. Environmental organizations in general expanded their utilization of the media to promote environmentalism.

In 1976 the Sierra Club opened the Sierra Club Store on Polk Street in San Francisco. The store sold Sierra Club books and calendars, hiking guides, cards and maps, pictorial books, environmental publications, and nature gifts. In October 1977 the *Sierra Club Bulletin*, the monthly publication of the Sierra Club, sought a broader audience. A name change (from the *Sierra Club Bulletin* to a bolder, simpler *Sierra*), new page formats and typefaces, paper that better accommodated color photos, sophisticated graphics, more frequent publication and more general articles all aimed to make the magazine more interesting and effective to an ever-growing audience. Explaining the changes the editor, Frances

Grendlin, remarked, "We think it's time to reach a broader audience who might well be interested in participating as we do – as citizens – in helping to preserve the planet."[5] Grendlin continued:

> we've brought environmental thinking into the everyday consciousness of millions of people.... there are college students who obviously want to participate... and there are children who, as our next generation, should learn early the values that will strengthen their lives. Not only must our magazine have material that speaks to these people and others, *we must make ways for them to find us.*[6] [our emphasis]

On the agenda for the 1980s was the objective of increasing advertising revenue. For the greater part of 100 years, the *Sierra Club Bulletin* featured very few ads for products, reflecting the anticonsumerist sentiment and its comparatively small membership and circulation. The little advertising that did appear provided income that was directly related to the club's purpose. However, as more professionals joined environmental organizations and as membership increased substantially, the quantity of ads significantly increased, as had the opportunities to purchase merchandise. One-half of the magazine's content became income-producing advertising.[7] As circulation increased so too did advertising, because many businesses purchase advertising space only when a magazine has a circulation threshold of 500,000. Advertisements for "all-cotton shower curtains" and an "outdoors singles network," for example, were introduced as the magazine increased circulation and new merchandise was conceived. Sierra Club's Public Information Service statistics show that *Sierra*'s circulation jumped from 165,000 in 1977 to 350,000 by 1985 and up to 500,000 in 1990.[8]

### The 1980s: selling ideology or selling stuff?

Significant economic and demographic changes in the 1980s influenced environmental activism in unusual ways. Economic growth in the early and mid-1980s created a class of young, upwardly mobile professionals. These Yuppies became legendary and their stereotype familiar to most Americans: a Wall Street executive with a six-figure salary and an obsession with materialism. They exemplify many Americans' ambivalence to environmentalism: spending money and accumulating goods in ostentatious display, while simultaneously expressing sympathy for many environmental causes. "Designated wilderness areas," commented deep ecologist and critic George Sessions, "are seen by the new yuppie Sierra Clubbers, for example, as areas of superlative scenery and playgrounds for 'industrial tourism' rather than primarily as sanctuaries for wild ecosystems and unmanaged habitat for wild species."[9] It is difficult, however, to lay the blame solely on Yuppies, because it was environmental organizations that initiated new product lines and expanded travel programs, some available only to members, others sold at a discount (advertised as the "advantage of membership").

Writer and social commentator Paul Fussell wryly commented that late twentieth-century America in general held to the mentality of "I consume, therefore I am."[10] Increasingly large budgets and a flood of disposable income propelled a flurry of environmental entrepreneurialism. Direct mail campaigns were run using highly sophisticated computer technology, and mailing lists were exchanged among organizations to further increase memberships. Marketing aimed at the new wealth of the 1980s included product catalogs, publishing, expanded travel programs, credit cards, and "environmentally sound" investment consulting.

Perhaps the most tangible difference between the 1970s and the 1980s can be seen in the proliferation of promotional products and in their sophistication: the bandannas and belt buckles of the 1970s gave way to the VISA cards, videos, toll-free numbers, and computerized mailing lists of the 1980s. The maturation of environmental activism included new expressions of thought, action, and publicity. Slick environmental merchandising reflected both the changing cultural conditions and the growing sophistication and commercialization of environmental organizations. In the mid-1980s, the Sierra Club began its *Mail Order Service*, a catalog that featured books, calendars, audiotapes, T-shirts, posters, Christmas cards, stationery, and "graphic products and logo items." Generated revenues have consistently hovered around $100,000 yearly.[11]

"Imageability" became an important selling point. Postcards, knickknacks, and calendars all featured nature: alive, air-brushed, and framed. These items advertised the organization and helped promote a wider imageability, which in turn extended the organization's national reach. During the 1980s the Sierra Club excelled in appealing to a variety of constituencies by providing lobbying efforts, litigation expertise, and educational materials.

Although fragmentation and competition for membership among organizations characterized the 1980s, membership in all environmental organizations increased. The growth rate for the Sierra Club was approximately 30 percent during much of the 1980s:

| | |
|---|---|
| 1970 | 114, 330 members |
| 1980 | 181, 773 |
| 1981 | 246, 317 |
| 1985 | 362, 500 |
| 1990 | 629, 000[12] |

Budgets skyrocketed; the Sierra Club's grew tenfold.[13] By 1990, revenues for the Sierra Club exceeded $44 million. While membership dues and contributions accounted for over $29 million, more than $10 million came from outings, book sales and advertising.[14] The message of unyielding consumerism had considerable influence. By the mid-1980s leaders in many environmental organizations could agree on the following needs:

- to continue membership growth;
- to reach an even broader audience through advertising and merchandise; and
- to maintain a dialogue of challenge to the technological environmental metadiscourse.

Popularizing and promoting the environmental message had evolved into a permanent strategy. If the Reagan years were symbolized by BMWs, Norditracs, the Trump Towers, Perrier and the excesses of Jim and Tammy Baker environmental organizations countered with wilderness photography, tote bags, T-shirts, ecotourism, and their exclusive line of credit cards. Although the messages differed (or did they?) the medium remained the same: commodities.

We have focused on the increased selling of the reformist Sierra Club, but other more radical organizations also experienced growth. Radical environmentalists called for dramatically different environmental discourses which advocated sweeping political, economic, and cultural changes, but could they themselves escape consumerism?

Central to the radical critique is an attack on industrialism – mass production and mass consumption. Radicals call for a "materially simpler lifestyle for people in wealthy countries."[15] In addition, they believe that cultural accumulation means that technological and social progress can continue without limit, making all social problems appear ultimately soluble.[16] Greenpeace shares with other radical groups direct action, grassroots activism, the use of the media, and ecocentric philosophy.[17] Like the reformist groups, however, Greenpeace too has depended on mail solicitations and door-to-door fundraising. Despite ideological rhetoric to the contrary, these radical groups have also participated in the commodification of their message. Greenpeace sells T-shirts, low-flow showerheads, and tote bags. Earthfirst! sells bumperstickers, T-shirts, and airhorns ("for disrupting Wise Use meetings or just generally causing a distraction...only $35"). While Greenpeace's activist scope exceeds the Sierra Club's by 1990 it was an international organization with gross revenues of nearly $100 million.[18] In fact, by the end of the 1980s Greenpeace claimed over 1 million followers in the United States; the Sierra Club claimed 629,000. Although some observers have astutely criticized the Sierra Club for becoming Yuppified we must not ignore the fact that radical environmental organizations have been, to varying degrees, guilty of the same thing. Environmental organizations' members have found it difficult to battle certain myths embodied in the dominant discourse in US society, including those of progress (equated with growth), technological optimism and, perhaps the most virtuous (or virulent), the need to produce and consume. Environmental ideologies, whether radical or mainstream, are fraught with inconsistencies and contradictions.

## Environmentalism as Spectacle

If we are to understand the commercialization of environmentalism, we must look below the surface at the complex relationships between sign, image, commodity, and culture. In contemporary society there is an overwhelming flood of signs and images.[19] Signs and images have merged with commodity. Postmodern deconstructionists, such as Barthes, Eco and Baudrillard, have challenged us to recognize the duplicity of image (for what you get is not *just* what you see).[20] In other words by purchasing a T-shirt, car or video, you purchase more than just an object, you buy the concomitant message of materialism. Converting the public to environmentalism involves promoting environmental ideologies. Images, texts, and commodities express power and domination. Images, deconstructionists argue, cannot be "objective" nor can they be "true" representations. They are multilayered with meaning. Postmodern deconstructionists charge that we must look for hidden agendas in promotions, products, and advertising. In as much as products have a function they are an image. In addition to material products, environmental organizations have relied on media attention to help sell their ideological goals and capture support. Consider the media's role in disseminating environmental currency.

Nearly every US household has a color TV and VCR. A rich variety of films and nature documentaries for home VCR use furnishes a library to help construct environmental iconography. A partnership of sorts has formed. Television has been the predominant medium through which ecological disasters and environmental activism have been documented. Dramatic footage of Cuyahoga river in Ohio engulfed in flames, oil-soaked sea birds struggling in the Santa Barbara oil spill, and sewage and industrial wastes spilling into the Great Lakes confront us with a set of disturbing images. "The reporting of environmental occurrences inevitably deploys powerful cultural symbols – such as nature, the countryside and the historic heritage – symbols which are already endowed with strongly anti-industrial connotations."[21] Environmental groups use the media to publicize an environmental issue or disaster, thus offering a critique of the ethos and logic of advanced industrialism.[22] This is a challenge to the technological environmental metadiscourse.

In addition to television the environment has become a worthy subject in our nation's most important news magazines. *Time* captured the most attention by naming the "Endangered Earth" as "Planet of the Year" in lieu of its famous "Man of the Year" for 1989.[23] By Earth Day 1990, the news coverage was extensive, and we appeared to be at the crest of another wave of environmentalism; an unusual triad formed – environmental organizations, the media and corporate America. A grand spectacle, Earth Day 1990 enriched the coffers for everyone involved. Opportunities to participate were equaled or exceeded by the opportunity to buy commemorative T-shirts, posters, and other memorabilia. Products could be bought everywhere; from McDonald's nation-wide to the Greenpeace store in San Francisco. The trend toward the environment-as-product-as-spectacle has continued. Even the 1992 UN Earth Summit in Rio sold an "official poster" that could "be yours for only $19 if you act quickly by calling the toll-free number." Various media managers have helped sell environmentalism to Americans and have elevated both environmental ideology and products (especially that of tourism) to a socially desirable level. They have done so by manipulating images and emotions.

Environmental groups themselves have become formidable propaganda machines in the manipulation of language, images, and ideologies. The public debate over environmental issues has fallen conspicuously into the domain of ideology and propaganda. "The groups war against one another in the realm of imaginative use of language, and symbols – an ever popular human activity."[24] Environmental organizations send out mailings that loudly proclaim "Action Alert" and "Your Urgent Response Needed," hoping that these messages will be considered as "news." Their purpose, however, is often to solicit membership. Promoting the environment is not innocent of layered meanings and manipulations. "It is not exceptional, for example, for Friends of the Earth to be the source of several hundred press articles in a single month, and for its staff to give over a hundred interviews on radio and television in a year."[25] The decision to influence or create "news" is a choice that involves power struggles over language and image. Ultimately, these messages and images have been manipulated for profit.

### Environment as commodity

Messages are both denoted (information given) and connoted (secondary meanings of symbolic interpretation). "We never encounter (at least in advertising) a literal image in a pure state."[26] Images in many cases have replaced reality and truth, which worries some critics who see our landscapes and culture becoming parodies and exaggerations, mirroring theme parks, such as Disneyland. Michael Sorkin has noted that indirect commodification is a process by which nonsalable objectives, activities, and images are purposely placed in the commodified world.[27] Nature is repackaged; the intention is to reframe reality. As merchandising proliferates it becomes cliché, managed and staged. The original (a mountain, a lake, or an endangered animal) is substituted with a visual re-creation, captured in a time frame and with a purity to compensate for present-day failures and possible future degradation. Environmental merchandise, then, is a charade of nature. The artificial is mixed up in the real, and everything is a simulation of something, and thus images have lost their original meaning. This can be taken to an extreme: astro-turf replaces grass, plastic trees replace the real and living. The formal and controlled "wilds" of the Disneyland jungle ride are filled with the sounds of recorded bird calls.

Shrewd merchandising of T-shirts, mugs, earrings, and tote bags has plastered the icons of the Sierra Club and Greenpeace everywhere. More often than not the images depicted on merchandise are not of environmental catastrophes – polluted rivers or gasping fish – but of the pristine. Nature is captured in an image destined to be a commodity purchased via MasterCard. Do videocassettes, sleepwear, clocks, and calendars perpetuate the objectification of nature? If modernists sought to deanimate nature by making it an object to control, members of environmental organizations must be leery of joining in, regardless of their intentions. The phenomena of commercialization can transform nature into a spectacle. Merchandise introduces the capacity to learn about nature – the world of mountains, wilderness, and animals – without ever having direct contact, thus another paradox of environmental merchandising: it can evoke an intimacy at a distance.

Commodities have the power to illustrate the possibilities of life. In the age of hype, accumulating things can elevate self-esteem and social status. But consumption can replace action. Viewed critically, the production of merchandise is the logical expression of the technological environmental metadiscourse. Image and technology work together to produce merchandise. Machines paint mountain ranges on millions of mugs. A Sierra Club logo embroidered on a pair of sweatpants doubles the price. The earth itself has become a commodity. As social theorist Elinor Gadon has astutely observed, the icon of our time, the dramatic photograph of earth taken by astronauts from their spaceship in 1969, has "been mass-marketed, reproduced in every conceivable medium, even reduced in scale to a tiny bauble that can hang from a chain like a protective amulet to be worn around the neck or dangled from a rear-view mirror."[28] Even Greenpeace sells these baubles ("Earth-as-earrings"). This NASA picture, a symbol of our heroic journey into outer space, however, is a distancing image of the earth that confirms our separation from it and that affirms it as a product of our most advanced technology.[29] The NASA picture is an aesthetically powerful image of Mother Earth. The paradox, of course, is that the picture is possible because of our technological conquest of the planet. The variations of the product may be endless, but the message is the same: buy me.

Merchandise deludes. If we are committed to environmental principles, it makes our lives full of contradictions. Can we purchase merchandise, however green, without supporting the continuation of the dominant environmental discourse? If we buy one product, does this mean environmental organizations have become merely tools for selling commodities? As long as the desire for commodities stays strong, there seems no way out of the alliance of capitalism and culture. We must remember that when we purchase merchandise, even environmental merchandise, not only do we perpetuate the profits of some industry, but we also condone a set of ideologies (about the positive attributes of mass production and mass consumption) that are part of the dominant technological metadiscourse. Merchandise reveals our culture's unresolved tensions, conflicting values, and divided way of life. It does not help us begin to solve them.

## FURTHER READING

Christopher, Tom and Marty Asher. 1994. *Compost This Book: The Art of Composting for Your Yard, Your Community and the Planet.* San Francisco: Sierra Club Books.

Hawken, Paul. 1993. *The Ecology of Commerce: A Declaration of Sustainability.* New York: Harper Business.

Kempton, William, James Boster, and Jennifer Hartley. 1995. *Environmental Values in American Culture.* (Cambridge: MIT Press).

LaMay, Craig and Everette Dennis, eds, 1991. *Media and the Environment.* Washington, DC: Island Press.

Milbrath, Lester. 1996. *Learning to Think Environmentally: While There Is Still Time.* Albany, NY: State University of New York Press.

Oelschlaeger, Max, ed. 1992. *After Earth Day: Continuing the Conservation Effort.* Denton: University of North Texas Press.

*The Recyclers Handbook.* 1990. Berkeley, Calif.: Earth Works Press.

Rifkin, Jeremy, ed. 1990. *The Green Lifestyle Handbook.* New York: Henry Holt & Company.

# NOTES

1  The first wave occurred during the the last half of the nineteenth century (1870 to 1900) and was marked by the clash between conservationists and preservationists. Resource management, typified by Gifford Pinchot's sustainable yield, sustainable use program in the National Forest, prevailed over the preservationists and was represented by John Muir. Pinchot's resource management maintained the environment as a utility for people and became the enduring environmental paradigm.

2  We use the terms commodification and commercialization interchangeably, although some would argue there are subtle differences between them.

3  Michael McCloskey, "Twenty Years of Change in the Environmental Movement: An Insider's View," in *American Environmentalism: The US Environmental Movement 1970–1990*, eds, Riley Dunlap and Angela Mertig (Philadelphia: Taylor and Francis, 1992), 77–88.

4  David Brower, *Work in Progress*, (Salt Lake City, Utah: Peregrine Smith Books, 1991).

5  Frances Grendlin, "From The Editor: Sierra Looks Ahead," *Sierra* (October 1977): 4–5.

6  Grendlin, "From the Editor," 4.

7  Brower, *Work in Progress*, 7.

8  Sierra Club Public Information Service and various statistics and information gathered by this service (Sierra Club Headquarters, 730 Polk Street, San Francisco, Calif., 1993). The connection between membership and magazine circulation statistics is a complex one. Circulation stats usually lag behind membership, because one household may have many members but will receive only one magazine. In general, circulation grew at about the same pace as membership.

9  George Sessions, "Radical Environmentalism in the 1990s," in *After Earth Day: Continuing The Conservation Effort*, ed. Max Oelschlaeger (Denton: University of North Texas Press, 1992), 17–27.

10  Paul Fussell, *Bad: Or, the Dumbing of America* (New York: Simon & Schuster, 1991).

11  Sierra Club Public Information, membership statistics, 1993.

12  Sierra Club Public Information Service, 1993.

13  McCloskey, "Twenty Years of Change," 83.

14  Sierra Club Financial Report, "An Auditor's Report for 1992," conducted by Peat Marwick, Inc. (available by request from the Sierra Club Public Information Service, 1993).

15  Michael F. Zimmerman, "The Future of Ecology" in *After Earth Day: Continuing The Conservation Effort*, 172.

16   Bill Devall and George Sessions, *Deep Ecology: Living as If Nature Mattered* (Salt Lake City, Utah: Peregrine Smith Books, 1985).

17   Rik Scarce, *Eco-Warriors: Understanding the Radical Environmental Movement* (Chicago: Noble Press, 1990).

18   Scarce, *Eco-Warriors*.

19   Mike Featherstone, "Perspectives on Consumer Culture," *Journal of Sociology* 24 (1990): 5–22.

20   See the following works: Roland Barthes, *Image-Music- Text* (New York: Hill and Wang, 1997), Umberto Eco, *Travels in Hyper-reality: Essays* (San Diego: Harcourt Brace Jovanovich, 1986) and Jean Baudrillard, *America* (New York: Verso, 1988).

21   Philip Lowe and David Morrison, "Bad News or Good News: Environmental Politics and the Mass Media," *The Sociological Review* (February 1984): 79.

22   Ibid., 78.

23   Riley Dunlap, "Trends in Public Opinion toward Environmental Issues: 1965–1990," in *American Environmentalism: The US Environmental Movement 1970–1990*, 107.

24   John M. Culbertson, "Ecology, Economics and the Quality of Life," *Historical Ecology: Essays on Environment and Social Change*, ed. Lester Blisky (Port Washington, NY: Kennikat Press, 1980), 163.

25   Lowe and Morrison, "Bad News or Good News," 84.

26   Barthes, *Image-Music-Text*, 42.

27   Michael Sorkin, "See You in Disneyland" in *Variations on a Theme Park: The New American City and the End of Public Space*, ed. Michael Sorkin (New York: Noonday Press, 1992), 205–32.

28   Elinor Gadon, "Metaphors for Birthing: Towards a New Creation Story for the Age of Ecology," in *After Earth Day: Continuing The Conservation Effort*, 196.

29   Gadon, "Metaphors for Birthing," 196.

# Postscript

## Beyond Angst: Thoughts on the Paradox of Alternative Environmental Discourses In Practice

Let us end with a provoking paradox: unless you live in a cabin in the remote Montana wilderness, make your own clothes, grow your own food, and subsist on minimal resources, life as an environmentalist in contemporary US society is one of inevitable disparity, a cultural dissonance, between the articulation of an alternative environmental discourse (no matter how radical or cutting-edge) and the reality of living in an intensely consumerist capitalist economy. We end this book by attempting to resolve, in some measure, this paradox.

Although we have shown there are numerous alternative environmental discourses challenging the dominant discourse, they all share one common belief: society must change its attitudes about and its use of the earth. Thus any alternative environmental discourse promotes some message of economic, political, social, and environmental change. These messages are often displayed through images, symbols, art, videos, T-shirts, and tote bags. People are symbol users and symbol makers. We invent games and new technologies, we construct ideologies and we create images to reflect ideas. Images attract people's attention and help them build their perceptions of the natural world. These mental constructions then may be expressed to others through various media: landscape paintings, literature, poetry, photography. The arts have played significant roles in shaping our ideas about the natural world. Landscape painting in the United States, for example, has greatly influenced people's perceptions of their environment, both reflecting and creating cultural attitudes. Art and image have helped us interpret the environment, often with great emotional impact.

Graphic expressions (logos, photographs, paintings) can confirm ideas of the written word, making visions of the verbal. Merchandise can be cheap and puerile in concept, or it can help convey (or at least promote) a difficult set of ideas. Often nature is "fearfully difficult to set forth in spoken or written words.... to put into expressive form the qualities of the natural world and its significance to humanity requires a very special technique, craft, and sensibility – also a great compassion."[1] Mystical and emotional reactions to images can stir sympathy and compassion for other living and nonliving beings, thus beginning a process of reconnection.

Publicity campaigns have always been central to the environmental movement. Photography, in particular, has been instrumental in recording landscapes through "visual magic." Certainly the Sierra Club benefited greatly from its association with Ansel Adams and his photography. Its calendars and books featuring his dramatic and evocative photographs urged people to cherish the ideas of wilderness and were vital in the early days of popular environmentalism.[2] Adams believed that "photography of the environment as a whole should be positive, but truthful, revealing and discerning, and above all, *it should move people to action*" (our emphasis).[3]

Environmental organizations can use highly visual images to disseminate alternative discourses and have in fact become sophisticated partners with the media. Greenpeace, in particular, has made the most concentrated effort to use visual media to promote environmental protection and an alternative discourse. Image plays an important role in gaining wider public support; it also can challenge the dominant environmental discourse To radical environmentalists, dramatic action has been central to promotional efforts. Although leaders of radical environmental organizations have resorted to many of the same promotional strategies as the mainstream groups (such as mail campaigns, T-shirts and bumperstickers), they have added new ones, such as dramatic skits and protests to teach people about issues through mass media. Greenpeace members have chained themselves to effluent pipes, base-jumped off of smokestacks and run interference to protect schools of dolphins from tuna boats. Unlike reformist activists, Greenpeacers have become daredevils who constantly create new tactics.[4] Sitting down in front of a bulldozer or sitting up in a tree is intervention and protest, and these protests increase public awareness. Action can create tension, thus questioning previously unquestioned (or sacred) practices. Publicity does in fact work: "Earth First! successes and high media visibility began to attract newcomers from the ranks of urban anarchists, the Rainbow Coalition, labor organizers, and others with a 'social justice' background."[5] In fact, the long-term viability of environmentalism depends on its ability to move mass opinion.

Stills and videos are crucial tools that groups employ.[6] Some consider Greenpeace's organizational activities to be "protest theater." Greenpeace often exposes problems or practices that economic or political institutions want to keep secret. "Of course, Greenpeace is much more than a theater company, but its strength, and the element that differentiates it from other environmental organizations is the impact of its visual and theatrical activities."[7] Greenpeace is in the business of creating potent imagery. As important as image is, *so too is action*: "Like the best guerrilla theater, the daring escapades and visual images take a backseat to results in the Greenpeace résumé."[8] The efforts of Greenpeace at "protest theater" unearth issues that are a concern to everyone, including the perpetrators. *They are connecting the parts back to the whole.* "When we do a protest, so much energy is released because when we're down there plugging the pipes we're a part of them [the industrialists] they've denied."[9]

Merchandise, theater, and art engage people in alternative environmental discourses. Environmentalism and commodities hint that if you do not like the way things are going, you can always change the world around you. Begin small but think big. Reusable lunch bags and mugs counteract the modern throw-away mentality. Coloring books teach new ideologies to the children who will be the next generation's leaders. T-shirts, which run the gamut from confrontational to humorous to colorful, have become a popular mode of expression and a means of identification. For example, the radical group Earth First! resists being labeled as an organization (preferring to remain a "movement") by having no "membership"; the closest thing to membership cards are T-shirts with the clenched-fist logo and the motto "No Compromise in Defense of Mother Earth."[10]

Environmental organizations, although obviously impelled in part by the need to generate donations and membership, are motivated by a sense of justice. Billboards, radio, newspaper spots and murals express an optimistic belief that transformation of the environment and human consciousness is possible. As one reviewer commented:

> In contemporary American culture, the actions of Greenpeace are rarely considered art by those given to determining such matters. Interestingly, the more successful political theater is, the less important it becomes to those affected that it is called art.... But as the function of art in our culture drifts steadily toward becoming investment commodity and entertainment, it might well be worth the art world's time to expand its narrow definitions to include activities that have a function more in keeping with traditional art values – *creating images that have an impact on people's lives* [our emphasis].[11]

Direct action, public protests and civil disobedience, T-shirts and baseball caps are methods of presenting alternative humanity–environment relationships to people who have never considered them.

On the way to replacing the modern desire to master and possess there will be something in between, perhaps a "consumerism with a conscience" that elicits obligation and responsibility for the greater whole. It might be a type of consumerism that inspires activism and stimulates a reevaluation of our economic and cultural myths. Environmental merchandise is one way of expressing dissatisfaction. Although we have shown how powerful and pervasive concern for the environment has become in our society, environmental ideas need to become widespread in order to completely overturn the technological environmental metadiscourse. This will happen not by articulating a return to some Arcadian vision but by synthesizing modern premises and traditional concepts.[12] It would seem a difficult task for our culture to altogether abandon consumerism in the near future.

Environmentalists who struggle to implement their new discourses in social, economic and political realities often find themselves up against the ongoing resistance of a materialistic society.[13] As much as environmentalists can reinforce old habits of consumerism, they have the potential to articulate new ideas. As our world becomes increasing fragmented, environmentalism has become a unifying cause, evoking emotion and reconnection. Perhaps we should consider the phenomenon of the commercialization of environmentalism not as a sellout to the drive for consumption but as an attempt to alter the balance of power, the power of ideas.

If you were to attend a city council meeting to discuss construction of an incinerator wearing a Greenpeace T-shirt and a hat that sports an Earth First! slogan, chances are most people present would recognize your ideological attachments. In fact most people would assume, merely by looking at these "things," that you are skeptical of (maybe even hostile to) the technological solution to landfill space and sensitive to concerns about air pollution. And if the majority of the citizens present wore something similar, you can be sure the politicians would feel pressured in their decision making. The products you wear promote an alternative way of thinking about humanity–environment relationships.

In our intensely consumerist capitalist society, images contain many layers, and merchandise contains deeper dynamics than the obvious first- or second-layered message of consumerism. Advertising displays values; it signals to people what our culture depicts as important. Commodities are essentially advertisements that contain these implicit messages:

1  buy me! wear me! (the obvious message)
2  these environmental issues are important, otherwise why would we advertise/promote them? (the subtle message)

Although deconstructionists can easily criticize the obvious materialism at play here, we can also see the subtle, yet potentially powerful messages that this kind of merchandise conveys. We can look at merchandise not so much as a spectacle of consumerism but as an attempt to bridge or unify the modern ways of image display and as a revisionary perspective on the natural world. The messages conveyed in environmental merchandise have the potential to incite emotion. Rediscovery of the natural world shifts the previously trivial to the central. If T-shirts or posters evoke compassion – feeling on behalf of the larger whole of which we are a part – then perhaps this is constructive, not meaningless. Images can create a common ground while also celebrating diversity. Environmental merchandise is not just confrontation and persuasion; it may also be an affirmation.

*Accepting ambiguity and paradox*

Many environmentalists have not articulated the paradoxical situation in which they live, preferring to believe that it is all right to consume as long as they are aware of the quality and the quantity of products consumed. We have suggested wariness to the lure of materialism. Certainly merchandise, even environmental merchandise, expresses a set of values that belongs to the technological environmental metadiscourse. Irony accompanies environmental merchandise because the process of production often poses health or ecological hazards. Is the environment actually sacrificed to make environmental products? Does merchandise, which displays the message to preserve, contribute to environmental despoliation by encouraging us to explore, experience, and care? These are difficult questions with no neat and clean answers. Environmental organization officers could get sidetracked with the profitable business of commodity production, forgetting their criticism of consumerism and their long-range goals of social and economic transformation. If we are committed to environmentalism (especially the transforming or revolutionary ideologies of radical environmental discourses) we must avoid perpetuating a system of values that undermines our objectives.

For the past 20 or 30 years, environmental destruction wrought by the practices under the dominant discourse has encouraged new kinds of thinking. Deep ecology, social ecology, ecofeminism are recently articulated discourses that seek to replace the dominant discourse in which we operate. To environmentalists, the difficult question is how to begin the overwhelmingly huge task of transforming cultural values and economic and political institutions. The long-term viability of environmentalism depends on growth sufficient to influence mass opinion. Certainly engagement of ideas is part of the formula for change. Part of this process will involve image (advertising, art, merchandise) because it is through image that we can reach a mass audience. In the fall of 1992 the Sierra Club expanded the *Sierra*'s circulation to include a national distribution, and the *Sierra* now competes on supermarket newsstands, offering an alternative to the tabloids. Its national distribution may reach an even broader audience, spreading an environmental ideology to even more Americans. David Brower, considered by many to be a radical environmentalist, is not terribly concerned about overconsuming certain types of merchandise. He speaks glowingly of The Nature Company, a commercial chain of stores that offers merchandise of "high quality and great beauty"; posters, telescopes, and crafts emphasize environmental design and thoughtfulness.[14] He, like others, sees the positive connections and reenchantment that are made between people and the nature world.

Merchandise and commercialization is intertwined with politics and economics. It is also now intertwined with various environmental discourses. Logos, images, environmental art, photography, T-shirts, mugs, *are* commodities, and yet they play an important role in spreading the message of new cultural ideas. Ironically, environmental merchandise – a product of the material/consumer impulses of the dominant discourse – may ultimately undermine that discourse by activating a new consciousness and creativity. Maybe!

## NOTES

1 Ansel Adams, "The Role of the Artist in Conservation," in *The Horace M. Albright Conservation Lectureship* (Berkeley: University California College of Natural Resources, 1975), 8.
2 Vicki Goldberg, *Artnews*. 90 (1991).
3 Adams, "The Role of the Artist in Conservation," 6.
4 Rik Scarce, *Eco-Warriors: Understanding the Radical Environmental Movement* (Chicago: Noble Press, 1990).
5 George Sessions, "Radical Environmentalism in the 1990s," in *After Earth Day: Continuing The Conservation Effort*, ed. Max Oelschlaeger (Denton: University of North Texas Press, 1992), 23.
6 Vicki Goldberg, *Artnews* 90 (1991).
7 Steven Durland, "Witness the Guerrilla Theater of Greenpeace," *High Performance* 40 (1987): 31.
8 Ibid., 33.
9 Ibid., 35.
10 Scarce, *Eco-warriors*, 62.
11 Durland, "Witness the Guerrilla Theater," 35.
12 David Ray Griffin, "Introduction," in *Sacred Interconnections*, ed. David Ray Griffin (Albany: SUNY Press, 1990), 1–13.
13 Elinor Gadon, "Metaphors for Birthing: Towards a New Creation Story for the Age of Ecology," in *After Earth Day: Continuing The Conservation Effort*, ed., Max Oelschlaeger (Denton: University of North Texas Press, 1992), 187–203.
14 David Brower, *Work in Progress*, (Salt Lake City, Utah: Peregrine Smith Books, 1991).

# Index